CW01559165

The Trojan Horse of Tithing

Propiv Press
Lancaster, Pennsylvania, USA

The Trojan Horse of Tithing

How Tithe Traditions Have Undermined a Pure Gospel Message

By Jonathan Brenneman
www.gotoheavennow.com

The Trojan Horse of Tithing

How Tithe Traditions Have Undermined a Pure Gospel Message

General Editor: Arnolda Brenneman

Propiv Press, Lancaster, Pennsylvania, USA

ISBN: 9798666806562

Printed in the United States of America.

Contents

1. Let's Get Ready To Take On an Intense Topic! *1*

What Could Have Changed Derek Prince's Mind?...................1

Why Talk About Tithing? 2

My Anguish for the Church 4

What Does a Healthy Attitude Look Like As We Take On
This Subject? 6

Not Yet Time To Focus on This 7

Don't Pull Up the Wheat With the Tares!...............................9

Benny Hinn's Statements 12

How the Wheat and Weeds Are Being Separated Right Now
....13

How the Pentecostal Revival Started 14

Let's Get Started! 16

2. My Tithe Story *19*

My Introduction to Tithing 19

Why Was the Tithe So Different Than Any Other Jewish
Law? 20

Supporting the Family and Fighting the IRS 22

How I Stopped Tithing...24

Can I Still Boldly Approach the Father?...............................25

Afraid To Question 26

How I Began To Voice My Questions 27

A Painful Loss of Fellowship...28

The Holy Spirit Lifting and Strengthening Me in the Middle
of Hardship 30

Wanting Prayer and Fellowship 31

How We Bought a Business and Fell Into Fraud....................31

Confronting Injustice 32

"Your Tithe Must Not Be Right" 33

Tightening the Noose 34

3. Who's Teaching Salvation by Tithing? 37

Deception Starts Subtly 37

What Does Salvation Encompass? 40

Righteousness, Blessing, Salvation 44

Is the Blessing or Curse Hinged on Your Tithe? 45

Open Heavens...46

How Is Malachi-Based Tithe Teaching Leading Christians To Relate to God?...48

The Implications of Tithing as a Requirement for Church Membership...50

Dressing Up Tithing Doctrines As Grace Doesn't Make Them Any Less Deadly..51

4. Subtle Deception Paves the Way for Blatant Error ..55

Do You Realize How Many People Believe Your Eternal Destiny Depends on Your Tithe? 55

Christians Embrace a Book That Teaches the Tithe Secures Your Place in Heaven! 58

Does a Little Poison in Your Good Food Matter?.................59

Will Non-Tithers Go to Hell, or to a Sad, Dry Valley Between Heaven and Hell? 60

Christians Finding No Assurance of Salvation......................62

How Many Steps Have You Taken Towards Accepting This Error?...63

We Get Into Heaven by "Being Good Enough" so We Need To "Do Our Best While We Have a Chance?".......................66

Blatant Teaching of Salvation by Tithing Going Around the World on Christian Television....................................68

Demonically Inspired Rage 70

5. Is the Tithe "Law?" **73**

The Circumcision Debate of the Early Church and the Tithe
Debate of Today 73

"But the Tithe Came Before the Law" 76

Did Jesus Command Us To Tithe? 81

Was Melchizedek Jesus? 85

Did God Command Abraham To Tithe? Was Abraham a
Regular Tither? Did Abraham Tithe on His Own Income? ..91

Did Abraham Become Rich Because He Tithed? 92

How Do I Tithe to Jesus? 94

Abraham's Tithe Was Most Closely Related to the
Babylonian Tithe 96

If Abraham Tithed Based on an Eternal Moral Principle,
Why Didn't God Himself Follow That Principle in His
Instructions for Dividing Spoils of War? 99

**6. The Many Layers of Problems With Teaching a
Christian Tithe From Malachi** **100**

9 Layers of Irrationality We Must Plow Through To Use
Malachi as Support for Mandating Christian Tithing 100

1st Layer – Malachi Was Written to People Under the Law
....101

2nd Layer - The Tithe Pointed to Jesus and Is Fulfilled in the
New Covenant 103

3rd Layer – Nobody Is Tithing As Malachi Commanded ...104

4th Layer - The "Offerings" Malachi Referred to Included
Animal Sacrifices and Other Mandatory Gifts 107

5th Layer - The Tithe Was Israel's Income Tax 108

6th Layer - The Probable Context of Malachi Was the Priests
Stealing the Levite's Portion of the Tithes 109

7th Layer - Very Little of the Tithe Went to Priests 113

3

8th Layer - Most of the Tithe Wasn't Originally Supposed To Go to the Storehouse, and Did Not Maintain the Temple ..115
9th Layer-People Are God's Temple Now and Not a Building
....116

7. The History of Tithing 118
Did Jesus, Paul, or the Early Apostles Receive a Tithe? 118
The First Generations of the Church Clearly Did Not Practice Tithing 122
Contrasting the Christian Love Feasts to the Pagan Feasts and the Tithe of Hercules 126
What Did the Church Fathers Say About Tithes? 127
What Else Accompanied the Increased Emphasis on Tithing?
....129
The Protestant Reformation and Opposition to Tithes 130
Up to the Present Time 132
What Does the History of Tithing Tell Us? 135

8. You Break God's Commandments for the Sake of Your Tithing Tradition 139
Human Religious Tradition 139
Open Your Hands to the Poor and Do Not Oppress Them 140
Declaring What Would Have Helped Your Father or Mother Is Dedicated to God 143
Let No Debt Remain Outstanding Except for the Continual Debt To Love One Another 145
Don't Test the Lord Your God 147
Don't Cause Any of These Little Ones To Stumble 147
Give in Secret 151
Let Giving Be As Each Decides in His Heart, Not Under Compulsion 152
Welcome One Another As Christ Has Welcomed You 154
Do Not Show Favoritism 154

Don't Judge by Mere Appearances, but Judge With Righteous Judgment..155

9. "But Tithing Works!" **159**
"Just Try It!"...159
Confirmation Bias...159
Some Miracle Provision Testimonies Are Made up! 160
Are People Who Tithe More Likely To Be Rich or Poor?...161
What's the Goal of Our Faith?.....................................162
Seeking Life Through "Spiritual Principles" Apart From Christ Is Witchcraft! 165
Chicken Blood 168
When Christians Have The Same Mindsets as Idol Worshippers 169

10. Tithing Undermines Spirit-Led Giving **172**
Buzz Words and Propaganda Techniques 172
Tithing Is Paying, Not Giving......................................173
There Is No Kingdom-of-Heaven Tax! 175
100% Is God's! 177
You Are Responsible for Where You Give! 180
How the Tithe Supplants Spirit-Led Giving 182
The Difficulty of Getting the Most Generous People on Earth To Tithe!...186
The Context of "It's Better To Give Than To Receive" 189
Why Would So Many Church Planters Consider the Tithe a Hindrance to Multiplication? 190
But How Will We Pay for Things?....................................192
What Will Happen to Church Finances if We Stop Teaching Tithing? 196

11. Spirit-Led Giving..**199**
Two Widows Who Gave Out of Their Need 199
The Widow of Zarephath 199

The Widow's Mite 201

Sacrificial Giving Is Not Always Spirit-Led Giving.............202

The Macedonians' Giving 203

Give To Meet People's Needs...204

"I Gave Everything and God Provided!" 207

Are You Following Principles or Following Christ?............207

Hearing God's Voice...208

Sowing and Reaping 209

Give To Get? 212

12. Corrupted Wisdom and Jesus's Temptation.........213

"Adam's Sin in the Garden of Eden Was Failing To Tithe."

....216

"Cain Killed Abel Over the Tithe." 217

"The First Fruits Is the Tithe"..218

"1 Corinthians 16:2 Is About Tithing" 221

Jesus Referred to Tithing When He Said To Give to God

What Is God's 225

Have We Been Reading the Bible With an Agenda?............226

13. What About Ministerial Support?.........................227

The Cultural Background of Jesus's Teachings 227

Apostolic Ministry 231

Is "Double Honor" Double Money? 233

The Ecclesiological Implications of Mandatory Pastoral

Salaries...234

Support for Apostolic Workers Intentionally Put Them in

Dependency Rather Than in Power!......................................237

14. Good News for the Poor 239

Those in Humble Circumstances Should Take Pride in Their

High Position! 239

Viewing Poverty and Prosperity Primarily in Terms of

Relationship Rather Than Money 240

What Is a Poverty Spirit Versus Prosperity Mentality? 242
Many Tithe Teachings Promote a Poverty Spirit 244
Come, All You Who Have No Money! 246

15. When Not To Accept an Offering *249*
Don't Try To Approach God in the Same Way a Sorcerer
Communes With Evil Entities! 249
What Can I Do To Thank You? 250
Support From Unbelievers 251
Pride 252
If We Love the Lord's Flock, We Want To See Them Giving
As Led by the Spirit—Motivated by Love! 255

16. Mothers Are Pleading for Someone To Tell Their
Children the Truth *257*
The Old House Dream 257
Mom's Interpretation 258
My Thoughts 259

Recommended Reading *265*

About the Author *268*

Contact *270*

Chapter 1
Let's Get Ready To Take On an Intense Topic!

What Could Have Changed Derek Prince's Mind?

Derek Prince wrote over 80 books. They have been translated and published in over a hundred languages, and I've seen them in bookstores around the world. Years after his death, some of his books continue to be top sellers on Amazon in the Charismatic/Pentecostal category. His influence also continues through hundreds of recorded sermons and radio broadcasts, with more than 45 *"Derek Prince Ministries"* offices around the world.[1]

Derek influenced me when I was a teenager, and his writings reinforced everything I'd heard about the importance of tithing. Recently, I learned that he changed his position on the matter in 1989. I had known that he eventually admitted *"We fell into the Galatian error"* concerning the Shepherding Movement,[2] but until now, I'd never heard of him changing his position on tithing.

A Bible teacher from New Zealand, Graeme Carlé, wrote a book called *"Eating Sacred Cows."* It taught that the requirement of a tithe only applied to those under the Mosaic Covenant, yet the Mosaic tithe was a great example of how important vacations are. Graeme mentioned that he began to study the matter after hearing

---

[1] Online   https://www.derekprince.org/Groups/1000065822/DPM_USA/About/About.aspx Accessed November 3rd, 2019
[2] Prince, Derek. *Jubilee 1995 Celebration*, Pg. 9

a Bible teacher whom he highly respected, Derek Prince, talk about it.

Warren Smith of Derek Prince Ministries, New Zealand, confirmed that this book got into Derek's hands and he ended up ordering 20 copies for his international council to help them avoid burn-out. A quote from one of Derek's books confirms that he changed his position on tithing:

> **In the New Testament, God never establishes a specific law, like that of the Old Testament, requiring Christians to set aside for him a tenth of their total income. The covenant of grace does not operate through laws enforced from without, but through laws written by the Holy Spirit in the hearts of believers. In 2 Corinthians 9:7 Paul instructs Christians, "So let each one give as he purposes in his heart, not grudgingly or of necessity."[3]**

What could have changed Derek's mind?

Why Talk About Tithing?

Before getting into the meat of the matter, I'd like to address why we need to talk about this and how to approach it with a healthy attitude.

Some people ask *"Why do you need to talk about this?"* In fact, a friend who agrees that scripture doesn't teach tithing for Christians said *"Why talk about this? It won't bring you favor to minister in churches. After all, scripture doesn't prohibit tithing, and it's a model of giving that works well in our culture."*

I'm a missionary, and at times I've done the work of a pastor. I minister as a guest speaker at churches, and giving helps me financially. Sharing my position on tithing doesn't help me to get more opportunities to speak! Some people assume anyone who

---

[3] Prince, Derek. *Blessing or Curse You Can Choose*. 3rd ed. United States: Chose Books, 2006. Pg. 100

questions tithing must not want to give. If money were my motivation, I would have plenty of reason to teach tithing, not question it!

I have little reason to write a book like this other than love for the truth, care for the church, and concern for the purity of the gospel message we preach. I will make the case that:

- *A foundational gospel issue is at stake, and even tithe teachings that are supposedly from a "grace perspective" have fundamentally changed the way many people are attempting to relate to God.*
- *Tithing is a Trojan horse, a doctrine that is cloaked in good intentions but gives Satan a foothold in the church.*
- *The church has been regularly breaking many commands of scripture for the sake of its tithe tradition.*
- *A major justice issue is involved.*
- *The modern tithe is not even a helpful principle, is based on the Babylonian tithe, and contradicts the basic principles of the ancient Jewish tithe.*
- *The tithe is an unnecessary stumbling block that has hindered people from coming to Christ as well as causing many people to turn away from Christ.*
- *Our integrity is at stake. Will we handle God's word with sincerity and truth?*
- *The tithe undermines Holy Spirit-lead giving, generosity, and stewardship.*
- *Teaching the modern tithe tradition undermines the effectiveness of our witness for Christ.*

Vitor Azevedo, a Brazilian pastor whose church went from zero to 3,000 members in just a few years, preached a series called *"Jesus without anything else."*[4] He said to a friend of mine, a missionary,

---

[4]   Azevedo, Vitor *Jesus + O Dizimo?* Online: https://www.youtube.com/watch?v=bPl838jTwEQ&t=6s Accessed March 2nd, 2020

3

"I've taught my church that they need just Jesus, not Jesus and tithing. Should I put this on the internet with all my other messages?"

My friend Reinhard advised him, *"If you put this on the internet, I believe you will be terribly persecuted for it. If you're willing to be persecuted for the sake of the truth, put it up. If not, don't. If you put it up, you'll be persecuted, but it will set people free."*

Vitor said in tears, *"I would rather close down my church for lack of money than keep the people in this bondage."* He went ahead and posted the message.

All hell broke loose. People started taking snippets of his messages totally out of context and posting them on the internet, warning about him, and calling him a heretic. He was canceled from every single conference and speaking engagement.

Can you imagine a pastor of a large church, with so many speaking engagements, having any reason to question tithing other than caring for the truth and the purity of the gospel message? He saw that tithing teachings were hurting people!

Vitor Azevedo's integrity and courage to share his conviction revealed the hearts of many other leaders. Their persecution revealed the heart issues underlying the doctrine they preached. When they accused him of *"heresy"* for rejecting tithing, they revealed that their *"gospel"* was tithing. It was not, as Paul said, *"…nothing…except Jesus Christ and him crucified."*[5]

I love the churches and have several pastor friends I love dearly and pray for. I believe in supporting ministers, and I myself support other ministries. I care so much about this issue because I passionately love the church. My purpose is to partner with what the Holy Spirit is doing in the church, not to tear it down.

Some people say *"It's useless to try to convince pastors to change their minds about tithing."* I disagree. Godly leaders such as Derek Prince have already changed their positions on tithing. Some leaders who are currently teaching tithing do sincerely love

---

[5] 1 Corinthians 2:2

God's people and have the integrity to consider what I have to say and put truth before convenience.

Some readers may initially feel like I'm setting up the most extreme teachings about tithing as a straw man to attack. Please bear with me and keep reading. I'll make a strong case that even so-called *"grace based"* tithe teachings have caused destruction in the body of Christ to a shocking extent!

My Anguish for the Church

Romans 9:1-5 I speak the truth in Christ—I am not lying, my conscience confirms it through the Holy Spirit— I have great sorrow and unceasing anguish in my heart. For I could wish that I myself were cursed and cut off from Christ for the sake of my people, those of my own race, the people of Israel. Theirs is the adoption to sonship; theirs the divine glory, the covenants, the receiving of the law, the temple worship and the promises. Theirs are the patriarchs, and from them is traced the human ancestry of the Messiah, who is God over all, forever praised! Amen.

Why did Paul have such anguish over Israel? He saw God's blessing and work among his people. But they stumbled by pursuing the law as the way of righteousness, not by faith but by works.[6]

I relate to what Paul says here, although not quite to the point of wishing I myself were cursed and cut off. As Paul loved his people, I love God's people and have a burning passion for the Holy Spirit's work among the churches. I pray fervently for churches and pastor friends, with much gratitude for what the Holy Spirit is doing among God's people. I can barely visit a new church without soon being in tears. I frequently weep half of the time when I'm in a Christian meeting because I recognize what the

---

[6] Romans 9:31-33

Holy Spirit is doing. I see how the Holy Spirit is moving in people's lives, and I put all my heart and soul into agreeing with his work.

I don't want to live if not for Jesus and for his purposes for the church. My life's passion is for people to know and experience God's glory, seeing it manifest in and through the church.

Yet a serious issue has hindered the church from manifesting God's glory more fully, causing us to send a mixed message. The declaration of truth brings a manifestation of God's glory, but it only goes so far if the church then contradicts itself and teaches people to pursue by works that which is only available by God's grace.

Many say *"We aren't doing that. We teach tithing under grace."* It's not possible to teach *"tithing under grace"* any more than it is to teach *"circumcision under grace."* The same problems remain. God's glory is manifest in the nature and character of Christ. No matter how much we try to dress up tithing as *"grace,"* it still misrepresents who Christ is and how he relates to people.

I've shed so many tears in prayer over the tithe issue. God has commissioned me to strengthen the church and encourage pastors. Yet questioning or disagreeing with the tithe will often close doors to ministry opportunities. I've put much prayer into asking God for wisdom about how to discuss this, and I recently shared my position with two Brazilian pastor friends. Thank God they understood where I'm coming from!

If it were just about being *"successful in ministry,"* disagreeing with the tithing doctrine is one of the worst things I could do. But God measures success in a different way than men do. The fear of the Lord and love for the truth won't let me around this issue. Love for the church and a passion to see a greater manifestation of God's glory through the church compel me.

The gospel is worth giving our money and our whole lives for. We want to build up the church, see people to give generously, and see provision for ministries, but it must be by God's grace and not according to the law.

Chapter 1

What Does a Healthy Attitude Look Like As We Take On This Subject?

Although this isn't only a charismatic issue, I'm addressing it from a pro-charismatic, full gospel position.[7] Some critics of tithing have addressed the issue from a very critical, anti-charismatic slant.

I highly esteem several people and ministries that teach tithing. I'm so thankful, for example, for the blessing that has come through Bethel Church and Hillsong Church, even though I couldn't disagree more strongly about the tithe. Bill Johnson's teaching helped me get started in a life of miracles, and the worship music from Hillsong has been a huge blessing! As hard-hitting as I will get here in my disagreement about the tithe, please don't take this book as a condemnation of certain people or ministries.

I'm bringing up huge issues and making strong points. Yet I share not with an accusatory intent but as a humble plea, directed especially to charismatic leaders whom I love and respect. I hope to reach several leaders for whom I have the utmost appreciation and affection, leaders who have added so much to my life. I myself have been prone to error, as Peter was. I'm humbly entreating today's leaders to re-consider this issue. Consider the implications and the fruit of teaching tithing, because it's causing great harm to the cause of Christ. Common tithe teachings are a Trojan Horse for error that is leading millions of people away from Biblical Christianity based on faith in Christ. If we have strayed, let's return to unadulterated gospel truth. Let's get rid of the old yeast!

Galatians 6:1 (NRSV) My friends, if anyone is detected in a transgression, you who have received the Spirit should restore such a one in a spirit of gentleness. Take care that you yourselves are not tempted.

---

[7] "Full Gospel" is the belief that healing, deliverance, and provision are part of the gospel package.

7

1 Corinthians 5:6-8: (NRSV) Do you not know that a little yeast leavens the whole batch of dough? Clean out the old yeast so that you may be a new batch, as you really are unleavened. For our paschal lamb, Christ, has been sacrificed. Therefore, let us celebrate the festival, not with the old yeast, the yeast of malice and evil, but with the unleavened bread of sincerity and truth.

If you're starting this book in disagreement with me, I hope you'll listen to my plea with humility, consider my arguments, hear my experience, and hear my heart for the church. We're dealing with issues that can't be ignored. Will you approach this matter with sincerity and love for the truth?

If you're starting this book as someone who is already in agreement with my position, I encourage you to maintain an attitude of thankfulness for the church, not focusing first on what is wrong, but on what the Holy Spirit is doing to edify the body of Christ. Even as I share strong criticisms of the tithe doctrine, I write with excitement because the Holy Spirit is dealing with this issue in order to bring forth a greater manifestation of God's glory through the church.

Not Yet Time To Focus on This

When I first became convinced that the tithe doctrine was such a serious problem, talking about it cost me! Even though I continued to see Jesus heal people in daily life, at times I fell into the trap of self-pity and a negative focus. When I saw Jesus heal unbelievers, I was reluctant to refer them to a local church because I wasn't sure if it would do them more harm than good! I'd seen human religious tradition hurt people so much.

Then as I wrote the *"Heaven Now"* trilogy, I returned to a continual focus on what the Holy Spirit is doing and a healthy attitude of thanksgiving for the church. The truths I was writing about often brought a tangible manifestation of God's glory which I could physically feel as a weight on my body as I wrote.

For a few years, I wasn't at peace to address the tithe issue frequently or directly. Over the years several people had asked me to write a book about it, but I didn't have confirmation in my heart to do so. I still held the same firm conviction about it, and hinted at my position in my blog. I shed many tears over the issue in private as I prayed for the churches.

Why didn't I feel the peace yet to write a book on the tithe, even when people had asked me to? It may have partly been because of the need to guard my heart and not get distracted, staying focused on partnering with the Holy Spirit's work in the church. However, I think it was also because so many people weren't ready to hear it!

John 16:12 I have much more to say to you, more than you can now bear.

What was Jesus talking about here? I'm not totally sure, but I think it was partly a reference to the soon-coming end of the whole Jewish system as they knew it, revelation later given through Paul. It was too weighty for them at the moment. Even later, they could barely accept the idea that the gentiles weren't obligated to join the Jewish system to be saved. Imagine the idea that the whole system they know would end, even for them as Jews! Think of how weighty Paul's revelation would have been to them, that circumcision was unnecessary!

As I primarily focused on other things, the Holy Spirit was still working on people's hearts over the tithe issue. During that time period some teachers who had never taught tithing, such as Dan Mohler, grew tremendously in influence. A few friends and charismatic church leaders who had once taught tithing began reconsidering the issue and even changing their positions. Che Ahn of the Revival Alliance, for example, wrote:

There are many sincere Christians today who faithfully give the tithe because they believe it is mandated in Scripture, and that mandate is still valid today. I know, for I used to be one of them. I was taught to tithe from the time I first became a Christian as a teenager, and it never occurred to me to question the teaching. My wife and I have always given more than the tithe every year since we've been married. However, more recently, I find that my position is changing, due to what I believe is a deeper understanding of God's grace and its operation in our lives.[8]

The Scripture most commonly used to support this view is Malachi 3:8-10 "Will a mere mortal rob God? Yet you rob me. But you ask, 'How are we robbing you?' In tithes and offerings. You are under a curse—your whole nation— because you are robbing me. Bring the whole tithe into the storehouse, that there may be food in my house. 'Test me in this,' says the Lord Almighty,' and see if I will not throw open the floodgates of heaven and pour out so much blessing that there will not be room enough to store it.'"

Unfortunately, this teaching on the tithe from Malachi 3 frequently intimidates people, inducing guilt by telling them that if they don't tithe, they are robbing God and are under a curse. The passage is also frequently quoted out of context. As we discussed at the beginning of this book, when we take a text out of context, we are opening ourselves to a "con."[9]

---

[8] Ahn, Che. *Grace of Giving*. Bloomington, MN: Chosen Books, 2013. Kindle Location 3645

[9] Ahn, Che. *Grace of Giving*. Bloomington, MN: Chosen Books, 2013. Kindle Location 3691

Chapter 1

Don't Pull Up the Wheat With the Tares!

Soon after moving to Goiania, Brazil, I suddenly had the peace to write directly about the tithe. I came out with a few blog posts on it and I started this book. I felt peace and the same fire in my heart motivating me to write as with my other books. I was amazed that almost all the feedback from the blog posts was highly positive. Years ago, when I had first talked about this, people often reacted with great anger and accusation.

As those first few blog posts were coming out, a good friend from South Africa commented. He wrote: *"Abba showed me this in 2006 but said it was not the time yet. People were not close to being ready to hear this truth. He said people will ask privately and share. Over the years we have had many productive times in sharing around this but I have felt for a while that this will be the next big one."*

This confirmed what I had felt. Another friend, a missionary, likewise told me that he hadn't felt the peace to focus publicly on refuting tithing. Then, at about the same time as I did, he felt *"I can't hide this from God's people anymore."*

Besides people not yet being ready to hear the message, I feel there was another reason it wasn't yet time to write a book on tithing:

Matthew 13:24-30 Jesus told them another parable: "The kingdom of heaven is like a man who sowed good seed in his field. But while everyone was sleeping, his enemy came and sowed weeds among the wheat, and went away. When the wheat sprouted and formed heads, then the weeds also appeared.

The owner's servants came to him and said, 'Sir, didn't you sow good seed in your field? Where then did the weeds come from?'

'An enemy did this,' he replied.

The servants asked him, 'Do you want us to go and pull them up?'

'No,' he answered, 'because while you are pulling the weeds, you may uproot the wheat with them. Let both grow together until the harvest. At that time I will tell the harvesters: First, collect the weeds and tie them in bundles to be burned; then gather the wheat and bring it into my barn.'"

This may not be the exact context of the passage, but the principle applies. Sometimes ministers who have sincere love and minister in God's power get their roots entangled with weeds. It happened to Derek Prince, who later admitted to falling into the Galatian error. I think it's happened to all of us to some extent. Church history is full of revivalists and reformers who missed it big time in a certain area, yet God worked through them.

I needed to learn to focus on what God is doing and walk in constant thanksgiving for the church in order to avoid pulling up the wheat with the weeds. Sometimes what is wheat and what is a weed becomes more evident as they mature. The fruit of certain teachings has become more evident with time.

I recently heard a lady who disagrees with tithing saying that everybody who is teaching it is a wolf in sheep's clothing. Although I agree with her position on tithing, I felt like she was pulling up the wheat with the weeds. Scripture says to not rebuke an elder harshly, but to exhort him as if he were your father.[10]

Peter was a true apostle who walked with Jesus, preached the gospel, and healed the sick. He wasn't a wolf or a charlatan. Yet sometimes he majorly missed it! Not long after his grand revelation from the Father that Jesus was the Christ, Jesus said to him *"Get behind me Satan!"*[11]

---

[10] 1 Timothy 5:1
[11] Matthew 16:23

Furthermore, Peter got his roots entangled in the circumcision faction so that Paul confronted him in front of everybody.[12] At its root, the tithe issue is the same as the circumcision issue.

Many leaders in the church hardly realize the extent of the trouble tithe teachings are causing. Many have taught it because people they respect taught it to them and they've sincerely believed it and lived it. Some of those leaders have born much more fruit for God's kingdom than I have. Do you see why addressing this issue feels like a conundrum for me and I am only addressing it with much prayer? I don't want to tear down godly people who I consider *"fathers in the faith,"* or lump them together with charlatans, yet the major problems tithe teaching is causing can no longer be ignored. The fruit has now matured, and it's become evident that this teaching is a weed in God's garden.

Benny Hinn's Statements

Soon after I felt peace to start writing this book, Benny Hinn caused a stir by making some strong statements about the prosperity gospel.[13] Benny Hinn didn't say anything about the tithe. I don't know if he's open to reconsidering his position on it, but what he did say deals with the same underlying issues I'm addressing.

Here are Benny's main points in the video[14] which went viral and in two later interviews:[15]

---

[12] Galatians 2:11-14

[13] I am referring to what is popularly called the "Prosperity Gospel," which is the deception that says "Gain is godliness." I do believe, of course, that as the gospel spreads it promotes prosperity and lifts people out of poverty by restoring right relationships with God, self, and others. Nothing is wrong with prosperity. Where things go awry is when people begin to equate gain with godliness, show favoritism, teach that your tithe and giving are your covenant with God, and put the gospel up for sale.

[14] Online: https://www.youtube.com/watch?v=v3k9Z1byAVk Accessed December 20th, 2019

[15] Online: https://www.youtube.com/watch?v=IrryxmAfXIk Accessed December 20th, 2019
Online: https://www.youtube.com/watch?v=8qUQwmwC7Oc Accessed December 20th, 2019

- **He's correcting his theology,** and we need to know it. He doesn't believe what he used to and he reads the Bible differently than he did twenty years ago.

- **It's an offense** to the Holy Spirit to say *"give $1000"* or put a price on the gospel.

- He has taken offerings like that before but he will never again do so because the Holy Spirit is *"just fed up with it."* **Doing so *"hurts the gospel."***

- *"If I hear one more time 'break the back of debt with $1000' I think I'm going to rebuke them.* **I think that's buying the gospel, that's buying the blessing, that's grieving the Holy Spirit."**

- His statement has nothing to do with critics but with his own soul as he has been spending time with the Lord. He got distracted from his call and has grieved the Lord many times, and **doesn't want to get to heaven and be rebuked by God.** He wants to be known as an evangelist, not as a prosperity teacher.

- *"Give to get"* theology has hurt Christians, and if you're not giving because you love Jesus, don't give. He heard people talking about giving and prosperity and thought *"**Where is Jesus in all this?"***

I can't say how much it filled my heart with joy to hear Benny speak. I see the Holy Spirit's work in his heart and in the church, and it motivates me all the more to keep praying for the church. Some people are cynical about Benny's motives for speaking, and negative responses have come from both Charismatics and non-Charismatics. I didn't sense anything but sincerity as Benny spoke, and the negative responses saddened me.

Benny still believes that God wants to prosper us, as I also do. But his roots had become entangled with weeds and he now recognizes it. I don't believe it was just a coincidence that I felt the peace to start writing about the tithe right before Benny's statements went viral.

How the Wheat and Weeds Are Being Separated Right Now

Several preachers were quite upset with Benny for speaking out. I feel like I'm writing prophetically now. God is using Benny's statements to reveal the motives of people's hearts, and it is beginning a time of separating the wheat from the weeds. Some are in ministry for selfish motives. Others teaching tithing sincerely love the Lord and his people. They are wheat, but they've gotten their roots entangled with weeds.

I watched one preacher in particular who was furious. He rebuked Benny, going on and on about how Satan would attack the church's finances through Benny's repentance, and claiming Benny had fallen into error. As I saw that preacher speak, I was sure he was demonized. Yet he claims to have seen Jesus personally, face to face, regularly.

I fear the Lord. I'm careful not to prematurely judge a minister's motives. I've made that mistake before, and I'd rather believe the best. But I have no qualms about saying this:

If you have seen Jesus, your countenance reflects it. My Baptist grandmother's face was glowing and she looked ten years younger after she fell on the ground and had a vision in which Jesus took her to the Father. Although I haven't had a vision like my grandmother did, I have also seen Jesus with the eyes of my heart as he healed people. I've felt like Jesus was standing beside me and I couldn't stop weeping. I know how seeing Jesus changes a person.

Yet that man's eyes and countenance looked like those of a murderer in a mug shot after being taken in by the cops, not like somebody who had seen Jesus. I could easily see that he was a liar and a charlatan. His response to Benny revealed what was really in his heart.

I knew very little about that preacher before seeing his angry response to Benny Hinn. But when I said *"His countenance looks like that of a murderer, not of a person who's seen Jesus,"* my friends told me that allegations of sexually predatory behavior were coming out of the woodwork against him. I wasn't surprised.

The Lord is going to continue laying bare the secrets of men's hearts, and a greater separation is happening now between the weeds and the wheat. People will see who's motivated by sincere love and who's in it for themselves.

How the Pentecostal Revival Started

The modern Pentecostal movement spread worldwide through a black preacher named William Seymour and the Azusa Street revival, but it started a few years earlier. Charles Parham was preaching on the Baptism of the Holy Spirit.

William Seymour sat outside the door in the hall and listened. He wasn't able to participate in the *"altar times"* of seeking God with everybody else. But he received from God through a preacher who had him sit outside the door because of his dark skin. Is that hard to understand?

God worked through a preacher who practiced segregation, a human tradition for which many churches of that day broke God's commandments. The Holy Spirit's work through Parham's life doesn't justify segregation. Imagine the humility it took for William Seymour to learn and receive from God through that imperfect minister! The great thing is that the Pentecostal revival which spread as a result became one of the greatest movements towards breaking down racial barriers.

I've felt confused at times as I've seen the Holy Spirit move in places with obvious problems. The tithe issue has caused so much trouble, undermining a pure gospel message and hurting the cause of Christ. Yet the people who fanned the flames in my heart for missions teach it, as well as those who got me started ministering healing. Sometimes I've felt like William Seymour, receiving much from certain ministers in spite of the elephant in the room! At that time, it was racism and segregation. Today it is financial manipulation.

In some places where I've learned and been blessed, I've heard someone stand up and imply that giving money could help a person to receive their healing. What an abhorrent practice! Some people, reacting to such manipulation, think divine healing must be fake and so they reject what God is doing. I know so well that Jesus heals people, but it grieves me how money issues become a stumbling block to make people cynical and hinder them from receiving from God.

Ministries can have miracles and a mighty work of the Holy Spirit, but be totally wrong in a certain area. This has often happened throughout church history! God is working mightily in the church today, but we've missed it big time when it comes to the tithe tradition. Critics have sometimes wanted to pull up the wheat with the weeds. They don't have the humility to see what God is doing in spite of what's wrong. Others have mistaken the Holy Spirit's move as an endorsement on wrong doctrines and abusive practices.

Paul rejoiced that the gospel was being preached, even if sometimes it wasn't even for the right motives. Some people had malicious motives in preaching, but they were still sharing the gospel and it bore fruit! The message that Jesus saves and heals will always bear fruit, and it often has in spite of the messenger!

Philippians 1:15-18 It is true that some preach Christ out of envy and rivalry, but others out of goodwill. The latter do so out of love, knowing that I am put here for the defense of the gospel. The former preach Christ out of selfish ambition, not sincerely, supposing that they can stir up trouble for me while I am in chains. But what does it matter? The important thing is that in every way, whether from false motives or true, Christ is preached. And because of this I rejoice.

Some preach the gospel with wrong motives. Some have good motives but have been drawn into hypocrisy or double-mindedness concerning their message, like the apostle Peter was. Some are now realizing that their roots got entangled with weeds.

Let's Get Started!

First, we're going to focus on how common tithe teachings have undermined a pure gospel message of salvation by grace through faith in Christ. This especially applies to any teaching saying Christians must tithe based on Malachi 3. We will then present numerous insurmountable arguments and rebuttals to any position that claims tithing has relevance to Christians today or that the modern tithe is anything more than a tradition of men. That evidence, when fully considered, makes arguments for the modern tithe-tradition look absurd.

Then we'll examine multiple scriptural commands that many churches are breaking for the sake of their tithe tradition. We'll make the case that tithing shouldn't even be taught as a good principle to guide our giving, and that it actually undermines Spirit-led giving. We'll also look at the related issue of *"sowing and reaping."* We'll examine the underlying heart-issues behind these teachings. Finally, we'll deal with the subject of ministerial support which is so closely related to the tithing discussion.

In many places, I simply give the scripture references in the footnotes for my statements instead of including the whole texts in this book. This helps us to keep moving as these are fairly straightforward facts about tithes from the scripture and anyone who wants to study further can verify these facts by checking out the scripture references.

Even though we are bringing serious error and injustice to light, I encourage you to have the humility to receive from God through people and movements that don't have everything right. When you see weeds, respond with humility and prayer so as not to rip up the wheat with the weeds. Don't just recognize what the enemy has sown, but continue to recognize what God is doing!

I am remaining in an attitude of prayer with thanksgiving for the church. Great change is already happening, and I'm so excited about it!!

Chapter 2
My Tithe Story
My Introduction to Tithing

I found out that God exists when I was about 8 years old, through a supernatural healing. A few years later, I went to a Christian camp for kids. We heard how Jesus died for our sins so we could be clean and right with God, and then rose again so we could have victory and be free from the power of sin. The atmosphere was heavy with God's glory. We wept as God revealed his love to us. Soon after, I was born-again and found peace.

I started sleeping with my Bible under my pillow so I would remember to read it the next day. I had already read nearly all the Bible cover-to-cover for the first time when I was 7 years old, and had never gotten the idea from the Bible that a Christian was supposed to tithe.

I'd read the Mosaic law about the tithe, along with many boring rituals, animal sacrifices, and strange regulations. I had known since I was 7 years old that the priest's clothes could not have wool in them, men couldn't shave the sides of their faces, Israelites had to kill a lot of animals, and men had to get cut where it hurt and suffer for days so they could be in covenant with God! I wondered why the tithe was different than any of the other things in the Old Testament that we didn't do anymore. I saw many New Testament passages telling me I wasn't bound by that Mosaic law:

Romans 7:6 (NRSV) But now we have been discharged from the law, having died to that wherein we were held; so that we serve in newness of the spirit, and not in oldness of the letter.

Romans 10:4 (NRSV) For Christ is the end of the law so that there may be righteousness for everyone who believes.

Ephesian 2:15 (NKJV) …having abolished in His flesh the enmity, that is, the law of commandments contained in ordinances.

Colossians 2:14 (NKJV) …having wiped out the handwriting of requirements that was against us, which was contrary to us. And He has taken it out of the way, having nailed it to the cross.

I soon heard in church that the tithe wasn't just another Hebrew law but was the way we made a covenant with God. They said Abraham tithed before the law so God made him rich! But their arguments didn't make sense to me. Having first read Genesis when I was seven years old, I noticed that God blessed Abraham and made him very rich long before he ever tithed. He also was circumcised and offered animal sacrifices before the law. Was I supposed to sacrifice animals too because Abraham did that before the law?

Why Was the Tithe So Different Than Any Other Jewish Law?

Nevertheless, my parents taught me to tithe on my allowance and I heard a lot about the importance of tithing in church. My grandmother, who gave me my first Bible, was a tither. I wanted so much to please God and do what was right. Since people I respected told me so much about tithing, I figured it must be important.

I heard in church that our tithe belongs to God and withholding it is robbing God. I heard that the church is the storehouse and you have to give a tenth of your money to the church and also give offerings. You could give offerings wherever you wanted, but the tithe had to go to the local church. Giving to missions and to the poor only came after your tithe.

You could also be guilty of robbing God if you didn't give enough in offerings, since scripture commands us to give to the poor and missions as well as tithing. After all, Malachi said the people robbed God *"in tithes and offerings."* You would be under a curse for robbing God if you didn't tithe, but if you did, the floodgates of heaven would open. We couldn't test God in anything else, but we could test him by tithing!

Malachi 3:8-11 Will a mere mortal rob God? Yet you rob me. But you ask, "How are we robbing you?"

In tithes and offerings. You are under a curse—your whole nation—because you are robbing me. Bring the whole tithe into the storehouse, that there may be food in my house. "Test me in this," says the Lord Almighty, "and see if I will not throw open the floodgates of heaven and pour out so much blessing that there will not be room enough to store it. I will prevent pests from devouring your crops, and the vines in your fields will not drop their fruit before it is ripe," says the Lord Almighty.

I started making money during a brief period of living in the utter despondence of guilt and condemnation, afraid I had committed the unforgiveable sin and lost my salvation. I went to New York to work for three weeks when I was 12 years old, and then I started delivering newspapers. I was a generous kid, although perhaps not so wise with my hard-earned money. I often blew most of it buying soda, ice cream, and snacks for all the kids in the neighborhood.

Then that year Anne and Charles Stock, who had been to the Toronto Airport church, held revival meetings at our church. God touched me, and I wept as I felt his love come on me physically and tangibly. I remember the sound of weeping mixed with laughter as people repented and felt the joy of being reconciled to God. Soon after I went on a mission trip and determined once and for all that I wanted to be a missionary and live my whole life for Jesus.

I never would have thought up all the reasoning I'd heard about tithing from reading the Bible for myself as a child, but I wanted very much to make sure I was doing the right thing. I was now reading a chapter of Proverbs every day. Proverbs really enforced the importance of being teachable, submitting to my parents and elders, and listening to wisdom. I'd repented from the sin of rebellion and I never wanted to go back to it. I wanted to be a missionary and live for Jesus. So even though the reasoning behind tithing didn't seem logical, I thought *"better to be safe than sorry!"* After all, I didn't see anything wrong with tithing, and I figured it was a way of showing I honored God!

Since I'd been a shoplifter when I was younger, I thought it right to go back to the stores I'd stolen from and make restitution before I would think about a tithe. I first did that with money from my paper route, going from one store to another, confessing my sin, and offering them money for approximately the value that I thought I'd stolen from them. Boy was that scary, but I felt so much better after doing it!

After that, I began to tithe faithfully. I wanted to do it as worship to God, and I started with joy, giving offerings to missions on top of it. It wasn't hard for the first few years, because I was a kid and didn't have any real expenses.

Supporting the Family and Fighting the IRS

As I grew older, I went on many mission trips and saw Jesus do wonders! I finished school and started working in construction when I was 17. Soon after, some difficult times came. After returning from a trip to Belize, I had to support the family for a time. (My parents were also tithers at the time. They reimbursed me for the support I gave some years later.) I was 18. In the year I began to support the family, I only made about $14,000. It felt like there were holes in my pockets and something always went wrong just when I thought I was going to have enough.

I didn't understand why it felt like I was financially cursed. I was tithing! Could it be that I was robbing God in offerings by not giving enough on top of my tithe? Malachi said they robbed him in *"tithes and offerings."* I did give to missions and other causes on top of my tithe. I wanted to give even more to other causes, but I didn't because my tithe came first. Maybe the windows of heaven weren't being opened because I was robbing God in offerings by not giving enough on top of the tithe, because I wasn't cheerful enough, or because I worried about having enough when I gave. Maybe…maybe…maybe…

But I kept deciding to stand firm and keep testing God with my tithe, believing he would open the windows of heaven. I still felt guilty, because I felt like the problem couldn't be on God's side and I must not have enough faith if I had lack. I was trying to have faith. I was stressed about money all the time, and my bank account overdrew over some little thing several times, adding bank fees to the financial burden.

When I was 20, I had an experience with God in which I began to understand the incarnation. I saw Jesus in such a way that I felt like I had barely known who he was and barely understood the Gospel before. It set me on a path of rapid spiritual growth, and my life began to be marked by miracles and healing.

During that time, the IRS audited me and questioned if I had really supported the family to be able to take the deductions I claimed. I believed I should have sufficient evidence, but it was not enough for them! The dispute continued for several years. I kept encouraging myself, holding on, and declaring victory. I got a CPA who said he believed we could win this case.

Up to and during my second trip to Russia, the manifestation of God's glory increased greatly. I became so aware of God's presence that it felt like currents of love flowing through my mouth and hands. I could feel his glory like a weight that rested on me. I would sometimes stretch out my hand and feel currents, like electricity, flowing out. I often knew what physical problems people had without them telling me, and they were healed. It felt like I was in heaven for weeks at a time, daily feeling the physically tangible manifestation of God's glory and seeing miracle after miracle.

Soon after the second trip to Russia, the IRS sent me a notice of a lean on my house for more than $14,000. The penalties and interest had so inflated the amount that it was more than I'd even earned during one of the years in question!

I'd bought that house when I was 22, spending about $2,500 to close the deal. It wasn't even habitable when I bought it, but I began fixing it up and I moved in. I'd worked so hard for the house and now I could lose it if I didn't pay $14,000!

I felt sick in the stomach and couldn't sleep because of the stress. I threw myself even more into healing the sick. I felt like I was rich because *"Jesus lives in me and I can touch people and see them healed."* I knew that the IRS could take all my money and possessions away, but they couldn't take Jesus away or stop me from giving away his riches. Ministering healing helped me to deal with the stress by getting my focus off of myself and my own problems.

I soon realized the CPA had completely dropped my case and stopped talking to the IRS, all the while telling me we could win the dispute and acting like he was working on it. While this was going on fees and interest were accruing. It had been years of one setback after another, and this felt like the straw that broke the camel's back.

How I Stopped Tithing

It became a matter of paying my bills or paying the tithe. By that time, I'd come to think that the tithe was extremely important. I was afraid I was backsliding if I didn't pay my tithe. I'd been taught that the tithe was *"first fruits"* and should be paid before anything else as a sign of trust, or else I was a thief and stealing from God.

But what could I do? I knew God was real and I loved him. Scripture also said to owe nobody anything except for the continuing debt to love each other,[16] that the borrower is the slave to the lender,[17] and if you are a slave and can get your freedom, do so.[18] Would it honor God if I paid a tithe and didn't pay my electric bill? Was I sinning no matter what I did in that situation?

I could no longer tithe. I had no strength left. I'd tried to believe and test God, but maybe my faith had failed. I still knew he was real and good. After being healed and seeing him heal so many people, there was no doubt of that.

The year before, my Christian accountant had told me how blessed I would surely be for how high of a percentage of my income I gave. And I had just challenged the church in Russia to tithe as I took the offering.

I stopped tithing. I wasn't sure if I was sinning or not when I did, but ironically, it felt like the windows of heaven opened when I stopped. I got some good-paying side jobs and relief came from the financial distress. It was as if God was saying *"I'm not condemning you and I care about your situation."* For so long when I was tithing, it felt like there were holes in my pockets.

Can I Still Boldly Approach the Father?

When I stopped tithing, I struggled with feeling like I no longer had the same boldness to approach the Father. I had been living in such bliss and joy! But now it felt like I was being a disobedient

---

[16] Romans 13:8
[17] Proverbs 22:7
[18] 1 Corinthians 7:21

Christian and wasn't right with God. Was I now cut off from that joy and glory because I didn't feel like it was right to tithe and not pay the electric bill, after having tithed *"by faith"* before and ending up with an overdrawn bank account?

Yet my heart was the same! I still loved the Lord with all my heart and I still wanted to give. My heart burned to see people be healed and encounter Jesus. God knew my situation and it wouldn't honor him to pay a tithe and not pay my bills on time.

I told only a few people. My two closest friends were shocked. They fully knew the circumstances, yet acted as though I was backsliding and my relationship with the Lord was falling apart. Their reaction was very difficult and I never would have expected it! I thought, *"Is this really what God's heart is like? It can't be."*

Their reaction made me think and question all the more. Why should tithes affect my relationship with God in such a way? Was my salvation and communion with God based on a tithe, or on the blood of Jesus? Scripture said I could approach the Father with boldness and confidence because of Jesus's redemptive work, not because I'd paid a tithe.

The Christians around me would have NEVER said that you were saved by the tithe. They would have called that error. Yet they practically acted as if we were saved by it. That was especially clear to me because I'd come to understand salvation as so much more than just a ticket to heaven. It included healing, wholeness, peace with God, and full access to the Father. I knew many other Christians around me would be ashamed to approach the Father or walk in intimacy with him if they hadn't paid their tithes. I thought *"Isn't paying for intimacy called prostitution?"*

Before, I would have NEVER said I was saved by tithing. Yet now, after having walked in such glory, why did I feel ashamed to approach God without a tithe?

Chapter 2

Afraid To Question

I'd already pushed aside so many questions throughout the years. Many people whom God had used in my life emphasized the importance of the tithe, and I was afraid to say they might be wrong. I was on the fence for a while. I had more and more questions, yet I was still afraid to ask them. I noticed so much arrogance, judgment, and accusation from the church towards anybody who had a financial struggle.

These were people I wouldn't have expected such an attitude from, but it seemed like an evil force took hold of them when they talked about someone's financial difficulty. It was all connected to their views on tithing. If the person didn't tithe, they must be struggling because they were cursed for not tithing. If they were tithing and still having difficulty, they must be a bad steward in some other way such as not giving enough over the tithe, tithing with the wrong attitude, or spending too much.

Couldn't a person be trying to do their best, honor God, and be a good steward of their money, yet face a financial trial? What about the apostle Paul, who at times was hungry and thirsty and without clothing?[19] Was he in need because of lack of faith or poor stewardship? Shouldn't we help people in need rather than self-righteously heaping condemnation on them?

I didn't think of most Christians around me as *"radicals"* on prosperity teaching. When they were themselves, they would deny they believed all financial difficulty was the result of someone's irresponsibility. It was as if they did not remember what they had said when that evil power came over them, as if it had been a different person who spoke so judgmentally. A person having no recollection of something they just said or did is common with demonic activity, and I realized I was bumping into a demonic stronghold of self-righteousness.

---

[19] 2 Corinthians 11:27

The words and behavior of many Christians I interacted with showed that in practicality they regarded the tithe as necessary to approach God. When the issue came up, something came over them and they were no longer themselves!

Specific situations I saw brought up more questions. I realized how many struggling Christians felt like they were falling away from the Lord if they missed a tithe to pay their bills. I knew a widow who, although she was careful with money, had been through hard circumstances and was deep in debt. She felt bad that she couldn't pay the whole tithe, yet her family needed to live and buy food. I thought *"Is this the gospel?"*

People were gossiping, saying she was having trouble because she was being a poor steward of her money. Wasn't the church supposed to help those in need? Why did the tithe doctrine lead to heaping condemnation on top of their struggles instead of relieving them?

How I Began To Voice My Questions

Questions kept presenting themselves to me. I put them aside but they kept surfacing again. Even people I thought highly of, wonderful people, became uncharacteristically angry and judgmental when discussing tithing. Something came over them.

I went to a seminar on church planting with YWAM church planting coach Brian Hogan. He talked about lightening the burden of what we call *"church"* that we bring to other cultures, stripping off all of our Western ideas of what church is and looking at the essentials of what the Biblical model really is. One of the things he mentioned was the tithe. He said *"We don't teach tithing. We teach giving and generosity."*

Brian said the tithe was under the law but under grace we give freely. He said if they had taught tithing to the churches they planted, the people would have actually given less. Grace can accomplish more than the law ever can!

Until then, I'd still had an underlying fear that only lukewarm Christians questioned tithing. Brian's seminar showed me there were on-fire Christians on the front lines of the gospel who didn't believe in tithing. It helped me to overcome the fear of asking questions so I could be honest with myself about the issue.

Finally, some months later, something clicked! As I read Galatians, I realized the circumcision issue which the early church struggled with was identical to the tithe issue of today. Everything Paul wrote in reply to the circumcision faction was just as applicable. It was a deadly error!

I wrote a list of 32 questions about the tithe and showed them to people close to me. Nobody could answer them in support of tithing. Several people close to me changed their positions when they saw my questions and examined what the Bible said. My parents, who had taught me tithing, said *"Wow, you're right. We can't support the idea that the tithe is for today, or that the Bible teaches anything for Christians but generous giving as we are able and willing."*

A Painful Loss of Fellowship

Now being convinced that the tithe as I had been taught was really at odds with justification by faith, I took the list of 32 questions to my pastor. My concerns had to do with the very foundations of my faith and essential gospel matters that I could not in good conscience ignore. He didn't attempt to give anything more than weak answers to one or two of my questions, but he said how much he disagreed and *"we can no longer support your ministry."* It was so painful, as this was the church that lit and fueled the fire for missions in my heart; that prayed for me when I went on mission trips. I was totally *"ruined"* for anything but being a missionary and seeing Jesus heal people. I'd invested everything into it.

If it was just about getting my church to back me, I could have easily said *"OK, I believe in tithing."* But I couldn't lie to myself. Truth has always been vital to me, and this was about much more than the amount we give. It was about justification. Everybody would deny that, but it was the main issue. Did I receive the blessing and get included in God's family by giving a tenth of my income, or by hanging my life on Christ? Was Jesus's redemptive work sufficient to break every curse and put me in right standing before the Father, or was it not enough unless I paid a tithe on top of it?

Many unbelievers were being healed and experiencing supernatural signs as I prayed for them and talked about Jesus. I saw about 20 New-Agers healed in just one day and shared the gospel with them. I would weep because I wanted to bring the gospel to more people. At the time, I had an invitation from Muslim friends to visit them and stay in their house for a few months. It was a country in Central Asia where Christianity is illegal and many people have never heard the gospel. I'd already shared the gospel with them, and Jesus healed one of them from chronic stomach pain. She felt a heat come on her belly as I prayed, and the pain left.

I knew that if I went, their family members and friends would be healed. I had the invitation and I wouldn't have to pay for food or lodging while I was there. I spoke enough Russian (their second language) to pray for people and talk about Jesus. I was willing to risk the danger of going there. If I got caught proselytizing, maybe I would just be fined or kicked out of the country for sharing the gospel rather than imprisoned as a native might be. What could be a better opportunity than this to bring the gospel to those who hadn't heard it?

But I would have had to pay my travel and pay the mortgage on the house when I was gone. I was broke after returning from a 7-week mission trip and a 3-week trip after that. I regretted buying a house. I struggled, feeling like maybe I just needed to have more faith for finances. I still hadn't completely broken free from feeling that *"something is terribly wrong with YOU if you face a financial need."*

I was in a position that few others were in to bring the gospel to a nation closed to evangelism, but it felt like my hopes of ever receiving missionary support were nearly crushed. My pastor would not even ask the church to stand behind me in prayer. Even on the applications for short-term mission trips I'd taken, they always asked if I was a tither. I had proudly checked the box *"Yes."* I still fellowshipped at church, but except for the youth group I could now only have spectator status, on probation as a supposedly *"disobedient Christian."* What could I do? This was no longer a matter of if I gave more or less than 10%. It was a matter of conscience. How could I lie to myself about a matter that was so clear, or accept a means of obtaining God's blessing other than faith in Christ?

After I got married, I moved to Brazil in spite of great difficulty. A scaffold collapsed under me before I went. I was bedridden for several weeks and only made about $15,000 that year. There was one problem after another. I spent thousands on the move and documents. I couldn't legally work in Brazil when I first came here. I understand why the Israelites shared their tithe with the foreigners in their land![20] If Christians were under the Mosaic tithe that Malachi refers to, Brazilian Christians should have been sharing their tithes with me!

I had maintained a connection with believers when I was in the US, but I had very little trust for churches in Brazil and didn't believe they would accept me because of my beliefs. (Which were and continue to be quite orthodox, but do not include tithing.) I continued to minister healing to neighbors and people I met, but I sometimes worried that they might end up worse if I sent them to a church.

After a few years, I started attending a small Baptist church that was marked strongly by sincere love with no manipulation. I could feel from a distance that it was different, before I even attended. I felt a glory there that I didn't feel in many charismatic

---

[20] Deuteronomy 14:28-19

churches, and it reminded me of how I encountered God's love when I first got saved. I started giving there because the pastor was not teaching tithing.

The Holy Spirit Lifting and Strengthening Me in the Middle of Hardship

In 2015 and 2016, I started writing the books God had put on my heart years before. As I wrote, I felt God's glory coming on my body tangibly again as I had before. I wrote with many tears. God softened my heart, bringing me back to a place of joy, and restoring me to the commission he'd given me to encourage pastors. He brought me back to a place of thanksgiving for the church and focusing first on the work of the Holy Spirit in the congregations. I turned from self-pity to living in love, and I saw an increase in miracles, even over Facebook messenger.

I also started teaching a group of Christians weekly, and for about a year I got a word of knowledge for healing for every new person that visited (to the best of my memory), and they were healed. I made friends with some pastors in Brazil. I've prayed for them and wept and rejoiced at seeing what God was doing in their congregations. In the few times I've gotten to speak to other groups of Christians here, more than once I was not aware of anybody who asked for healing ministry leaving without being healed.

We took in Edgar, an old man who was being robbed, and cared for him until he died. We faced death and kidnapping threats for helping him. Some of my Facebook friends rallied to help us care for Edgar's needs during that time. I had to lift him by the armpits and help my father-in-law to bathe him, clean his poop, and change his diaper. I vomited more than once because of the smell, but I had great joy in helping the old man. At times during the last few years, I felt so hard-pressed that I didn't know if I would live or die. I resolved that as long as I lived, I wanted to live for Jesus.

Wanting Prayer and Fellowship

When I was visiting the US in 2017, I met with the pastor of the church that had been my home congregation in the US. I had never stopped attending there until I moved to Brazil. I shared our difficulties and asked him to agree to disagree about the tithe, but to put us on the prayer list with the other missionaries. He said they couldn't join with me in that way if I didn't believe in tithing.

I was working hard, risking my life and using my resources to help an old man, facing a kidnapping threat against my daughter, seeing Jesus heal people on the street, at the snack bar, in their homes, and in church, but often at the end of my rope. Yet he still seemed to think I was a stingy and disobedient Christian, and I couldn't persuade him to put us on the prayer list!

I know many of the people in the congregation would have loved to pray for us, and I'm so thankful for all the Facebook friends who prayed for us and helped us to care for Edgar. I even think that the assistant pastor would have agreed to pray for us as missionaries if I'd talked to him first.

How We Bought a Business and Fell Into Fraud

I just wanted to preach and strengthen the churches, but my job teaching English via the internet is mostly at night and on weekends. I was barely ever able to attend the Baptist church on Sundays. I wanted my wife to no longer have to leave early in the morning for work, face highway robberies, and come home late at night. I wanted my daughter to have time with her mom. I wanted to have more to give to ministries I believe in. So, we borrowed money, promising to pay it back with the sale of my house in the US, and opened a franchise here in Brazil. It was a kiosk in the mall, and the financial statements we had received showed that it was already making a small monthly profit.

As we were opening the franchise in late 2017, I was visiting the US and several people gave strong prophesies about financial justice. I thought it meant that God was restoring us with the business we were opening. Now I think it was because God saw that we were in the process of being robbed.

We had a great struggle to keep the business open and got more and more in debt to pay the bills. I hadn't imagined it could lose money so fast! We took out loans to convert the kiosk to a store so as to offer more services. After over a year, some friends in the US prayed for us. My eyes opened, and I realized the kiosk was not viable when we bought it. The salesperson had lied to us.

I went to the shopping center and asked for the figures the business had reported to them before we bought it. Their figures were almost 10,000 reais per month lower than the financial statements the salesperson had shown me before we bought the business. Contrary to the balance sheets the franchise had shown us, the shopping center's figures showed that the business had been losing money quickly. When I saw this, I thought I had a solid case for criminal fraud, but unfortunately it is often difficult to get justice through Brazil's legal system.

I started emailing the franchise with questions, and they soon sent me financial figures for the months before we bought the business – including months their salesperson had told us they didn't have figures for, due to a robbery. Thus, the franchise itself proved to me that their salesperson had lied by giving me information their representative had hidden by telling us it was unavailable before we purchased the business.

Confronting Injustice

I had heard the franchise founder was a Christian and a God-fearing woman, so I sent her a respectful message on Facebook showing the evidence of wrong, such as differing financial statements, pleading for help, and asking her to meet with us at their headquarters, a four-hour drive from our house. The franchise had also forced us to use an out-of-state architecture firm which did not send anybody personally to see the location of the store they were doing a blueprint for. The blueprint was full of errors which had cost us many thousands of reais, putting us deep in debt and increasing the cost of the job about 50,000 reais over what was estimated. We brought it with us to show the errors.

I asked her to help us in view of the situation, since the franchise had caused us great financial damage. I thought it could very well be possible that she really was a God-fearing person. If so, she would certainly help us, seeing that her salesperson had lied to us and the franchises' errors ate up our remaining capital. We were already way behind on what we owed the franchise, and they were calling my wife all the time to collect on past-due franchise fees.

The franchise owner responded nicely and said she would certainly be there, but she was not there when we arrived. We reminded her staff that we drove four hours to be there because the franchise founder had promised to be at the meeting, so they contacted her and said she was coming later.

We had the meeting, showing the evidence of fraud, showing the blueprint for the store which was all wrong, and playing an audio clip of the manager who was there before we purchased the business, saying the problem was always lack of movement and sometimes the place only attended to one or two people a day. (It would have had to average well over twenty people a day to have made the figures in the financial reports we'd seen.) The staff's eyes were wide when they heard the audio clip, but nobody responded.

Then the founder of the franchise entered. She refused to hear any of our complaints, although I had sent her the evidence earlier. She put all the blame on us and on our manager for the business failing, then promised very nicely to help us.

"Your Tithe Must Not Be Right"

At the end, she sent everyone else out to have a personal meeting with us, saying she was speaking no longer as a businessperson but as a fellow believer. The first thing she said was that she had been in the same position, and God showed her that her tithe wasn't right and her relationship with her husband wasn't right, and she would never prosper until she got those things right. And so, she told us that we would never prosper until we got our marriage and our tithe right.

How did she know if we were tithing or anything about our marriage? Do you see the depth of deception and self-righteousness? One of the greatest deceptions in the church is that people's standing with God can be measured by their financial position. This lady's franchise had lied and defrauded us in the sale of the business and then directly caused many thousands of reais in losses with the blueprint and construction. Nevertheless, she assumed her financial standing was evidently God's blessing because of her tithe, and our struggle obviously must mean we were not tithing.

Her response, unfortunately, is all too similar to the response of many staunch tithers when I tell them that I believe the Biblical pattern is generosity that is not under compulsion or of necessity. It is immediate judgment, overflowing with self-righteousness, as if the only reasons one could not believe in tithing were lack of faith, lack of commitment to God, being a freeloader, or stinginess.

Few seem to be willing to seriously engage with what scripture actually says about the subject, or to even be aware that there have been many Christians who have given generously and risked their lives for the gospel without believing in tithing.

Tightening the Noose

I confronted the franchise owner and someone else in her business more directly, calling out lies and injustices. We had been trying to sell the business for a low price to someone who didn't have debt, so we could pay our employees. But instead of recognizing the injustice of the situation and helping us, the franchise just kept trying to make more money off the deal.

One lady came to my wife, asking her if it was true that she was selling the business because she was moving to the US to get married. What a preposterous fabrication the salesperson told her!

Chapter 2

We had told the franchise we didn't want them lying to sell our business and we had increased the number of clients enough through advertising so that it could be profitable for someone without debt. But the franchise's salespeople continued to lie and defraud others, and the owner still thought she was blessed because of her tithe and we must not be right with God because of our financial straits.

How did she respond to my message which called out the lies and fraud directly and pleaded with her for justice? She blocked me on Facebook and the franchise threatened more fines.

I didn't know what to do. I was in a new city and didn't know Christians there, still working nights and weekends, but wanting to be involved in the church. I missed my new friend Pastor Jorge and other people in Rio. Our employees hadn't received their full salary, and it cost even more to fire them. I thought I should have a solid legal case of fraud against the franchise, but my wife consulted with lawyers and they said that I could actually go to jail and they could charge me with fraud. When I declared my assets as we bought the business, I apparently must not have understood that I was only supposed to declare a house as an asset if it didn't have a mortgage.

As of the second edition of this book, several financial miracles have changed our situation considerably. But judge for yourselves. Did I get in such a position because I stopped paying a tithe? Was I stingy? Did I just not know how to trust God? Or could it be that people's hearts, love, and giving can't be measured by a percentage? Could it be that some people are rich because of fraud, and some people are poor because of injustice?

Could it be that God judges by so much more than a percentage of our money, he sees our hearts, and giving could be risking your life to rescue an old man, then cleaning his poop and caring for him, not just money?

It could be going to minister healing to people when you don't have money for the trip but love compels you. It could be buying diapers and milk for a homeless mother. And it could just be going into a very difficult situation because love is compelling you and you believe God sent you.

Chapter 3
Who's Teaching Salvation by Tithing?

Deception Starts Subtly

I'm convinced that common tithe teachings undermine the very foundations of the gospel and seduce Christians away from relating to God through Jesus. Of course, almost everybody who teaches tithing would deny that they are teaching salvation by tithing. The more recent trend is claiming to teach *"tithing by grace."* Realizing some of the inherent problems with the more traditional tithing message, more people are saying they teach tithing without the curse.

The logical conclusion of most modern tithe teachings is salvation by tithing. Even many who claim to teach *"tithing by grace"* are continuing to teach salvation by tithing. I can already see some people's eyes rolling, thinking I'm blowing this thing way out of proportion! We are going to come face to face with serious issues that cannot be ignored. As shocking as it seems, this is an area of widespread deception in the body of Christ. There is mainstream acceptance even of statements blatantly teaching salvation by tithing.

Satan is a serpent. He brings in a lie and packages it to look like truth. Deception starts subtly. Few people would go from believing *"By grace you have been saved, through faith"* to *"Your tithe gets you into heaven."* It takes a number of steps to get there.

2 Corinthians 11:2-4 (NRSV) I feel a divine jealousy for you, for I promised you in marriage to one husband, to present

you as a chaste virgin to Christ. But I am afraid that as the serpent deceived Eve by its cunning, your thoughts will be led astray from a sincere and pure devotion to Christ. For if someone comes and proclaims another Jesus than the one we proclaimed, or if you receive a different spirit from the one you received, or a different gospel from the one you accepted, you submit to it readily enough.

Satan is quite happy if we give lip service to a truth while living and thinking according to a lie. It's called being double minded. Even if most Christians would deny that tithing gets them into heaven, how many are fundamentally relating to God on the basis of their tithe, or their works, instead of on the basis of Christ's work? I would have never have said I believed in salvation by tithing, but I was ashamed to approach God without my tithe!

Here's one example of how deception starts subtly: you've probably heard this widespread teaching, but may not have stopped to carefully consider the implications of what you were hearing. Maybe you'll listen to those messages again with new ears.

It says the bread and wine Melchizedeck gave to Abraham were communion elements, Jesus's body and blood, and Abraham made a covenant with God by his tithe so he could eat the bread and wine. It says *"the tithe is the covenant."* Many who have accepted this teaching are trying to relate to God as if the tithe was their *"covenant connection"* to him.

Kenneth Copeland teaches this. The pastors of the church I attended loved him. They would categorically deny teaching salvation by tithing, but they acted like I was out of covenant with God when I stopped tithing. They also decided I could no longer be in covenant with them! That is cognitive dissonance.

Charisma News recently published an opinion article entitled *This Tithing Myth is Robbing the Church's Widows and Poor People.*[21] Most of the responses to the article in Facebook comments were

---

[21] Online: *https://www.charismanews.com/opinion/80291-this-tithing-myth-is-robbing-the-church-s-widows-and-poor-people* Accessed March 13th, 2020

cries of *"heresy"* or *"blasphemy,"* or *"sad to see this in Charisma."* I asked several people why they thought the article was so bad. Their responses reveal how many of them think that tithing is the gospel.

One man said *"It's the activator in our covenant with God. It's the curse breaker."* He then linked me to Kenneth Copeland's website to help me better understand tithing and covenant.

That is a typical response of many who think tithing is a fundamental of the Christian faith. I reminded him that the New Covenant is between Jesus and the Father, and we partake of its benefits by identification with Christ through faith. If you have to tithe to take communion or have a covenant with God, you are saved by tithing.

Faith is the activator, and the blood of Jesus breaks the curse. If we need the tithe to activate our covenant with God or break the curse, faith is void and Jesus's blood is insufficient.

> **Romans 3:24-25 (NRSV) …they are now justified by his grace as a gift, through the redemption that is in Christ Jesus, whom God put forward as a sacrifice of atonement by his blood, effective through faith.**

Lest anyone say *"Don't dismiss the principle because of abuse,"* many teachers claim to teach tithing by grace, yet they are still teaching people relate to God on the basis of their tithe. No matter how much you try to dress up tithing as *"grace,"* it still misrepresents how God relates to us. I fully agree with Matthew Narramore:

> **The doctrine of tithing cannot be held by people without affecting their whole understanding of life in Christ. It colors their view of every individual subject, such as righteousness, grace, salvation, and blessing. It distorts the message of the finished work of Christ. It neutralizes the power of the New Covenant. It detracts from the glory of being a son of God in Christ, seated with him at the Father's right hand, and reigning in life. It diminishes God's goodness, it is a**

hindrance to his working, and it is inferior to the relationship that he expects to have with his sons.[22]

What Does Salvation Encompass?

I hold the *"full gospel"* position on salvation. That is to say, a scriptural understanding of salvation includes so much more than a ticket to heaven. It includes wholeness, healing, peace, provision, deliverance, and most of all, full access to approach God the Father and experience continual communion with him by grace. Communion with God produces the fruit of holiness.

Many Charismatic preachers are inconsistent in their definition of salvation. They preach the *"full package"* of what salvation includes, and I agree. They categorically deny that they are preaching salvation by tithing. But then they say you obtain blessing, provision, and wholeness through your tithe, because they have suddenly switched their definition of salvation from *"full gospel"* to *"a ticket into heaven."* They teach that you get your ticket into heaven by grace alone, but you only get the *"full package"* of salvation by your tithe.

When Benny Hinn called giving $1,000 to get a breakthrough *"selling the gospel,"* he recognized what should be obvious to anybody who holds a full-gospel position. If you believe God's blessing is part and parcel of salvation, then it logically follows that trying to obtain God's blessing with money is trying to obtain salvation with money.

Ephesians 2:8-9 (NRSV) For by grace you have been saved through faith, and this is not your own doing; it is the gift of God— not the result of works, so that no one may boast.

Many of us know this as a foundational verse about salvation, and agree that anybody who teaches otherwise is teaching a false gospel. However, we sometimes miss the fact that *"salvation"* here

---

[22]Narramore, *Matthew E. Tithing: Low-Realm, Obsolete & Defunct.* Graham, NC: Takoa Pub., 2004. Chapter 10

is more than a ticket to heaven upon death. The word *"salvation"* in Ephesians 2:8 is *"sozo"* in Greek. The meaning of *"sozo"* is practical, and the gospels often translate it *"healed"* or *"made whole."*

Scripture does apply *"sozo"* to being born-again, but the Bible also often uses it in the context of physical healing or in other ways. Everyone who touched Jesus was made whole (sozo).[23] God saved (sozo) Paul from a shipwreck.[24] The scriptural uses and contexts for this word are foundational for those of us who believe the *"full gospel"* message.

Scripture speaks of salvation as past, present, and future. Being born again and forgiven is salvation in the past. Jesus dealt with sin once and for all by the sacrifice of himself. God's present deliverance and the practical application of his grace in our lives is salvation present. If you need to be delivered or healed now, the scriptural promises of salvation apply. Receiving our resurrected, glorified body is salvation future. Salvation past, present, and future are all by grace and not of works.

According to scripture, the righteous are already surrounded with God's favor,[25] and those in Christ are already blessed with every spiritual blessing in heavenly places![26] Scripture says we must continue in God's grace the same way that we first received it. If it's not the way you first received God's grace, it's not how you continue in God's grace!

Galatians 3:1-5 You foolish Galatians! Who has bewitched you? Before your very eyes Jesus Christ was clearly portrayed as crucified. I would like to learn just one thing from you: Did you receive the Spirit by the works of the law, or by believing what you heard? Are you so foolish? After beginning by means of the Spirit, are you now trying to finish by means of the flesh? Have you experienced so much in vain—if it really

---

[23] Mark 6:56
[24] Acts 27
[25] Psalm 5:12
[26] Ephesians 1:3

was in vain? So again, I ask, does God give you his Spirit and work miracles among you by the works of the law, or by your believing what you heard?

Colossians 2:6-9 (NKJV) As you therefore have received Christ Jesus the Lord, so walk in Him, rooted and built up in Him and established in the faith, as you have been taught, abounding in it with thanksgiving. Beware lest anyone cheat you through philosophy and empty deceit, according to the tradition of men, according to the basic principles of the world, and not according to Christ.

Some say *"You're just overreacting to abuse, but that doesn't negate the principle. We don't preach the curse. We preach God's grace. There is no condemnation for not tithing. Failing to tithe won't bring a curse on you. But all the blessings for tithing certainly apply!"*

If you didn't first receive Christ by tithing, then don't try to *"get your miracle"* or *"get your blessing"* now with a tithe. If you didn't initially get God's blessing by tithing, neither do you continue in God's blessing now by tithing. Galatians 3:5 includes financial miracles—we receive them by believing God's word, not by the works of the law.

Larry Burkett wrote that the tithe isn't law, because there is no punishment for not tithing. Yet he said God will withhold his blessing if you don't tithe![27] Isn't that a punishment?

Trying to obtain the blessing by your tithe is the same error as trying to avoid the curse by your tithe. It is beginning by the Spirit and trying to finish in the flesh. Colossians talks about those who would cheat us according to the *"tradition of men"* and the *"basic principles of this world"* so that we would fail to live *"according to Christ."* Today's tithe is a *"tradition of men,"* differing vastly in both practice and principle from the tithe under the Mosaic law. And if

---

[27] Burkett, Larry. *Giving and Tithing - Includes Serving and Stewardship.* Moody Press, 1999. Pg. 36

you are relying on the tithe as a *"basic principle"* by which to obtain blessing, you are not living *"according to Christ."*

1 Corinthians 1:19-20 (NKJV) For the Son of God, Jesus Christ, who was preached among you by us—by me, Silvanus, and Timothy—was not Yes and No, but in Him was Yes. For all the promises of God in Him are Yes, and in Him Amen, to the glory of God through us.

If the promise is *"yes"* for you in Christ, it is not according to your tithe. Romans 11:6 says that if it is according to grace, it cannot be by works or grace would no longer be grace. Consider Romans 8:*32:* "He who did not spare his own Son, but gave him up for us all—how will he not also, along with him, graciously give us all things?" How then can it be that we need to give a tithe to receive God's promises? Don't be taken captive by the traditions of men and the basic principles of this world!

Many teachers rightly say getting into heaven is *"by grace, through faith, and not of works."* Yet they go on to teach that we get God's present blessing, healing, provision, or deliverance by works. When you understand that a biblical view of salvation includes healing, deliverance, and every other promise of God in Christ, it follows that such a preacher is teaching salvation by tithing. He may say you'll get into heaven someday by God's grace, but he's teaching people to relate to God practically and presently through their own self-righteous works.

Salvation is by grace through faith, and not of works, from the beginning to the end. God's grace transforms us, manifests God's nature through us, and empowers us. It brings us healing, deliverance, provision, and blessing. We continue to receive God's grace in the way we first received it. If you didn't first receive God's grace by tithing, you don't continue to receive it by tithing. If you didn't get saved by tithing, you don't continue in your salvation by tithing either.

Some preachers suggest giving money in the offering can release a person's healing or get them closer to it. Yet the Bible teaches healing as part and parcel of salvation, just as the forgiveness of sins is. Jesus paid for it with his blood.

The Catholic Church used to sell *"indulgences."* People gave money to the church for their sins to be forgiven. When we understand that healing is just as much a part of salvation as forgiveness is, we should understand that suggesting anyone can obtain healing by giving money is equal to selling indulgences.

The tithe doctrine has paved the way for other errors. In one of the ministries that has had the greatest impact on my life, a conference speaker said *"I'm not saying you can buy your healing but..."* He went on to suggest that *"sowing a seed"* could help you receive your healing. Those who believe the full gospel must recognize this as no different than saying *"I'm not saying you can buy your forgiveness but sowing a seed can help you to receive it."* Yeah right!

I wished I could speak with the leaders of this ministry and say *"You've imparted so much to my life that I can never thank you enough. I appreciate you, but you're in bed with serious error. How can you allow a speaker to say such a thing without rebuking them in the fear of the Lord? How can you invite a speaker back who teaches such a thing?"*

Let's examine the implications of some of the most common teachings about tithing and how they logically lead to salvation by tithing, subtly seducing people away from relating to God through Christ. We'll then see how these steps have led to more blatant teachings of salvation by tithing.

Righteousness, Blessing, Salvation

Righteousness is being made right with God. Jesus is our righteousness, and scripture says we receive righteousness by faith, apart from the law. Any righteousness apart from Christ is as good as filthy rags.[28] These teachings are foundational throughout the New Testament.

> **1 Corinthians 1:30-31 (NRSV) He is the source of your life in Christ Jesus, who became for us wisdom from God, and righteousness and sanctification and redemption, in order that, as it is written, Let the one who boasts, boast in the Lord.**

> **Titus 3:5 (NRSV) He saved us, not because of any works of righteousness that we had done, but according to his mercy, through the water of rebirth and renewal by the Holy Spirit.**

Here's the important thing: righteousness and blessing are inseparable. You can't be righteous and cursed. If you are righteous, you have God's blessing. Since Jesus is our righteousness, we obtain God's blessing through what Jesus has done, and not through any works of our own.

> **Psalm 5:12 (NRSV) For you bless the righteous, O Lord; you cover them with favor as with a shield.**

> **Proverbs 10:6 (NRSV) Blessings are on the head of the righteous.**

> **Psalm 112:6 (NRSV) For the righteous will never be moved; they will be remembered forever.**

All God's promises are yes in Christ. If you're in Christ, the promises of God are yes for you. You can't be in Christ and cursed. If you are in Christ, you are blessed with every spiritual blessing in heavenly places.[29]

---

[28] Isaiah 54:6
[29] Ephesians 1:3

Is the Blessing or Curse Hinged on Your Tithe?

I grew up hearing, based on Malachi 3:8-10, that I'd be abundantly blessed if I tithed and gave offerings, but I'd be cursed if I didn't. There are multiple layers of problems with using Malachi to teach a tithe for Christians today, and we'll deal with them in another chapter. For now, let's consider the implications of the blessing or curse hinging on your tithe.

Scripture teaches righteousness and blessing go together. Therefore, if we try to attain the blessing or avoid the curse by tithing, we are trying to be justified by tithing. We may say we believe we're justified through Jesus's work alone, but the way we are practically relating to God is now through our tithe.

The gospel says we are delivered from the curse and receive the blessing because of what Jesus did. Trying to obtain the blessing by your tithe is the same error as trying to avoid a curse by your tithe. Don't be deceived into trying to attain through works that which Jesus has already attained for you. Galatians is crystal clear that this issue of the blessing or the curse boils down to justification. The blessing or curse could only be hinged on your tithe if you were justified by tithing. But you aren't! Don't let anybody subject you to a curse that Jesus has redeemed you from.

Galatians 3:10-14 (NRSV) For all who rely on the works of the law are under a curse; for it is written, "Cursed is everyone who does not observe and obey all the things written in the book of the law." Now it is evident that no one is justified before God by the law; for "The one who is righteous will live by faith." But the law does not rest on faith; on the contrary, "Whoever does the works of the law will live by them." Christ redeemed us from the curse of the law by becoming a curse for us—for it is written, "Cursed is everyone who hangs on a tree"— in order that in Christ Jesus the blessing of Abraham might come to the Gentiles, so that we might receive the promise of the Spirit through faith.

I've often heard it taught that we receive the blessing of Abraham by tithing. That's essentially the same error as it would be to teach that the blessing of Abraham came through circumcision. It came through faith, apart from tithes or circumcision.

Vitor Azevedo, the Brazilian pastor we mentioned earlier, shared the story of a woman who thought she got cancer because she didn't pay her tithe. Sadly, there are now millions of Christians who think like her due to Malachi-based tithe teaching.

Open Heavens

The other way the misapplication of Malachi's words undermines foundational gospel truth is that Christians are told their tithes open the heavens over them. Many have taught this without realizing or fully considering the scriptural implications of their teaching. Whether the teaching that tithing opens the heavens is shared knowingly or in ignorance, it still fundamentally changes how Christians seek to relate to God. What is an open heaven, according to scripture?

The book of Hebrews describes the Jewish temple and sacrificial system and then explains how all of these things were patterns of the *"true realities"* in the New Covenant. It teaches that the true Most Holy Place, which Jesus entered on our behalf, is heaven itself.

Hebrews 9:24 For Christ did not enter a sanctuary made with human hands that was only a copy of the true one; he entered heaven itself, now to appear for us in God's presence.

The next chapter continues:

Hebrews 10:19-22 Therefore, brothers and sisters, since we have confidence to enter the Most Holy Place by the blood of Jesus, by a new and living way opened for us through the curtain, that is, his body, and since we have a great priest over

the house of God, let us draw near to God with a sincere heart and with the full assurance that faith brings.

When it says we have confidence to enter the Most Holy Place, Hebrews isn't speaking of the Jewish temple but of the same Most Holy Place that Jesus entered—heaven itself! When we approach God's *"throne of grace,"* we enter heaven! Scripture is absolutely clear here that our open heaven is the torn body of Jesus! A scriptural understanding of an open heaven shows it corresponds to salvation and access to God's presence by grace.

Therefore, to teach we can attain to an open heaven through tithing is to teach salvation through tithing. To say that tithing opens the heavens is to put the tithe in the place of Jesus's sacrifice and what it accomplished. Don't try to attain by tithing that which Jesus attained for you by dying. His torn body is the open door to heaven now; full access to God and to every blessing that is part and parcel of salvation.

Jesus said that God makes his sun rise on the evil and the good, and sends rain on the righteous and unrighteous.[30] He said that God is kind to even the ungrateful and the wicked.[31]

It's absurd to teach that God would curse (or *"withhold blessing"* from) a righteous person for not tithing when he blesses even the unrighteous out of his magnanimous heart! Keep continuing in your salvation in the way you first received it! Good works are the fruit of having received God's life, and not a means of attaining it.

How Is Malachi-Based Tithe Teaching Leading Christians To Relate to God?

Most pastors deny they teach salvation by tithing. Yet if your teaching leads people to relate to God presently on the basis of their tithes, you actually are teaching salvation by tithing and

---

[30] Matthew 5:45
[31] Luke 6:35

contradicting the message that leads to the manifestation of God's glory in and through the church.

I thought I went to one of the least legalistic and most grace-based churches I knew, but when I got into a pressing situation, I realized that I didn't feel like I could approach God in the same way since I wasn't paying my tithe. I knew many other Christians would feel the same. That was when I started to question what I was basing my relationship with God on.

Others, even from *"grace-based"* churches, have suddenly found they felt a tremendous amount of confusion, guilt, and condemnation over this issue when they were in a pressing situation. One person from a *"grace-preaching"* church had disagreed with me so strongly about the tithe just two years earlier. She broke down crying because she was in a pressing financial situation and felt so much guilt and condemnation about struggling to pay her tithe. Even though she was tithing, it was such a burden every time that she couldn't do it with joy and then felt condemned because she was trying so hard to do it joyfully and felt she couldn't so she was a bad Christian.

I could relate to her. When I was tithing, I'd been taught that giving only started beyond my tithe. So, I always felt like I wasn't giving enough. After all, Malachi said *"You've robbed me in tithes and offerings."* I hadn't considered that the tithes Malachi talked about were crops and livestock and the *"offerings"* Malachi referred to included animal sacrifices. I was always wondering at what point my offerings were enough. Have you ever been there? You always try harder and it's never enough. That is not the gospel I first received!

In his video *"Tithing will kill you,"*[32] Pastor Bertie Brits shares his testimony of how tithing totally changed how he related to God and to other people. He began to judge other people's relationship

---

[32] Brits, Bertie *Healing For The Financially Abused (Tithing Will Kill You)* Online https://www.youtube.com/watch?v=VcyYnrQp7YA. Accessed December 3rd, 2019. Also in his book: Brits, Bertie. *Jesus Is the Tithe: the Message of God.* South Africa: Bertie Brits, 2019. Chapter 2.

with God by their financial situation. Instead of the compassion he previously showed for the poor, he wondered what they were doing wrong.

He was soon *"sowing"* so much on top of his tithe that his girlfriend was stealing from the restaurant she worked at so as to give him plates of food! He lost his joy and no longer saw God as a caring Father. When none of his tithes or sowing and reaping worked as he'd been promised they would, he kept wondering what he was doing wrong, redoubling his efforts, increasing his sowing, trying to be more joyful about it, trying to root out any unbelief that must be underlying, and feeling all the more insufficient.

I can testify that he's right on. The tithe teaching changed how I related to God exactly as he describes, and I've seen it in the lives of many other people. I can relate to Bertie as to how zealous I was for the things of God. It's often the most zealous people who take the teaching the most seriously who get burnt out on it and then, hopefully, realize the fundamental errors. As Bertie describes, even if you are tithing, the accompanying teaching puts you in a place where whatever you do is never enough. The teaching says you are not even giving until it goes beyond the tithe, so unless you give significantly beyond the tithe you are *"sowing sparingly."* So, if you are *"reaping sparingly"* you must also be robbing God in offerings.

There are two sides to this coin. I was a young man who had spent a lot of money on mission trips and was in the position of being the main provider for my family for a time after I just started working. For many people who are in a tough position like that, the tithe teaching bears the fruit of guilt and condemnation. For many others, the fruit is religious pride and self-righteousness.

I was recently listening to Reverend Mike Kola Ewuosho sharing his view on the tithe.[33] Although he insisted that the tithe isn't what makes us accepted by God, he said, *"The tithe is gospel."* He also teaches that the tithe is the fruit of faith, and we are

---

[33] Debate between Rev. Ewuosho and Dr. Russel Earl Kelly Online: https://www.youtube.com/watch?v=okw70Ron6CQ Accessed August 7th, 2019

justified by faith. These are typical statements of many who teach tithing. I've heard them often. Now if the tithe is gospel, the logical implication is that those who don't tithe haven't accepted the gospel. If the tithe is of faith, the implication is that those who don't tithe don't have faith. (Although Jesus referred to the tithe not only as law but as one of the lesser matters of the law,[34] and scripture says "The law is not of faith."[35]) According to scripture, faith is what makes us acceptable to God.

For many people such as myself and my friend from a *"grace-preaching"* church who broke down crying, a blessing came with the financial difficulty. Being in such a hard position made us realize how guilty we felt without our tithe, and thus we examined the foundation of our faith in Christ. We would have never thought we were relating to God on the basis of our tithe until we tried approaching him without a tithe.

The Implications of Tithing as a Requirement for Church Membership

A church may categorically deny teaching salvation by tithing, but if their acceptance or non-acceptance of people into fellowship (or even good standing for leadership) hinges on a tithe, consider what that implies. Remember that a scriptural understanding of salvation includes full access to approach Father God without shame.

We are ambassadors of Christ and the body of Christ on the earth. If the church's acceptance of someone into fellowship depends on the tithe, the church is essentially telling people that being accepted by Christ depends on the tithe. If the church's approval depends on a tithe, the implication is that God's approval depends on a tithe. If the church's qualification for ministry depends on a tithe, the implication is that Christ's qualification for us to obey his call depends on our tithe. And thus, in all

---

[34] Matthew 23:23
[35] Galatians 3:12

practicality, this teaches people to attempt to approach God based on their works rather than on Christ's work. Who are we to reject someone whom Christ has received?

Although it's hard to be sure how many churches are doing so, some are telling their people not to take communion if they haven't paid their tithes. That clearly implies that our means of salvation, Jesus's blood and body, are not given freely but only to those who pay. Thus, Christ's work on our behalf is no longer effective by grace through faith and those churches might as well be selling indulgences.

Dressing Up Tithing Doctrines As Grace Doesn't Make Them Any Less Deadly

I recently listened to a sermon by Joseph Prince, one of the world's most influential grace preachers, called *God's Plan to Prosper You in The End Times.*[36] He teaches that God's plan to provide for us and our families is through the tithe. He states that tithing is God's way of protecting us and our possessions, as well as enriching us in every area of our lives. (*"Every area"* includes the spiritual and emotional aspects as well as financial, since he includes marriages, parenting, family, and relationships.)

Prince says tithing is not out of obligation but then quotes Malachi with the interpretation *"non-tithing Christians are God-robbers,"* which is another example of cognitive dissonance. If failing to tithe is robbing God, tithing is an obligation. Prince implies that people will see God's glory on us because we tithe, and teaches that tithing opens the heavens over us and delivers us from the curse that came on Adam and Eve in Genesis. He tries to dress up the tithe as grace by saying that God doesn't curse us for not tithing, but failure to tithe puts us under the curse on the ground

---

[36] Prince, Joseph. God's Plan to Prosper You In The End Times. August 26, 2018. Sermon notes online: https://www.josephprince.com/sermon-notes/gods-plan-to-prosper-you-in-the-end-times Accessed December 18th, 2019

because of Adam's sin. (Is the threat of remaining under a curse *"obligation?"*)

Prince says that we return to God by giving tithes and offerings, which implies that we are away from God without tithes and offerings. No wonder my friends acted as if I was backsliding by failing to pay a tithe! And no wonder I felt like I couldn't approach God without my tithe! This is some of the most *"grace-based"* teaching in the charismatic church on tithing, and it's still deadly!

I don't have anything against Joseph Prince any more than I have against the apostle Peter, who got carried away with the circumcision faction. I'm pointing out that my concerns aren't just with some extremists who take tithing *"too far."* The modern tithe teaching, especially the Malachi-based version, is poisonous at its roots. The subtitle on Prince's sermon notes says *"Jesus our Passover Lamb is the reason we can be protected, healthy, and blessed."* True. Then he goes on to teach that our tithe delivers us from the curse of Adam's sin and brings God's protection and blessing.

Stop for a minute and think about that. The tithe delivers us from the curse of sin? If we need the tithe to deliver us from the curse of Adam's sin, then Jesus's blood wasn't enough to completely accomplish it or to completely undo the effects of Adam's sin. If that were the case the first Adam (in Genesis) would be greater than the last Adam (Jesus). If we need tithes to experience prosperity in every area including our relationships, marriages, and family life, the blood of Jesus was not enough to fully bring redemption to these areas. Those who claim to teach *"grace tithing"* have messages full of doublespeak and are continuing in the same error.

If we, as full-gospel believers, understand that protection, health, blessing, and deliverance from the curse of sin are part and parcel of salvation and then we say we have to tithe to get them, we are presenting salvation by tithing. My Bible says that the blood of Jesus is enough for God to reconcile all things to himself!

Colossians 1:19-20 For God was pleased to have all his fullness dwell in him, and through him to reconcile to himself all things, whether things on earth or things in heaven, by making peace through his blood, shed on the cross.

Notice that Prince talked about redemption through Jesus's blood, but then talked about the need to tithe in order to actually experience that redemption. I remember reading Jehovah's Witness literature a few times. It talks about a lot of orthodox truth, like Jesus as the Lamb of God dying for our sins. People put their guard down and start to listen, and they don't realize as they go on how truth starts to be distorted. If you haven't been warned and don't yet know about all their teachings, some of which the literature does not immediately present, it takes discernment to recognize the deception creeping in.

Similarly, tithe teachings come cloaked in good intentions. People warm up to the error without fully considering what it implies. Orthodox statements bring their guard down. But like a cold-blooded frog in a pot on the fire doesn't feel any difference if the temperature is raised slowly, they begin to increasingly accept error. What was implied now is stated blatantly. Soon it is not only your financial blessing, but your entrance into heaven that is secured by the tithe. And if the frog is suddenly snatched out of the nearly boiling water, the sudden change in temperature makes it feel as if the pot of boiling water was the norm, was right, and something is dreadfully wrong outside of it.

I don't have to wait long when I question the modern tithe tradition for people to come out of the woodwork saying things like *"Tithing is Christianity 101,"* and *"You're teaching heresy!"* Or even worse, *"You're on the highway to hell!"* These statements prove they have come to see tithing as a foundation of the Christian faith, a doctrine as fundamental as the deity of Christ or the resurrection from the dead.

The abundance of people who make such statements shows the extent of the problem in which many Christians are building their house on tithes instead of on Christ, the only true foundation that can be laid.[37] If so many make such accusations against another Christian who questions tithing, imagine how many more feel that they themselves would be in hell if not for their tithes but they can now make it into heaven because of their tithes?

The specific issue of the controversy in Galatians was circumcision, but the broader issue was the law. The specific issue today is now tithing, but the broader issue is exactly the same.

Galatians 5:7-9 You were running a good race. Who cut in on you to keep you from obeying the truth? That kind of persuasion does not come from the one who calls you. "A little yeast works through the whole batch of dough."

Matthew 16:6-8, 11-12 "Be careful," Jesus said to them. "Be on your guard against the yeast of the Pharisees and Sadducees." They discussed this among themselves and said, "It is because we didn't bring any bread." Aware of their discussion, Jesus asked, "You of little faith, why are you talking among yourselves about having no bread? ... How is it you don't understand that I was not talking to you about bread? But be on your guard against the yeast of the Pharisees and Sadducees." Then they understood that he was not telling them to guard against the yeast used in bread, but against the teaching of the Pharisees and Sadducees.

Do you think I'm blowing this out of proportion? Let's consider the extent to which the yeast is already working through the whole batch and this slippery slope starting with subtle deception has led to the acceptance of blatant and explicit teachings of salvation by tithing. It only takes a little bit of leaven, a little bit of subtle error dressed up as truth, to work through the whole batch of dough. What I'm about to share still shocks me, but it's only the tip of the iceberg and it causes me great concern for the state of the church.

---

[37] 1 Corinthians 3:11

Chapter 4
Subtle Deception Paves the Way for Blatant Error

Do You Realize How Many People Believe Your Eternal Destiny Depends on Your Tithe?

I was just reading the reviews of a few books on tithing on Amazon. One review said *"Of course no Christian believes that you are saved by tithing."* Maybe she didn't read the other reviews of the same book, or maybe the next one I saw was posted after hers was. Another review just a little after hers contained multiple statements that failing to tithe, or not believing in tithing, would send you to hell.

> For those who oppose the tithe the devil is gonna laugh in your face as he drags you into hell and throws flames on you and cuts you into pieces.

> So, when anybody claims that Mat. 23:23 was only addressed to the Pharisees and not us, then that is a damn lie from Hell. (Damn lie because it will damn you to Hell if you believe, live, or teach that lie.)

> …don't let Satan nor false teachers deceive you and fool you into thinking that "the tithe has been done away with." Not only is the church hurt but you yourself are also hurt and you even lose the salvation that Jesus worked so hard to give you

when you were first born again…don't let Satan, nor false teachers, steal your crown of eternal life.

Robbing God of his tithe…is an eternally serious sin and crime against God.

If you don't pay the tithe or teach others that the tithe no longer applies—then you are going to hell.

This is about your eternal life here. We are not discussing matters of only losing rewards. We are talking about your very soul. We are talking about everlasting damnation. We are talking about Heaven and Hell here.

These statements were all taken from a one-star review of Dr. Russel Earl Kelly's excellent book, *"Should the Church Teach Tithing?"* These are only a few quotes. The author of the review went on and on with similar rants, even saying those who teach that tithing is Old Covenant will suffer hotter fires in hell. He referred to a book called *"Hell Testimonies"* by Mike Peralta, which claims that many people are in hell for not tithing. He posted this as a review of multiple other books which he probably never read. It only shows as a verified review on Dr. Kelly's book.

Many of you might initially assume a guy writing like that is just a wacko, an extremist who believes things that very few people would actually teach. I would have assumed the same, but when I started questioning tithing, I was shocked to learn how many Christians actually think like him. You also may be shocked when you realize the extent to which this false gospel of salvation by tithing has gained ground in the church.

One American pastor recently wanted to discuss tithing with us, but we were unable to continue with a rational and respectful conversation. He continually stated that non-tithers were unsaved and destined to hell, rather than engaging in any biblical discussion. I am still shocked by how often this line of thinking comes out when discussing tithing.

Many Africans, and especially Nigerians, are well-acquainted with the issue. Pastor Enoch Adeboye leads the Redeemed Christian Church of God, with branches in 110 countries and 5 million members in Nigeria alone. He has said bluntly, *""Anyone who is not paying his tithe is not going to heaven, full stop."*[38]

Pastor Adeboye then warned his pastors and leaders that they would also go to hell for sending other people to hell if they failed to warn their congregants that failing to tithe faithfully would send them to hell. He told a story about a pastor who was in hell for not teaching about tithing. He taught the leaders that any non-tithing member would get the whole church in trouble with God, open the door to witches and wizards, and bring God's curse on the congregation like Achan brought trouble on all of Israel.[39]

Adeboye's claim that Adam got kicked out of Eden for not tithing seems to suggest that his teaching of salvation by tithing, like Creflo Dollar's teaching, was based on Kenneth Copeland's doctrines about tithing. The leaven Jesus warned against entered with Copeland and earlier teachings, and we see how it worked through the whole lump in Creflo Dollar and Enoch Adeboye's teachings.

Some people say *"Oh, Adeboye is in Africa, and they are crazy over there."* They fail to consider that his doctrine's origins are in the United States, and it is coming full-circle. He has churches all over the world including in the US and UK.

Dr. Abel Damina is a famous African preacher who until recently was known for his heavy emphasis on tithing and give-to-get messages. Then around the same time as Benny Hinn's statements were going viral, Dr. Damina shared his personal story of turning away from such teaching, saying the whole nation should be outraged that a man would stand up and say *"Anyone who does not pay a tithe will not make heaven."* He continued *"You render the blood of Jesus useless. You render the sacrifice of Christ*

[38] *Nigerians Debate Giving 10% of the Income to the Church.* Online: https://www.bbc.com/news/world-africa-43286733
[39] Online: *https://www.facebook.com/RONALDWROBEY/videos/10216909828204217/*

useless. You render the finished work of Christ useless. And you want me to keep quiet!...You reduce the work of Christ to 10%! Is that how stingy a man can be, equating Jesus to 10%? Fatal error!"[40] In another sermon which YouTube later removed, Dr. Damina confessed he had no assurance of salvation while he was teaching tithing and give to get. He finally recognized the error!

I recently saw a video of an African pastor punishing his church members for not paying their tithes.[41] Dozens of people laid face down on the ground as the pastor went around, whipping each one with a stick. While that sounds extreme, it is not a far cry from the teaching of leading western ministers, who have called non-tithers God-robbers and threatened them with curses or even eternal damnation for their failure to tithe. After all, I'd rather have someone whip me with a switch than have God curse me!

Will western leaders consider the enormity of this issue worldwide, that there is now major controversy over whether a person can make it into heaven without a tithe? They are only taking the error we discussed in the previous chapter, imported largely from American teachers, to its logical conclusions. And the notion that tithes help secure your place in heaven has also gained unbelievable acceptance in the United States!

Christians Embrace a Book That Teaches the Tithe Secures Your Place in Heaven!

I realize many people don't like the word *"heresy"* since it's been so misused to bash people who have different beliefs on non-essential issues. But when any teaching says that there is a way to the Father except through Christ, or another way to be saved, *"heresy"* is an

---

[40]*Dr. Abel Damina Takles Pastor Adeboye On Tithe Principles* Online: https://www.youtube.com/watch?v=KXbD11_BolU&fbclid=IwAR0YQAr2qzNawRDs7ml OhqdNuAG2WlHcNAnyld-nPcSo9dlsiHulqEcXm24 Accessed November 15th, 2019
[41] *Pastor Beating Members For Not Paying Tithes* Online: https://www.facebook.com/bajanmass/videos/10162603508660282/ Accessed December 15th, 2019

appropriate word. The apostle Paul treated such teaching very seriously, as we see in the book of Galatians.

As an example of how the subtle deception we discussed in the last chapter has opened the way for blatant error to spread, consider several passages from the book *"Heaven is so Real."* Consider what this book teaches and how quickly and easily it gained widespread acclaim in mainstream Christianity.

An imprint of the world's leading Charismatic/Pentecostal publisher published it. The pastor of the biggest church in the world at that time wrote the forward. It became an international bestseller, selling over a million copies, and becoming the #1 bestseller in South Korea. It was translated into more than 40 languages, and the Spanish version won the Harold Kregel 2008 Book of the Year award for *"most inspiring and impactful book"* during the Spanish Evangelical Products Association Awards in 2009.

Charismatic Christians raved over it, including people I know. I don't know how I myself read it the first time as a young teenager and did not see the blatant error. It clearly teaches salvation by works, especially that your eternal destiny hinges on your tithe.

Does a Little Poison in Your Good Food Matter?

Many Christians accuse the Jehovah's Witnesses of preaching a false gospel because they teach salvation by works. I agree, yet the false teaching of salvation by our own works in *"Heaven is so Real"* comes through even more clearly than in the Jehovah's Witness literature. The Jehovah's Witness literature has many statements teaching that Jesus died as the atonement for our sins, but they are mixed with teaching salvation by works.

If a Jehovah's Witness says *"We teach salvation by grace. We teach that Jesus died for our sins,"* Christian pastors respond, *"Yeah, but you also teach that only 144,000 elite believers have a heavenly hope and only those of that group can partake of the communion bread and wine, so that most don't dare take communion.*[42] *You teach that one must qualify for baptism by works like proselytizing and suggest that preaching enough is a requirement for obtaining salvation."*

Not for one moment would we imagine that saying something about Jesus's atonement excuses such error, or say *"A little poison isn't anything to worry about. There's a lot of good food in the Watchtower Magazine. In fact, the Jehovah's Witnesses teach that Jesus is the Lamb of God and died for our sins."*

Jehovah's Witnesses are widely considered by evangelicals to be wolves in sheep's clothing, teaching a false gospel of salvation by works because they teach that the few who make it into heaven secure their place by teaching and proselytizing. So how is it that *"Heaven is so Real"* teaches your place in heaven depends on your tithe, and it becomes a widely acclaimed international bestseller?

How is the first doctrine considered *"heresy"* while the latter is acceptable, unless there's an underlying heart issue that makes us want to overlook the latter error? Even if you personally find the doctrine that your tithe secures your place in heaven to be appalling, I want to make the case to you of how much this error has infiltrated the Pentecostal/Charismatic culture.

Will Non-Tithers Go to Hell, or to a Sad, Dry Valley Between Heaven and Hell?

I know many readers will imagine I'm taking something way out of context and extrapolating far-fetched conclusions, as many anti-charismatic *"heresy hunters"* do. Far from it! *"Heaven is so Real"* teaches salvation by tithing repeatedly and explicitly, claiming that

---

[42] Conklin, Paul K. *American Originals: Homemade Varieties of Christianity.* The University Of North Carolina Press, 1997. Page 160 https://books.google.com.br/books?id=NDrqCQAAQBAJ&pg=PA150&lpg=PA150&dq=14 4,000+who+make+the+most+converts&source=bl&ots=qzGj5bQ1W6&sig=ACfU3U1m0s_ lltwqOK-iE7hU-SUkKQkl7g&hl=pt-BR&sa=X&ved=2ahUKEwij2IDd6brmAhV1GLkGHfWiDE0Q6AEwDXoECA0QAQ#v=o nepage&q=144%2C000%20who%20make%20the%20most%20converts&f=false

God taught it directly to the author. Consider a few quotes for yourself:

> **Many Christians are poor and have problems in their lives because their hearts are not right with me and they don't tithe. Any Christian who doesn't tithe will not be blessed because they love money more than My Word. Those who love money more than My Word will never see My kingdom. You already know where they will be at the end.**[43]

The words *"My Kingdom"* in the context of the book refer to heaven. It is saying that non-tithers will never get into heaven. What is *"where they will be at the end"* referring to? Two previous passages give a clue:

> **I looked out over a brown and lifeless valley. Everywhere there was brown. The whole region seemed to be filled with dead grass.**
>
> **I noticed multitudes of people who were wearing sand-colored robes roaming aimlessly in the vicinity of the pit's yawning mouth. Their heads were hanging low and they looked very dejected and hopeless.**
>
> **"Who are these people, Lord?" I asked.**
>
> **"They are disobedient 'Christians.'"**
>
> **"How long will they have to stay in this barren, lifeless place?"**
>
> **"Forever, My daughter. The only ones who will enter My kingdom are the pure of heart-My obedient children."**

---

[43] Thomas, Choo. *Heaven Is So Real!* Expanded Edition. Charisma House, 2003. Kindle Locations 2023-2025

This passage reinforces the teaching that non-tithing (*"disobedient"*) Christians will never make it into heaven. Instead of saying they will go to hell, it seems to say they will exist in eternity at the edge of hell's pit, dejected and hopeless. Yet another passage in the book seems to say they will be thrown into the lake of fire:

> **He took me to another high mountain from which I could look down into another endless valley where a multitude of people dressed in gray-colored robes were wandering about in an apparent mood of dejection. Their robes reminded me of the gowns worn by hospital patients.**
>
> **The people looked weak and lost, and their gray faces matched the color of the robes they were wearing. They stared at the ground in front of their feet as they walked around in circles, aimlessly and hopelessly. This place was mostly men with just a few women.**
>
> **"Who are these people, Lord?"**
>
> **"They are the sinful Christians."**
>
> **"What is going to happen to them" I wondered aloud.**
>
> **"Most of them will go to the lake of fire after judgment."[44]**

When *"Heaven is so Real"* talks about sinful Christians, it says very little about sins like persistent sexual immorality. But it mentions failure to tithe more than anything else, along with lack of church attendance, not praying enough, and vague references to *"loving the world."*

---

[44] Thomas, Choo. *Heaven Is So Real!* Expanded Edition. Charisma House, 2003. Kindle Locations 1083-1087

Christians Finding No Assurance of Salvation

I've responded to various messages from people living in torment and doubting their salvation, and even if they can ever be saved. They're suffering mental torment because they are relying on their own works for salvation and they can never be good enough. I encourage them to call on the name of the Lord, receive Christ's righteousness as a free gift, and enter communion with God through the free gift of righteousness so as to bear the fruit of righteousness.

When I see the widespread acceptance of a book like *"Heaven is so Real"* among Charismatic Christians, I think *"It's no wonder that so many people are living in torment and bondage, never being able to trust in Christ's work or experience any assurance of salvation."* Few realize how many Christians either feel that they're right with God because they pay a tithe, or live in constant guilt and condemnation if they don't. Is that the gospel? Is it what Jesus died for?

It's not only non-tithing Christians who are having trouble finding assurance of salvation. It's many tithers. If Dr. Abel Damina, a famous pastor who talked all the time about tithes, all the while had no assurance of salvation, then imagine how many churchgoers are in the same boat!

The nature of the teaching is that you can never do enough. It's not only tithes, it's tithes and offerings, so how do you know when your offerings are enough? Many tithe teachings imply that if you are tithing and struggle financially, you aren't doing it in faith or from your heart. If it doesn't count to get you temporal blessing because you aren't doing it well enough, it must not count to get your eternal blessing or build up your house in heaven either! (Another article which the author's website links to shares a vision from a Presbyterian minister which teaches that your tithes provide building material for your house in heaven.[45])

---

45 Park, Yong *Getting Into Heaven* Online:
http://www.divinerevelations.info/documents/pastor_park/ Accessed December 8th, 2019

This isn't a minor or non-essential issue. I'm making my disagreement with tithing public because we are dealing with teaching that's incredibly destructive. The apostle Paul said *"But even if we or an angel from heaven should proclaim to you a gospel contrary to what we proclaimed to you, let that one be accursed!"*[46]

One lady began to doubt her salvation and felt oppression come all over her when she read *"Heaven is so Real."* She asked the Lord why and he said *"This book isn't from me. Trust in what Jesus has done for you, and throw this book out."* She then doubted if she was really hearing the Lord's voice, but she finally experienced peace when she threw it away. Likewise, my mother felt such a demonic heaviness when she read the book that she threw it on the ground and started stomping on it, saying *"Satan, you're under my feet!"*

How Many Steps Have You Taken Towards Accepting This Error?

What paved the way for the evangelical church to widely accept such blatant error? It was the subtle error of the most common tithe teachings, disguised as truth. It was only a little bit of leaven. The book *"Heaven is so Real"* only had to take the tithe teaching a little bit beyond what many pastors were already teaching in order to get to the point where your eternal destiny now hinges on your tithe. Many of the tithing messages we find in a quick YouTube search explicitly state that non-tithers are going straight to hell.

Being led astray into false doctrine happens in steps, and it begins with a heart-compromise. In this case that compromise is teaching tithing because we want it to be true and using logic that we wouldn't apply to anything else, even when the weight of scripture and church history is against it.

Some people say *"We would never teach salvation by tithing. You're just reacting to some fringe extremists."* This error is not on

---

[46] Galatians 1:8 (NRSV)

the fringe, but is now mainstream. How did *"Heaven is so Real"* become a bestseller among evangelical and charismatic Christians? If you still think I'm exaggerating or just lifting words out of context, consider yet another quote:

The Lord is very unhappy with people who are not tithing. The Lord showed and told me clearly that whoever doesn't tithe will not see His face because they love money more than Him.

The tithe is 10% of whatever your gross pay is, not your net pay. God doesn't need our money, but he wants every believer to bring the tithe to His house so the church can do God's work. Offerings are love gifts for the needy and a giving of thanks to God's house and different areas of ministry. All of God's work requires money. Anyone who is able to do these things faithfully will be blessed by Almighty God the most because it is obedient and shows love. These two things are very important commands of God.

If you truly want to be with Jesus forever in heaven and have a blessed life while you are on this earth, please pay close attention to what the Lord says. I have a responsibility to write the truth of God's words. I wrote this as clearly as I can so new believers and some Christians who are confused about the tithe and offering can fully understand.[47]

Again, it states that nobody will see God's face without tithing. It primarily defines obedience as giving tithes and offerings. *"Obedience"* has become a buzz-word for tithing, even though **there is no place in scripture that God has ever commanded gentile Christians to tithe**, and the modern tithe differs vastly from the Mosaic tithe which God commanded under the law.

---

[47] Thomas, Choo. *Heaven Is So Real!* Expanded Edition. Charisma House, 2003. Kindle Location 3073-3080

Then the book says you need to pay close attention to this if you want to be with Jesus forever in heaven. What is it saying to pay close attention to if you want to make it to heaven? The whole context leading up to this statement talks about nothing but tithes and offerings.

The Lord told me that the only ones who are truly saved are those who live according to His commandments and walk in His Holy Spirit.

Whoever believes in Him must love Him with their whole heart and have fellowship with other Christians. God also expects them to attend church and pay their tithes and offerings. Those who are unable to attend church must give their tithes and offerings to the local church or any other church.[48]

This quote comes under the heading *"Marks of salvation."* Talking about obeying God's commandments and walking in the Spirit, the whole thing is about paying tithes and offerings, church attendance, and praying enough!

Here again the book is very clearly saying that those who don't tithe aren't saved. They aren't Christians; not part of God's family. I've shared my experience when I stopped tithing. Is it any wonder that my closest friends reacted as if I were backsliding, although I loved the Lord and was trying to honor him in the best way I could? How do so many people experience what I did in good churches, even in so-called *"grace churches"* that *"teach tithing by grace?"*

With tears, I write this plea to the pastors of churches I love. Many of you say *"We'd never teach tithing in such a legalistic way,"* yet people in your own churches have had experiences similar to mine. There are people in your own churches who feel ashamed to

---

[48] Thomas, Choo. *Heaven Is So Real!* Expanded Edition. Charisma House, 2003. Kindle Location 3475-3482

approach the Father without a tithe, or feel like they can approach the Father boldly because they come with a tithe. Could it be that you have been lured into compromising with a false gospel?

The teaching of tithing is legalistic at its very root, and a little leaven works through the whole batch.[49] If you say *"I teach tithing but I'd never say it secures your place in heaven,"* I ask you to re-read the last chapter and ask yourself how many steps you've taken towards that very error. Even if you will never teach explicitly that tithing secures your place in heaven, it only takes the next generation to go a step further by taking your teaching to its logical conclusion. It may seem shocking, but it is already happening.

We Get Into Heaven by "Being Good Enough" so We Need To "Do Our Best While We Have a Chance?"

One of the foundations of the Christian faith is salvation by grace through faith in Christ, not of works, lest any man should boast.[50] Yet *"Heaven is so Real"* could not be more explicit in teaching salvation by works, and mainly, by tithing faithfully.

Whoever wants to be with the Lord Jesus forever must work for his salvation daily, all the days of his life.[51]

Here is a quote from the front page of the author's website:

He said, He is giving people a chance to know what it takes to enter His Kingdom through this book. Remember, none of our salvations are secure until the end. We must do our best while we have a chance.[52]

Where is this teaching leading Christians? Here are two reader testimonials from the revised and expanded edition of the book:

---

[49] Galatians 5:9, 1 Corinthians 5:6
[50] Ephesians 2:8+9
[51] Thomas, Choo. *Heaven Is So Real!* Expanded Edition. Charisma House, 2003. Kindle Location 3058
[52] Online: www.choothomas.org Accessed July 12th, 2019

I know that in talking to her, I want to be good enough to join her (Choo) in this glorious kingdom she has told me so much about.[53]

How has such doctrine made its way into mainstream Christianity? This reader concluded that she hoped she could be good enough to get to heaven! If we get into heaven by being *"good enough,"* we've disposed of the gospel message and our *"Christianity"* is no different than any other religion. How could the world's leading Charismatic/Pentecostal publisher share such a statement as an endorsement of the book rather than being grieved at how it is leading people away from Christ? This deception came in through the Trojan horse of the common teachings about tithing that we discussed in the previous chapter.

I tell you humbly that this book is next to the Holy Bible to know our Lord Jesus and his coming.[54]

Many critics of the charismatic movement accuse us of putting personal revelation on the same level as scripture. This is usually a straw-man argument. Yet the author of *"Heaven is so Real"* actually does treat her book as if it were scripture, saying she transcribed the words exactly as Jesus told her.[55] From the quote above it's apparent that some of her readers do too. Similarly, **many of today's churches teach the modern tithe as if it were scripture, even though it contradicts scripture on many points and it's indisputable that the first generations of the church did not practice it.**

We as Charismatics often tend to dismiss criticism because we've heard so many attacks with false accusations and faulty reasoning coming from *"heresy hunters."* I minister healing and my

---

[53] Thomas, Choo. *Heaven Is So Real!* Expanded Edition. Charisma House, 2003. Kindle Location 10

[54] Thomas, Choo. *Heaven Is So Real!* Expanded Edition. Charisma House, 2003. Kindle Location 197

[55] Thomas, Choo. *Heaven Is So Real!* Expanded Edition. Charisma House, 2003. Kindle Location 2369

life has been dramatically impacted by people closely connected to the much-criticized Toronto revival and the so-called *"NAR."* (New Apostolic Movement.)

I rejoice when people tremble, weep, shake, scream, or fall as the Holy Spirit touches them. I've written to refute the accusations that these are usually manifestations of a *"kundalini spirit."* I love the sound of wailing mixed with laughter and screams as people cry aloud to Jesus.

I am by no means a critic of the charismatic movement. I'm speaking up with great appreciation for many Charismatic Christian leaders, full of thanksgiving for the church, and saying *"We are really missing it here with the tithe teaching and in danger of being led astray. You haven't realized the implications of this teaching or where it is leading. Let's not start in the Spirit and end up in the flesh."*

It's remarkable to me is that even much of the non-charismatic criticism of *"Heaven is so Real"* says little or nothing about the really serious error in it, which is teaching salvation by works. Rather, it complains about the way the author shook and danced!

The mainstream acceptance of *"Heaven is so Real"* shows me that the false doctrine of salvation by tithing is drawing far more Christians astray than cults like the Jehovah's Witnesses are. I've known more Christians who've talked excitedly about *"Heaven Is So Real"* than I've known who got entangled in the Jehovah's Witnesses.

If tithing faithfully and working hard for our salvation every day for the rest of our lives is what gets us into heaven, we have nullified the gospel. The difference between the other major religions of the world and Christianity is that they try to qualify for salvation based on their religious works, but we preach Christ crucified and salvation by grace through faith in him.

Blatant Teaching of Salvation by Tithing Going Around the World on Christian Television

As more evidence of how easily Charismatic Christianity has embraced teaching that blatantly says your tithe gets you into heaven, consider a few quotes from Creflo Dollar. If I'm not mistaken, at the time he had a larger TV audience than any other preacher in the world.

This isn't about picking on Creflo Dollar. He developed a friendship with Andrew Farley, a pastor who teaches against tithing, and even had Andrew speak at his church. After a few years, Creflo changed his tone and publicly apologized for some of his earlier teaching that led people into bondage. He taught so-called *"grace-tithing"* for several years. But finally, about two years after the first edition of this book, Creflo made a clean break with tithe teachings, told people to throw out everything he ever wrote on the subject, and taught that tithing is irrelevant for Christians.[56]

My point is the extent to which a false gospel of salvation by tithing has made its way into mainstream Christian culture, and how easily Charismatic Christians have embraced it. Creflo was only saying what the teachings we have examined in the previous chapter logically imply.

The tithe is the covenant. [57]

If you take the time to tithe and tithe correctly, it's impossible to go to hell, because if you're doing all that, the tithe will keep you in heaven. The tithe will keep you in the presence of God. [58]

---

[56] Dollar, Creflo. The Great Misunderstanding Online: https://www.youtube.com/watch?v=zOSboAvyy9E Accessed August 21st, 2022
[57] Dollar, Creflo. Online: https://www.youtube.com/watch?v=NLsDNxZcOa8 Accessed December 16th, 2019
[58]Dollar, Creflo. Online: https://www.youtube.com/watch?v=NLsDNxZcOa8 Accessed December 16th, 2019

It's impossible to get healing or deliverance or any other promise in the word of God except through the tithe. [59]

In fact, Creflo joked about handing guns to the ushers, lining up all the non-tithers, shooting them down at the count of three *"Jesuses,"* then throwing them into a mass grave out back so that God could come to church.[60] He said, *"I'm serious. That's what they deserve if not for God's grace."*

It didn't shock me that somebody said some really stupid things, but it shocked me how many Christians I found defending such statements and even laughing at the comment about shooting down all the non-tithers and throwing them in a mass grave!

Christians' high level of acceptance of a preacher saying such things astounded me. Creflo was one of the most influential people in Christian culture, yet I heard very few Charismatic Christians, much less leaders, show even a hint of concern. Rather, if the subject was brought up, many people would go to any length to justify his words!

By the way, I can't even tell you how many non-tithers I've seen Jesus heal as I laid hands on them, and I myself was in financial distress and not giving a tithe to my local church! The statement that people can't be healed or delivered without a tithe is just laughable to me. Yet sadly, all too many Christians wonder if it's true.

Creflo's statements didn't really go a whole lot further than what some of the other teachers who've done the most to promote tithing have said or strongly implied.

Demonically Inspired Rage

The hatred and anger evident in the joke about shooting down non-tithers is perfectly consistent with the self-righteous and

---

[59] Dollar, Creflo. Online: https://www.youtube.com/watch?v=NLsDNxZcOa8 Accessed December 16th, 2019

[60] Dollar, Creflo. Online: https://www.youtube.com/watch?v=NLsDNxZcOa8 Accessed December 16th, 2019

furious responses of many Christians if anybody so much as questions if tithing is the biblical model for Christians' giving today. I've experienced this again and again. It shows that so much more than being a minor doctrinal disagreement, it is a case of demonic deception.

I know some pastors will be shocked and have trouble believing me when I talk about how pervasive this level of hatred and self-righteous judgmentalism has become. I guess you would hardly know if you've never questioned the tithe. I was also shocked when I encountered it.

Consider how eager Christians were to embrace and defend one of the world's most influential preachers joking about shooting down non-tithers and throwing them in a mass grave. You can hardly imagine the extent of damage such teaching has caused in the body of Christ, especially in poverty-ridden places like Africa where it has reached.

Ministers who didn't blink an eye when Creflo explicitly taught salvation by tithing were furious when he recently repented. Their anger at his repentance revealed their hearts. Charisma magazine even published an article accusing him of heresy.[61]

One friend of mine, a pastor and a godly man, became so angry when I questioned the tithe that he later came back and apologized. He didn't know why he acted so irrationally and out-of-character. It was like something came over him. He was a godly man, but had a demonic stronghold rooted in tithe teachings. Another friend who became very angry when I talked about tithing heard the Holy Spirit respond *"The reason you are so angry is because what he's saying is true."*

We have heard the same testimony from other people. Bertie Brits tells of a man who wrote a book on tithing. It was endorsed by well-known leaders and about to be published. Then he heard

---

[61] Morgan, Jamie. Pastor, Revivalist Calls Out Creflo Dollar for Anti-Tithing Pronouncement. https://charismamag.com/spriritled-living/pastor-revivalist-calls-out-creflo-dollar-for-anti-tithing-pronouncement/ Accessed August 21st, 2022

Bertie preaching that the tithe has no value for Christians today. He became furious, thinking it was righteous indignation. And the Holy Spirit said, *"You are furious because everything Bertie is saying is true."* He repented.[62]

Irrational rage is a manifestation of a demonic stronghold. It's one of the strongest manifestations of a religious spirit of self-righteousness. Speaking the truth confronts the lie the demon is holding on to and stirs up resistance. There are godly men and women who have a demonic stronghold that was built up by today's tithe teachings. If you want to consider the matter from the perspective of scripture or history, they suddenly change and act way out of character. It's a demon manifesting.

I recently shared Johnny Enlow's experience[63] with their members giving more when they taught free-will giving rather than tithing. *"Dumb A**," "stupid," "liar," "go to hell"* and similar phrases soon appeared repeatedly in the comments, followed by *"Jesus is Lord."* Many of the people who behave like this when the mask comes off are pastors and leaders.

Some of them have had real salvation experiences and even powerful ministries. Peter was a true apostle who walked with Jesus, had a powerful ministry, and healed the sick. Yet he was led astray by the circumcision faction, and Jesus told him *"Get behind me Satan"*[64] not long after his glorious revelation that Jesus was the Christ. That's how quickly it's possible to flip from truth to error.

With great love for the church and thankfulness for all the Holy Spirit has done in the charismatic movement, I'm telling you, teaching that the tithe is the door to God's blessing is satanic. You may have taught that and had a powerful ministry, seen the sick healed, and even experienced revival. Yet none of that is God's

---

[62] Brits, Bertie. *Money Crucified-The Tithe Eating Tithe* Starting 24 minutes and 48 seconds into the video. Online: https://www.youtube.com/watch?v=8mzICkJqltE Accessed December 20th, 2019

[63] Enlow, Johnny Up for Discussion Episode 11. Is tithing Biblical? https://rumble.com/v1fs6qt-up-for-discussion-episode-11-is-tithing-biblical.html?fbclid=IwAR25ZNA7fyz06BSISpQRdnVD1S8VhyuoF0hsqQ-rx3fuXIQV6Ze7Af479Ds Retrieved August 21st, 2022

[64] Matthew 16:23

endorsement on all you do or teach. People walking in power have been caught in error as well as financial and sexual scandals many times. Miracles and deliverance in a ministry don't justify false teaching that puts the tithe in the place of Jesus's redemptive work.

Today's teaching about tithing has opened up many people to demons of self-righteousness and false religion. Some people are even defrauding others and think their wealth is a sign of God's blessing because of the tithe. The few stories I share in this book are just the tip of the iceberg. These issues are pervasive in the church today and it is major deception!

Chapter 5
Is the Tithe "Law?"

The Circumcision Debate of the Early Church and the Tithe Debate of Today

For a time, I no longer believed the tithe was the biblical standard for giving, but I wanted to avoid making a fuss about it. Then as I was reading the book of Galatians, I suddenly realized that the tithe debate of today is identical to the circumcision debate of the early church. Just as there were apostles and leaders on each side of the circumcision debate in the early church, there have been leaders on both sides of the tithe debate today.

As I share in this chapter, some people may continue to have objections such as *"We never said anybody was saved by tithing. We just teach that it's the fruit of faith and obedience to God."* I know. I once believed in tithing and would have heartily rejected the notion that anybody is saved by tithing. But I realized I was deceiving myself. Imagine somebody saying *"We don't teach salvation by circumcision. We just teach that it's the fruit of faith and obedience to God."* They would still be falling into the error of the Galatians.

Acts chapter 15 tells us more about the controversy which was the backdrop to the book of Galatians. Although the focal point of the controversy was circumcision, the broader issue was whether the Gentile Christians should be required to obey the Jewish law.

Acts 15:1-2, 5-12 (KJV) And certain men came down from Judea and taught the brethren, saying, Except ye be

circumcised after the custom of Moses, ye cannot be saved. And when Paul and Barnabas had no small dissension and questioning with them, the brethren appointed that Paul and Barnabas, and certain other of them, should go up to Jerusalem unto the apostles and elders about this question.

But there rose up certain of the sect of the Pharisees who believed, saying, it is needful to circumcise them, and to charge them to keep the law of Moses. And the apostles and the elders were gathered together to consider of this matter. And when there had been much questioning, Peter rose up, and said unto them, Brethren, ye know that a good while ago God made choice among you, that by my mouth the Gentiles should hear the word of the gospel, and believe. And God, who knoweth the heart, bare them witness, giving them the Holy Spirit, even as he did unto us; and he made no distinction between us and them, cleansing their hearts by faith.

Now therefore why make ye trial of God, that ye should put a yoke upon the neck of the disciples which neither our fathers nor we were able to bear? But we believe that we shall be saved through the grace of the Lord Jesus, in like manner as they. And all the multitude kept silence; and they hearkened unto Barnabas and Paul rehearsing what signs and wonders God had wrought among the Gentiles through them.

This is just one place where the New Testament clearly teaches against requiring a tithe from God's people. The apostles concluded that requiring gentile Christians to follow the Jewish law was *"making a distinction"* that the Holy Spirit did not make, testing God, and putting a heavy yoke on the disciples that *"neither our fathers nor we were able to bear."* As we go, we'll see that even the tithe of the Jewish law was a light burden compared to the tithe of today's tradition.

Acts 15 alone makes it absolutely clear that the apostles did not teach the Gentile believers to tithe. The only things of the law that they asked the Gentile Christians to keep were abstaining from food offered to idols, from blood, from things strangled, and from fornication. Of those, the only one with much relevance to most of us today is abstaining from fornication.

Acts 15:19-32(KJV) Wherefore my sentence is, that we trouble not them, which from among the Gentiles are turned to God: But that we write unto them, that they abstain from pollutions of idols, and from fornication, and from things strangled, and from blood. For Moses of old time hath in every city them that preach him, being read in the synagogues every sabbath day.

Then pleased it the apostles and elders with the whole church, to send chosen men of their own company to Antioch with Paul and Barnabas; namely, Judas surnamed Barsabas and Silas, chief men among the brethren: And they wrote letters by them after this manner; The apostles and elders and brethren send greeting unto the brethren which are of the Gentiles in Antioch and Syria and Cilicia. Forasmuch as we have heard, that certain which went out from us have troubled you with words, subverting your souls, saying, Ye must be circumcised, and keep the law: to whom we gave no such commandment: It seemed good unto us, being assembled with one accord, to send chosen men unto you with our beloved Barnabas and Paul, Men that have hazarded their lives for the name of our Lord Jesus Christ. We have sent therefore Judas and Silas, who shall also tell you the same things by mouth.

For it seemed good to the Holy Ghost, and to us, to lay upon you no greater burden than these necessary things; That ye

abstain from meats offered to idols, and from blood, and from things strangled, and from fornication: from which if ye keep yourselves, ye shall do well. Fare ye well. So when they were dismissed, they came to Antioch: and when they had gathered the multitude together, they delivered the epistle: Which when they had read, they rejoiced for the consolation. And Judas and Silas, being prophets also themselves, exhorted the brethren with many words, and confirmed them.

Besides testing God and putting a heavy yoke on the gentiles, those who wanted to impose the Jewish law on gentile Christians were *"troubling"* them and *"subverting their souls."* Demanding a tithe does all of that. It makes distinctions between God's people that God himself does not make. **The modern tithe tradition puts a heavy yoke on Christians that did not even exist under the law.** It troubles believers and subverts their souls by changing how they seek to relate to God.

"But the Tithe Came Before the Law"

Of course, we've heard *"The tithe isn't law. It came before the law."* Yet nobody applies this argument consistently. This and every other argument that the tithe is not of the law can also be applied to circumcision and animal sacrifices. Abraham also was circumcised and offered animal sacrifices before the law. Did the apostles in Acts 15 determine that circumcision was an *"eternal moral principle"* and the *"fruit of true faith for all believers"* because it predated the law? No! The tithe question of today is no different than the circumcision issue of the early church. In fact, *"it's the fruit of faith"* would be a stronger argument for circumcision than for tithing. At least scripture expressly says that circumcision was the sign of Abraham's faith, even though it is the faith that matters, not circumcision.

Dr. David Croteau notes that that besides circumcision, the closest issue we can find to the tithe issue is the levirate law. This was the law that said if a man died childless, his brother should sleep with his wife and raise up children for him.[65]

Like tithes, this law was found in many cultures around the world before the law of Moses, and it was incorporated into the Mosaic law. Yet we don't know anybody who tries to claim that the levirate law is an *"eternal moral principle"* because it predated the Mosaic law, just as we don't know anybody who says circumcision is an *"eternal moral principle."* Imagine if somebody today claimed he needed to sleep with his childless brother's widow! We'd never say he is *"acting under grace"* because he is following the *"eternal moral principle"* of the levirate law that predated Mosaic law. We'd call it absurd!

By calling circumcision *"law"* when circumcision came before Moses, Galatians makes it clear that relating to God through the law or grace came long before Moses. It goes back to the garden of Eden. The tree of life was the knowledge of God. John 17:3 says *"This is eternal life, that they may know you."* The tree of life bears the fruit of holiness flowing out of communion with God. It is grace.

The tree of the knowledge of good and evil was the law that brought death. Here's a short excerpt from *"Present Access to Heaven."*[66] It contrasts the old law we have been freed from with the new law we have in Christ, and shows the correlation between these two laws and the two trees in the garden. The statements are compiled directly from scripture.

The veil 2 Corinthians 3 speaks of is the Old Covenant law that was done away with. The law was good,[67] but it was powerless to justify us[68] or bring us into the knowledge of the Lord; through it came the knowledge of sin,[69] and not of righteousness. Since the law did

---

[65] Croteau, David A. *You Mean I Don't Have to Tithe?: a Deconstruction of Tithing and a Reconstruction of Post-Tithe Giving.* Eugene, Or.: Pickwick Publications, 2010.
[66] Brenneman, Jonathan. *Present Access To Heaven.* Lancaster, PA: Propiv Press, 2016. Pages 52-55
[67] Romans 7:12, 16
[68] Galatians 2:16, 3:11

not lead to the knowledge of the Lord, but to the knowledge of sin, it was from the *"good"* part of the tree of the knowledge of good and evil.

Just like the fruit of the tree of the knowledge of good and evil did, the law brought death.[70] Rather than freeing from sin, the law caused sin to multiply,[71] aroused our sinful passions,[72] and revived sin.[73] The law was flawed,[74] and perfection was simply not attainable through it.[75]

The old law was abolished[76] and became obsolete [77]because it was weak and ineffectual,[78] and a better hope was introduced, through which we may now approach God[79] and enter heaven itself.[80] This was a new law, the law of the Spirit of life in Christ,[81] the Spirit of God dwelling in man; the knowledge of the Lord.

This law of life was not in letter, but was written on our hearts by the Spirit of God. Unlike the old law which was of the tree of the knowledge of good and evil, this law was the knowledge of the Lord which was made possible through the forgiveness of sins. Under this new commandment, we love as God loves, because we have received God's love and that love has become our nature.

John 17:3 (NRSV) And this is eternal life, that they may know you, the only true God, and Jesus Christ whom you have sent.

Jeremiah 31:31-34 (NRSV) The days are surely coming, says the Lord, when I will make a new covenant with the house of Israel and the house of Judah. It will not be like the covenant

---

[69] Romans 3:20
[70] Romans 7:5, 9-10, Romans 8:2, 1 Corinthians 15:56
[71] Romans 5:20
[72] Romans 7:5
[73] Romans 7:9
[74] Hebrews 8:7
[75] Hebrews 7:11+19, 10:1
[76] Ephesians 2:15
[77] Hebrews 8:13
[78] Hebrews 7:18
[79] Hebrews 7:19
[80] Hebrews 9:24, 10:19
[81] Romans 8:2

that I made with their ancestors when I took them by the hand to bring them out of the land of Egypt—a covenant that they broke, though I was their husband, says the Lord.

But this is the covenant that I will make with the house of Israel after those days, says the Lord: I will put my law within them, and I will write it on their hearts; and I will be their God, and they shall be my people. No longer shall they teach one another, or say to each other, 'Know the Lord,' for they shall all know me, from the least of them to the greatest, says the Lord; for I will forgive their iniquity, and remember their sin no more.

2 Corinthians 3:5-6 (NRSV) Not that we are competent of ourselves to claim anything as coming from us; our competence is from God, who has made us competent to be ministers of a new covenant, not of letter but of spirit; for the letter kills, but the Spirit gives life.

We had to die to the old law, which was of the tree of the knowledge of good and evil, to live in the new law, the knowledge of the Lord. This knowledge of the Lord comes by justification through grace[82] and produces grace.[83]

This law, of the knowledge of the Lord through grace, is Christ's new commandment that we love as he loves us.[84] This law empowers us. This is the law of righteousness and of being led by the Spirit of God. Let's look at some scriptures which contrast the law of the old covenant with the new law of grace and righteousness which we have received:

Romans 6:14 (NRSV) For sin will have no dominion over you, since you are not under law but under grace.

---

[82] Romans 3:24, Titus 3:7
[83] 2 Peter 1:2
[84] John 13:34

> **Romans 7:4 (NRSV) In the same way, my friends, you have died to the law through the body of Christ, so that you may belong to another, to him who has been raised from the dead in order that we may bear fruit for God.**

> **Romans 10:4 (NRSV) For Christ is the end of the law so that there may be righteousness for everyone who believes.**

> **Galatians 5:18 (NRSV) But if you are led by the Spirit, you are not subject to the law.**

One reason Christians presently experience much less than heaven's reality, struggling with sin and lacking in power, is that they have been bewitched into following the old law that is in letter but not in the knowledge of the Lord through grace. Just as we first received salvation through grace, we must continue in it by grace.

> **Galatians 3:1-5 (NRSV) You foolish Galatians! Who has bewitched you? It was before your eyes that Jesus Christ was publicly exhibited as crucified! The only thing I want to learn from you is this: Did you receive the Spirit by doing the works of the law or by believing what you heard? Are you so foolish? Having started with the Spirit, are you now ending with the flesh? Did you experience so much for nothing?—if it really was for nothing. Well then, does God supply you with the Spirit and work miracles among you by your doing the works of the law, or by your believing what you heard?**

> **Galatians 3:10 (NRSV) For all who rely on the works of the law are under a curse...**

> **Galatians 5:4 (NRSV) You who want to be justified by the law have cut yourselves off from Christ; you have fallen away from grace.**

When Adam and Eve sinned and became aware of their nakedness, they tried to cover themselves with leaves. Then God killed an animal to cover them with the animal skin. The leaves were symbolic of their own works, but the animal God killed pointed to Jesus, by whose perfect sacrifice we would be clothed in God's righteousness. The leaves pointed to the tree of the knowledge of good and evil, but the animal skin pointed to the free gift of righteousness which puts us in communion with God, by which we eat the fruit of the tree of life.

The point is that the law and grace go back to the two trees in the garden of Eden. Galatians refers to the son of the slave woman and the son of the free woman as the two covenants, and the story it is referring to happened long before the Mosaic law was given. There's no sense in saying that the tithe, the levirate law, circumcision, or anything else were not of the old law that brings death because they came before Moses.

The law of sin and death is externally imposed, but under the law of life, holiness comes from the inside out as the fruit of communion with God. The law which brings death is in letter, such as a percentage of your money. Under the law of life, circumcision or uncircumcision is nothing. Giving more or less than 10% of your money is nothing. The only thing of any value is faith expressing itself through love.

Galatians 5:6 For in Christ Jesus neither circumcision nor uncircumcision has any value. The only thing that counts is faith expressing itself through love.

Boasting in a percentage is boasting in the flesh and in outward appearances, just as is boasting in circumcision. Scripture records both wicked men who were circumcised and gentiles who were uncircumcised but commended for their faith. The argument Galatians makes is that Abraham was justified before he was circumcised, and so it was really his faith that mattered. Galatians rejects the notion that all who have faith then need to be circumcised to show that faith.

Likewise, 10% is absolutely worthless as a measure of people's hearts. **Some tithers are defrauding others and are thieves, and some people are giving less than 10% of their money to a local church but living 100% for Jesus**. May I not boast of anything except the cross of Christ!

Under the law of sin and death, the motivations are guilt, trying to measure up, and trying to do well enough to gain God's blessing and avoid punishment. The law of life works from a place of rest, having already been made righteous, delivered from the curse, and abundantly blessed. It's life flowing from participation in God's nature.

Did Jesus Command Us To Tithe?

Let's look at the argument that claims Jesus said we should tithe. If it were valid, by the same logic we must adhere to animal sacrifices and the levirate law today.

> **Matthew 23:23-24 (NRSV) Woe to you, scribes and Pharisees, hypocrites! For you tithe mint, dill, and cummin, and have neglected the weightier matters of the law: justice and mercy and faith. It is these you ought to have practiced without neglecting the others. You blind guides! You strain out a gnat but swallow a camel!**

Who was Jesus talking to? Scribes and Pharisees, who were under the law, before his death and resurrection which inaugurated the New Covenant, and before the destruction of the temple which brought a final end to the Old Covenant. Of course, it was right for the Scribes and Pharisees to tithe!

Those who say the tithe is *"not law"* should note that in this passage, Jesus not only referred to the tithe as the law, but as one of the lesser matters of the law. If Jesus was affirming the tithe for gentile Christians in this passage, he also affirmed animal sacrifices and the levirate law. Where?

> **Luke 5:14 (NRSV) And he ordered him to tell no one. "Go," he said, "and show yourself to the priest, and, as Moses commanded, make an offering for your cleansing, for a testimony to them."**

Jesus said this to a man whom he cleansed of leprosy. What was the offering Jesus was referring to?

> **Leviticus 14:1-7 (NRSV) The Lord spoke to Moses, saying, "This shall be the ritual for the leprous person at the time of his cleansing: He shall be brought to the priest; the priest shall go out of the camp, and the priest shall make an examination. If the disease is healed in the leprous person, the priest shall command that two living clean birds and cedarwood and crimson yarn and hyssop be brought for the one who is to be cleansed. The priest shall command that one of the birds be slaughtered over fresh water in an earthen vessel. He shall take the living bird with the cedarwood and the crimson yarn and the hyssop, and dip them and the living bird in the blood of the bird that was slaughtered over the fresh water. He shall sprinkle it seven times upon the one who is to be cleansed of the leprous disease; then he shall pronounce him clean, and he shall let the living bird go into the open field."**

Similarly, in Matthew 5:23-24, Jesus commands to be reconciled with your brother before offering your gift at the altar. The gift he was talking about was an animal sacrifice, yet none of us would dream of taking this passage and saying *"Jesus affirmed animal sacrifices in Matthew 5. It was a given, what they were supposed to be doing, therefore all Christ followers must offer animal sacrifices."* How could we conclude that such logic is absurd when applied to Matthew 5 and animal sacrifices, yet is valid when applied to Matthew 23 and tithing? It shows that maybe we are reading the

Bible with an agenda and looking for something to confirm what we already want to believe.

I once posted on Facebook that we must be circumcised and offer animal sacrifices because both came before the law, and Jesus condoned animal sacrifices in the New Testament by his command to the leper. A friend, a Lutheran minister, thought I was serious. As Paul did in the book of Galatians, she argued vehemently to the contrary! I explained that I fully agreed with her position and her reaction was quite appropriate, but I was posting facetiously to make a point. Why would we reject such logic without a thought when it comes to circumcision or animal sacrifices, yet embrace it in order to argue tithing? When she understood my point, she commented that she fully agrees with my position on tithing, as did Martin Luther.

If Jesus was affirming the tithe for gentile Christians in Matthew 23, he was also affirming animal sacrifice for gentile Christians in Luke 5 and Matthew 5. We read Luke 5 and Matthew 5 and conclude that Jesus was talking to a Jew under the Jewish law and not to us. How can we then read Matthew 23 and not realize the same thing?

I have so often heard the argument in favor of tithing *"Jesus didn't say anything against the tithe. He never abolished it."* Let's read what Jesus said about another matter right before Matthew 23:

Matthew 22:23-30 (NRSV) The same day some Sadducees came to him, saying there is no resurrection; and they asked him a question, saying, "Teacher, Moses said, 'If a man dies childless, his brother shall marry the widow, and raise up children for his brother.' Now there were seven brothers among us; the first married, and died childless, leaving the widow to his brother. The second did the same, so also the third, down to the seventh. Last of all, the woman herself died. In the resurrection, then, whose wife of the seven will she be? For all of them had married her."

> **Jesus answered them, "You are wrong, because you know neither the scriptures nor the power of God. For in the resurrection they neither marry nor are given in marriage, but are like angels in heaven."**

Jesus didn't abolish Levirate marriage or say anything against it in this passage, just as he didn't say anything against the tithe in Matthew 23. He told them they were wrong concerning the resurrection, not Levirate marriage. If we use the argument that Jesus *"accepted"* the tithe, why don't we apply the same reasoning to Levirate marriage and continue to teach it today?

Just say we consider all this, but choose to ignore it and stick to the same reasoning we've always used to support our dogma that the tithe is not law and Jesus affirmed it for the church today, even though we're unwilling to apply the same logic to any other matter in scripture. We must then consider: What was the tithe that the scribes and Pharisees gave?

It was a tenth of their garden herbs, and not money! We cannot ignore the Old Testament scriptural context for the tithe Jesus was talking about. **According to the Jewish law, the tithe was always food. It was illegal to give money in place of your tithe, unless you added a fifth to redeem it! In that case it was 12%.**[85] The law said you could sell the food if the trip was too far to carry it all, but when you arrived at your destination you must use the money to buy food again.[86]

That's why Jesus didn't have Peter tithe on the four-drachma coin he took from a fish's mouth in Matthew 17:27. It was a significant amount of money, about four days' pay for a skilled worker, and Jesus had Peter give it wholly for the temple tax. **This story highlights what both the Old Testament and Jewish historians agree on: money was not tithed.**

I hear people saying *"You just don't want to give. If you were generous, what would it matter?"* That's not the point. The point is

---

[85] Leviticus 27:31
[86] Deuteronomy 14:24-26

integrity with how we handle scripture and even historical facts. Why would we lie to ourselves?

We have to go through layer after layer of irrationality to support the modern tithe tradition. If you ignore one issue, multiple others remain that are even stronger. Some insist that the tithe is not law. Some insist that we are still under the old law, even though our freedom from that law is one of the primary themes of the New Testament. Even if you convince yourself of that, you then have to consider that the modern tithe is not based at all on the tithe under the law, but contradicts it in even the most basic principles. *The closest thing to the modern tithe is the Babylonian tithe that God warned his people about even in the Old Testament!*

Was Melchizedek Jesus?

Ancient literature and archeological evidence point to the fact that the nations around Abraham practiced tithing the spoils of war to a king.[87] Hebrews chapter 7 uses the ancient knowledge of this tradition to make the argument that, since one who was lesser would tithe to one who was greater, the priesthood of Melchizedek is greater than the Levitical priesthood.

Some have attempted to extract an argument from Hebrews chapter 7 that Christians today are supposed to tithe, yet the chapter doesn't say that anywhere and is not even about money. The whole point is arguing the supremacy of Jesus over the law.

Hebrews 7: 1-8 (NKJV) For this Melchizedek, king of Salem, priest of the Most High God, who met Abraham returning from the slaughter of the kings and blessed him, to whom also Abraham gave a tenth part of all, first being translated "king of righteousness," and then also king of Salem, meaning "king of peace," without father, without mother,

---

[87] You can easily find information about this with a Google search of "Babylonian tithe." Here is one article with quotes from ancient writings:
http://nazarenespace.ning.com/profiles/blogs/tithing-amp-slave-wives-in Accessed July 29th, 2019

without genealogy, having neither beginning of days nor end of life, but made like the Son of God, remains a priest continually.

Now consider how great this man was, to whom even the patriarch Abraham gave a tenth of the spoils. And indeed those who are of the sons of Levi, who receive the priesthood, have a commandment to receive tithes from the people according to the law, that is, from their brethren, though they have come from the loins of Abraham; but he whose genealogy is not derived from them received tithes from Abraham and blessed him who had the promises. Now beyond all contradiction the lesser is blessed by the better. Here mortal men receive tithes, but there he receives them, of whom it is witnessed that he lives.

I recently was listening to Joseph Prince preach on this. He pointed to the words *"there he receives them,"* saying *"It's present tense! This means tithing is for today!"*

The KJV and NKJV use italics when words were added by the translators but are not in the original text. The words *"receives them"* are in italics. The pronoun *"he"* is referring to Melchizedek, who received tithes in the past from Abraham, as the passage says just a little earlier.

Earlier in that sentence it says *"Here mortal men receive tithes."* This is very clearly speaking of the Levites and Priests, since the temple was still standing when Hebrews was written. The Jewish system continued until the destruction of the temple, and the first Christians were Jews. Scripture indicates that the Jewish Christians continued to keep the law until the destruction of the temple, while, as we saw in Acts 15, they determined not to hold gentile Christians to the Jewish law.

The *"mortal men"* receiving tithes when Hebrews was written were Levites and Jewish priests, not church leaders or any non-Levites. This is one of the reasons that **until recently it was** *"universally agreed"*[88] **that the early church did not take tithes.** For church leaders to have received tithes, the early church would have needed to add a fourth tithe to the three that were, according to most scholars, already in effect. Jesus himself was of the tribe of Judah, not a Levite, and thus not qualified by the law to receive a tithe. Until the destruction of the temple, Christianity was considered a sect of Judaism, and Jewish Christians continued to observe Mosaic law.

Prince argues that Melchizedek was Christ pre-incarnate. Starting from this assumption, he then uses words that were not in the original text but added by translators to argue that Christ receives tithes today. Again, I ask, *how can we go to such lengths based on assumptions not stated in scripture, from a passage which is not even about giving, and ignoring the historical context, to argue that tithing is God's command for today's church?* Are we approaching the subject with sincerity and truth, or are we just trying to find support for the way we want to do things?

The idea that Melchizedek was Christ pre-incarnate is extremely dubious. Scripture says that he was like the Son of God, not that he was the Son of God. Consider D.W. Burdick's commentary:

The verb aphomoioo always assumes two distinct and separate identities, one of which is a copy of the other. Thus Melchizedek and the Son of God are represented as two separate persons, the first of which resembled the second.[89]

Psalm 110 also clearly distinguishes between Jesus and Melchizedek. It is speaking to Jesus in the second person, and speaks of Melchizedek in the third person.

---

[88] Hastings, James. *Dictionary of the Apostolic Church*. Edinburgh: Clark, 1915.*Tithes* Online: https://www.studylight.org/dictionaries/hdn/t/tithes.html
[89] *"Melchizedek," The International Standard Bible Encyclopedia – Revised*, G.W. Bromiley, Ed., Grand Rapids: Eerdmans, 1986, Vol. 3, p. 313

Chapter 5

Psalm 110:4 (NKJV) The Lord has sworn and will not relent, "You are a priest forever according to the order of Melchizedek."

Melchizedek was the priest of *"El Elyon,"* often translated in Hebrews as *"The Most High God."* Yet according to Dr. Russel Earl Kelly, the title *"El Elyon"* would mean *"Baal"* to any Canaanite, and was only later used by the Israelites as a title for the true God. When it says Melchizedek was the *"king of righteousness"* and *"king of peace,"* the original words are *"Salem"* and *"Zedek."* These were both lower gods in the Canaanite Pantheon. *"Salem"* was the goddess of the dawn as well as the name of a city, and *"Zedek"* was Jupiter, the god of justice. Dr. Kelly notes that, giving the extreme importance ancient cultures placed on knowing the name of a god, it is conspicuous that Melchizedek did not swear in the name of *"Yahweh God Most High"* as did Abraham.[90] Abraham identified Yahweh as the Most High God. Melchizedek did not.

I found Dr. Kelly's case to be convincing, but it was obviously a point of contention with many people. Some find it offensive that God would use a pagan priesthood as a type of Christ's priesthood. My thoughts were that the people of that day had very little revelation of who God was. Even Paul in the New Testament found a pagan altar to *"an unknown god,"* and Paul said *"What you worship in ignorance, I announce to you...."*[91] If Paul could use their altar as a springboard for announcing the gospel, I don't see why God couldn't use Melchizedek's priesthood as a type of Christ's. The Canaanites of the day didn't know that *"The Most High God"* was Yahweh. They thought it was one of their deities. Yet Abraham knew better. Scripture uses Melchizedek, a pagan priest, as a type of Christ's priesthood.

---

[90] Kelly, Russell Earl. *Should the Church Teach Tithing?: a Theologians Conclusions about a Taboo Doctrine.* New York: Writers Club Press, 2007. *Chapter 2: Genesis 14 Abraham, Melchizedek, and Arab Customs.* Also online, although in lesser detail: http://www.tithing-russkelly.com/id8.html Accessed December 15th, 2019

[91] Acts 17:22-31

Because of the questions people asked, I did some research myself and it strongly confirmed Dr. Kelly's conclusions. I found quite a bit of information that would be too overwhelming to share in great detail here. However, I learned that many scholars specializing in the region's history consider Melchizedek to have been a priest of pagan deities. The following confirms this, as well as explaining how Abraham used the term *"El Elyon"* immediately after his encounter with Melchizedek in reference to Yahweh, the true God.

Joseph Blenkinsopp explains that the very name *"Melchizedek"* is theophoric, denoting him as a worshipper of Zedek.[92] It can be translated either *"King of righteousness"*[93] or *"My king is Zedek."*[94] As to *"El Elyon," "El"* could refer to Yahweh or the Canaanite god El, and *"Elyon"* could refer to a certain Phoenician god but it was also a common epithet applied to different gods.

The clearest example of "Elyon" functioning autonomously is found in in the fragments of Sanchuniathon's "Phoenician Theology" preserved by Eusebius using Phylo of Byblos as his source. According to Sanchuniathon, a certain Elioun, called "Most High," dwelt in the neighborhood of Byblos, as well as his wife Berouth. To them was born a son, Epigeius or Autochthon, who was later called "Ouranos" (Heaven) and a daughter, "Ge." (Earth) Sometime later, Elioun died in an encounter with wild beasts and was there-upon deified. His children also became deities, and through the union of Ouranos and Ge, the god Kronos was born. Later, a union of Ouranos and his favorite mistress produced Zeus. (Demarous) With certain exceptions, this cosmology is

---

[92] Blenkinsopp, Joseph. *Abraham: The Story of a Life*. Wm. B. Eerdmans Publishing. 2015. Pg. 56.

[93] Gesenius, Wilhelm, Edward Robinson, Francis Brown, S. R. Driver, and Charles A. Briggs. *A Hebrew and English Lexicon of the Old Testament: with an Appendix Containing the Biblical Aramaic*. Boston, NY: Houghton, Mifflin and Company, 1906. Pg. 575.

[94] Van der Toorn, K.; et al. (1996). Dictionary of Deities and Demons in the Bible. Wm. B. Eerdmans Publishing. p. 560.

closely related to others in the ancient Near East. Texts such as the Hurro-Hittite "Song of Kamurbi" (also known as "Kingship in Heaven"), Hesiods Theogony, and various Ugaritic myths about El and Baal all display striking similarities to the ordering and functioning of gods in Sanchuniathon. [95]

So, the Phoenician god Elioun's children were named Heaven and Earth? This certainly gives some context to Melchizedek's identification of El Elyon as *"possessor of heaven and earth!"* Notably, Zedek was also a deity mentioned in the writings of Philo of Byblos and attributed to Sanchuniathon.[96] In fact, one hypothesis is that Zedek was an epithet of the god El.[97]

In contrast to the mixed evidence to support the identification of "Elyon" as autonomous, there is a wide range of evidence to suggest that "Elyon" was a common epithet in the West Semitic region, applied at different times and in different cultures to any god thought to be supreme.

The text continues, talking about the use of *"Elyon"* in reference to Baal, Zeus, and Isis. In summary:

Thus the epithet "Elyon" seems to have enjoyed a rich and widespread usage in the ancient West Semitic world. Not only was it associated with the "high gods" of different cultures,

---

[95] Toorn, Karel van der, Bob Becking, and Pieter Willem van der Horst. *Dictionary of Deities and Demons in the Bible*. Extensively Revised Edition. Wm. B. Eerdmans Publishing, 1999. Page 294 https://books.google.com.br/books?id=yCkRz5pfxz0C&pg=PA295&lpg=PA295&dq=el%20 elyon%20baal&source=bl&ots=aIswi1o_- o&sig=ACfU3U20siw5wifKoMDaHTR6FXJy5cOAwQ&hl=pt- BR&sa=X&ved=2ahUKEwjth_jHmqvmAhWwJrkGHddVDkMQ6AEwBXoECAcQAQ&fb clid=IwAR3Ij- fAnONbyYTzdAmqjnvwahK7d8fC_R3xSrbNDWbpFTEgcwTiFS71Or0#v=onepage&q=el &f=false

[96] Toorn, Karel van der, Bob Becking, and Pieter Willem van der Horst. *Dictionary of Deities and Demons in the Bible*. Extensively Revised Edition. Wm. B. Eerdmans Publishing, 1996, entry Zedek

[97] Bromiley, Geoffrey W. *The International Standard Bible Encyclopedia*. Michigan: Eerdmans, 1998. Entries Melchizedek, Adoni-Zedek https://en.m.wikipedia.org/wiki/Sydyk

but it could also be used within the same culture for different gods as one ascended in significance to become the "Most High God."[98] As to the meaning of El, "El" may refer either to "God" (of Israel) or to Canaanite El.[99]

What stood out to me in the above quote is the term *"Elyon"* could be used in the same culture in reference to different gods as one ascended in importance over the other. In Genesis 14, Melchizedek simply speaks of *"El Elyon,"* but Abraham swears in the name of *"Yahweh El Elyon."*[100] Melchizedek did not know the name "Yahweh" that was revealed to Abraham, which in ancient times meant that he did not know Yahweh. *"The Most High God"* meant a different thing to a Canaanite worshipper of Zedek than it did to Abraham. Abraham made it clear that the true *"Most High God"* is Yahweh and not Zedek or any other!

These facts make it obvious that Hebrews speaks of Melchizedek figuratively, as a type of Christ, and not literally as Christ. After writing most of my book, I went back and read Dr. Kelly's full book. He further develops the case that Melchizedek was a pagan priest, making strong arguments and giving other

---

[98] Toorn, Karel van der, Bob Becking, and Pieter Willem van der Horst. *Dictionary of Deities and Demons in the Bible.* Extensively Revised Edition. Wm. B. Eerdmans Publishing, 1999. Pg.295 and 296 https://books.google.com.br/books?id=yCkRz5pfxz0C&pg=PA295&lpg=PA295&dq=el%20 elyon%20baal&source=bl&ots=aIswi1o_-o&sig=ACfU3U20siw5wifKoMDaHTR6FXJy5cOAwQ&hl=pt-BR&sa=X&ved=2ahUKEwjth_jHmqvmAhWwJrkGHddVDkMQ6AEwBXoECAcQAQ&fb clid=IwAR3Ij-fAnONbyYTzdAmqjnvwahK7d8fC_R3xSrbNDWbpFTEgcwTiFS71Or0#v=onepage&q=el &f=false

[99] Toorn, Karel van der, Bob Becking, and Pieter Willem van der Horst. *Dictionary of Deities and Demons in the Bible.* Extensively Revised Edition. Wm. B. Eerdmans Publishing, 1999. Pg. 296 https://books.google.com.br/books?id=yCkRz5pfxz0C&pg=PA295&lpg=PA295&dq=el%20 elyon%20baal&source=bl&ots=aIswi1o_-o&sig=ACfU3U20siw5wifKoMDaHTR6FXJy5cOAwQ&hl=pt-BR&sa=X&ved=2ahUKEwjth_jHmqvmAhWwJrkGHddVDkMQ6AEwBXoECAcQAQ&fb clid=IwAR3Ij-fAnONbyYTzdAmqjnvwahK7d8fC_R3xSrbNDWbpFTEgcwTiFS71Or0#v=onepage&q=el &f=false

[100] Green, Jay. *The Interlinear Bible: Hebrew - Greek - English; with Strongs Concordance Numbers above Each Word.* London: Hendrickson, 2011. Genesis 14.

examples of scripture using terms and names with negative meanings and origins, and turning them into positive spiritual meanings.[101]

Hebrews chapter 7 is actually a strong text for the annulling of tithing, used as an argument against it by many opponents of tithing in church history:

Hebrews 7:18-19 (NKJV) For on the one hand there is an annulling of the former commandment because of its weakness and unprofitableness, for the law made nothing perfect; on the other hand, there is the bringing in of a better hope, through which we draw near to God.

"The former commandment" includes Deuteronomy 12, 14, and 26, Leviticus 27, and Numbers 18, the tithe passages of the Old Covenant. Hebrews doesn't say *"the former commandment is a good principle to follow,"* or that it's a *"a good starting place for Christlikeness."* Rather, it's unprofitable, weak, and powerless to produce the nature of Christ manifesting through you. The tithe has no value for producing Spirit-led generosity.

Did God Command Abraham To Tithe? Was Abraham a Regular Tither? Did Abraham Tithe on His Own Income?

The facts we've just examined have already totally destroyed the argument that the tithe was not law. Nobody will apply the same logic to any other matter, and the tithe remains an external standard of doing by the letter in order to become something rather than living by the Spirit as the outflow of what we've become by grace.

Even so, let's consider a few more layers of irrationality which we will have to plow through if we are going to insist that we

---

[101] Kelly Pages 17-23, 28

should imitate everything Abraham did before the Mosaic law. First, *did God command Abraham to tithe? Can you show me where?*

Of course not! The position of the circumcision faction which Paul argued against in Galatians was at least much more defensible than that of the tithe faction, because at least Abraham was circumcised by God's command. He didn't even have a command from God to tithe. Abraham probably wasn't tithing by free will alone either, but in obedience to the local Canaanite laws.

Was Abraham a regular tither? Did he tithe on his personal income? Scripture only records him tithing once on the spoils of war, not on his own wealth. He was far from his own flocks and herds after pursuing the kings. In this story, found in Genesis 14, Abraham gave the other 90% to the king of Sodom. Should we also remit 90% to the king of Sodom, a type of Satan? How can we use Abraham's one-time spoils of war tithe in accordance with the tradition or law of the surrounding Canaanite nations as support to argue that *"Tithing is an eternal moral principle that came before the law, and all obedient Christians must now regularly give a tenth of their gross income to God."*

Did Abraham Become Rich Because He Tithed?

We've heard again and again that Abraham became rich because he tithed. But God blessed Abram (Abraham) and gave him the promises long before he gave a tenth to Melchizedek. Genesis 12 tells us of how God blessed Abram, and Genesis 13:2 tells us that Abram had become very rich with livestock, silver, and gold.

Many have pointed to Jacob's vow as another example of the tithe mentioned before the law. We don't know if Jacob ever fulfilled his vow, yet there was no command from God. Did he make his vow rashly? The Bible doesn't say, although it does warn against making rash vows. Some point out that Jacob made his vow in unbelief, ignoring everything that God had just promised him.

The very fact that it was a vow shows that it wasn't for everyone. Scripture records various types of vows in Leviticus 27 and in other passages, and we would never teach that any of those other vows are binding on all Christians today because someone in the Old Testament made them.

Scripture doesn't say if Jacob's vow pleased God, or if that kind of bargaining was another case of Jacob acting as the supplanter, as when he bargained for Esau's birthright. If he fulfilled the vow, we don't know how. Would it have been a burnt offering? That seems to be most likely, considering his culture. Nevertheless, let's look again at what Jacob said:

Genesis 28: 20-22 Then Jacob made a vow, saying, "If God will be with me and will watch over me on this journey I am taking and will give me food to eat and clothes to wear so that I return safely to my father's household, then the LORD will be my God and this stone that I have set up as a pillar will be God's house, and of all that you give me I will give you a tenth."

Notice that Jacob didn't tithe so that God would bless him. On the contrary, he promised God a tithe *if* God would first take care of him. Jacob's father had *already* blessed him with the blessings of Abraham in verses 3 and 4 of Genesis 28, and God himself *had already blessed him* in a dream, recorded in verses 12 to 15.

The point is that in the case of both Abraham and Jacob, God's promise and blessing came long before any mention of the tithe. This proves that neither the promise nor the blessing was contingent on the tithe. If it were so, God would not be faithful.

Talking about the promise brings us back to Galatians chapter three. I encourage you to read the whole chapter again with this in mind, but here is verse 18:

Galatians 3:18 For if the inheritance depends on the law, then it no longer depends on the promise; but God in his grace gave it to Abraham through a promise.

Teaching the promise of blessing depends on the tithe is precisely the error of the Galatians. There's no question in scripture that the promise came before and apart from any mention of tithes.

How Do I Tithe to Jesus?

Let's just ignore those problems for a moment and imagine that Melchizedek was the pre-incarnate Christ, God had commanded Abraham to tithe to him regularly, not just once, and we must do everything Abraham did. How would we tithe to Christ today? The most common teaching is that we give the tithe to Christ by giving it to the local church.

But how do we come up with that conclusion? Hebrews 7 talks about a change in the priesthood and an abrogation of the earlier commandment. Even if the tithe would somehow carry over to the new priesthood, who are the new priests? Besides Jesus, every one of us has been made a king and priest to our God?[102]

In fact, it was God's intention even for the nation of Israel that they should be a kingdom of priests. God said so when they came to Mount Sinai.[103] But they withdrew and told Moses *"We're afraid that we'll die if God speaks directly to us. So, you speak for him, and we will listen."*[104] Only after the people asking Moses to approach God for them did God give directions for the Aaronic priesthood, the Levites' duties, and the tithe to support them.

You might say *"Yes, we are all kings and priests, but not everybody is in full-time ministry."* Yet even under the Old Covenant, the majority of those who received the tithe were not in full-time ministry. The Levites received nine tenths of the tithe and they worked at the temple in two-week shifts.[105] Many of them were worship leaders or were involved in helps ministries.[106]

---

[102] 1 Peter 2:9
[103] Exodus 19:6
[104] Exodus 20:18-29
[105] 1 Chronicles 23 and 24
[106] 1 Chronicles 16:4, 37-38, 23:4-5, 28-31

And then what about those who are in full-time ministry, but are not *"the pastor"* of a church? What about those who are working 40 hours a week in ministry and 40 hours a week in a secular job? What about missionaries, or, in other words, modern-day apostles? What about those working for relief organizations, who are in full-time helps ministry?

And what do we do with the fact that the New Testament, in the original language, does not distinguish between pastors and elders?[107] It teaches a plurality of elders and nowhere states that there is one pastor for each congregation. Many common teachings of how to give the tithe to Jesus are based fully on arbitrary assumptions and human tradition, not on scripture.

There is, however, one way that scripture explicitly teaches we can give directly to Jesus:

Matthew 25:34-40 Then the King will say to those on his right, "Come, you who are blessed by my Father; take your inheritance, the kingdom prepared for you since the creation of the world. For I was hungry and you gave me something to eat, I was thirsty and you gave me something to drink, I was a stranger and you invited me in, I needed clothes and you clothed me, I was sick and you looked after me, I was in prison and you came to visit me."

Then the righteous will answer him, "Lord, when did we see you hungry and feed you, or thirsty and give you something to drink? When did we see you a stranger and invite you in, or needing clothes and clothe you? When did we see you sick or in prison and go to visit you?" The King will reply, "Truly I tell you, whatever you did for one of the least of these brothers and sisters of mine, you did for me."

The early church considered the poor the *"altar of God."*[108] I wonder how the vast majority of tithe-teachers, considering this

---

[107] I examined this in my book "I Am Persuaded."

scripture along with church history and even the use of the Old Testament tithe, can teach that your tithe goes to the *"local church"* and only after your tithe can you give to the poor, missionaries, or other ministries? There isn't one iota of Biblical support for it. The way churches distribute the tithe today falls far short of ancient Israel's instructions for distributing the ancient tithe.

In fact, the notion that we give our tithe to Jesus by giving it to the pastor is built on an ecclesiology that even many tithe-teachers fully reject.

Abraham's Tithe Was Most Closely Related to the Babylonian Tithe

We've mentioned that Abraham tithed according to the tradition, and probably law, of the Canaanite nations around him. Many ancient cultures had a tithe. The tithe that had the most in common with the modern tithe, and with Abraham's tithe, is the Babylonian tithe. You can find ancient references to this with a Google search of *"Babylonian tithe"* or *"Chaldean tithe."*

The Babylonian tithe differed from the Jewish tithe under the Old Covenant in that it was taken not only on crops and livestock but also on manufactured goods and money. The Jewish tithe applied only to the fruit of the land and livestock. This means that the poor hired laborer, who received his pay in money, would be compelled to pay the Babylonian tithe but he would be exempt from the Jewish tithe. The Jewish tithe provided for the orphan, the widow, and the Levite, who had no land of his own.[109] The Babylonian tithe oppressed the weak. The Jewish tithe was distributed according to specific instructions which God laid out in the law. The Babylonian tithe was received by a king and used as he saw fit. The Babylonian tithes went to a temple.[110] Most of the

---

[108] For example, see John Chrysostom's *Homilia 20.3* in *Epistulam 2 ad Corinthios*
[109] Deuteronomy 14:27-29
[110] Online: https://avalon.law.yale.edu/ancient/hammpre.asp Accessed November 22nd, 2019

Jewish tithe was eaten by the tither or went to the Levitical cities. Here are a few ancient references to the Babylonian tithe:

"…eleven garments as the tithe (on 112 garments)"

"…(the sun-god) Shamash demands the tithe…"

"four minas of silver, the tithe of (the gods) Bel, Nabu, and Nergal…"

"…he has paid, in addition to the tithe for Ninurta, the tax of the gardener"

"…the tithe of the chief accountant, he has delivered it to (the sun-god) Shamash"

"…why do you not pay the tithe to the Lady-of-Uruk?"

"…(a man) owes barley and dates as balance of the tithe of the **years three and four"

"…the tithe of the king on barley of the town…"

"…with regard to the elders of the city whom (the king) has **summoned to (pay) tithe…"

"…the collector of the tithe of the country Sumundar…

"…(the official Ebabbar in Sippar) who is in charge of the tithe…"[111]

---

[111] Taken from *"The Assyrian Dictionary of the Oriental Institute of the University of Chicago"* Vol. 4 " *E,"* compiled by Ann Wilson online: http://nazarenespace.ning.com/profiles/blogs/tithing-amp-slave-wives-in Accessed November 22nd, 2019

Scripture also talks about the Babylonian tithe! This is another one of those tithe passages that I've never heard mentioned in a tithe sermon:

1 Samuel 8:4-11, 15-18 So all the elders of Israel gathered together and came to Samuel at Ramah. They said to him, "You are old, and your sons do not follow your ways; now appoint a king to lead us, such as all the other nations have."

But when they said, "Give us a king to lead us," this displeased Samuel; so he prayed to the Lord. And the Lord told him: "Listen to all that the people are saying to you; it is not you they have rejected, but they have rejected me as their king. As they have done from the day I brought them up out of Egypt until this day, forsaking me and serving other gods, so they are doing to you. Now listen to them; but warn them solemnly and let them know what the king who will reign over them will claim as his rights."

Samuel told all the words of the Lord to the people who were asking him for a king. He said, "This is what the king who will reign over you will claim as his rights…He will take a tenth of your grain and of your vintage and give it to his officials and attendants. Your male and female servants and the best of your cattle and donkeys he will take for his own use. He will take a tenth of your flocks, and you yourselves will become his slaves. When that day comes, you will cry out for relief from the king you have chosen, but the Lord will not answer you in that day."

Israel embraced the Babylonian tithe when they rejected the Lord as their king, even though God warned them that it would lead to their oppression. Their desire to be like the other nations led further into idolatry and eventually to captivity in Babylon, whose ways they had embraced. In fact, scripture names the whore of

Revelation 17 and 18 as *"Babylon the Great,"* and warns God's people to come out of Babylon so as to not share in her judgements.[112]

How did we end up embracing a Babylonian tithe that goes to a king, curses the poor, and oppresses the weak? Abraham's tithe is no more of an example to us than was sleeping with his wife's slave woman to bear a child.[113] That practice, along with the tithe, was found in the code of Hammurabi,[114] ancient Babylonian law.

History is clear that the church began to mandate tithing only hundreds of years after Christ. It came along with several other changes that most of us don't view very positively, such as the mixing of Christianity with Roman politics and worldly systems.

If Abraham Tithed Based on an Eternal Moral Principle, Why Didn't God Himself Follow That Principle in His Instructions for Dividing Spoils of War?

Yet another point deals a crushing blow to the notion that Abraham's tithe followed an eternal moral principle which was written on men's hearts from the beginning.

Abraham tithed on what? The spoils of war. The Mosaic law gives instructions for dividing spoils of war in Numbers 31. The high priest received one one-thousandth of the spoils of war, and the Levites got one one-hundredth. It was much less than a tithe! If Abraham's spoils-of-war tithe were an *"eternal moral principle,"* surely God would have incorporated that *"eternal moral principle"* into his own instructions for dividing the spoils of war!

---

[112] Revelation 18:4
[113] Genesis 16:1-4
[114] Code of Hammurabi Online: http://mcadams.posc.mu.edu/txt/ah/Assyria/Hammurabi.html Accessed November 16th, 2019

Chapter 6
The Many Layers of Problems With Teaching a Christian Tithe From Malachi

9 Layers of Irrationality We Must Plow Through To Use Malachi as Support for Mandating Christian Tithing

> **Malachi 3:8-10 (NRSV) Will anyone rob God? Yet you are robbing me! But you say, "How are we robbing you?" In your tithes and offerings! You are cursed with a curse, for you are robbing me—the whole nation of you! Bring the full tithe into the storehouse, so that there may be food in my house, and thus put me to the test, says the LORD of hosts; see if I will not open the windows of heaven for you and pour down for you an overflowing blessing.**

Modern tithe teachings based on Malachi imply justification by tithing and lead people to practically relate to God on the basis of their tithes. This has led many people into one or both of the two manifestations of self-righteousness. The first is guilt, shame and condemnation, and the second is religious pride and self-justification.

There are multiple layers of problems with the most common arguments that tithing is relevant to the church today. Even if we get through the first layer of irrationality, many other serious logical problems continue to confront us.

1st Layer – Malachi Was Written to People Under the Law

Good Bible schools teach that one of the rules of hermeneutics (biblical interpretation) is asking *"who was this written to?"* Malachi was not written to us, but to Jews under the law who were commanded to tithe. One of the major themes of the New Testament is that we are not under the law.

Many passages in the Old Testament prophets concern the Sabbath, yet the vast majority of people who teach tithing from Malachi read the more numerous passages about the Sabbath, and say *"That was written to people under the law. We celebrate on Sunday, not Saturday, because it is when Christ rose from the dead."* In fact, many Christians consider Seventh Day Adventists to be a *"cult"* for their insistence on the importance of keeping the Jewish Sabbath.

Isaiah 58:13-14 (NRSV) If you refrain from trampling the sabbath, from pursuing your own interests on my holy day; if you call the sabbath a delight and the holy day of the Lord honorable; if you honor it, not going your own ways, serving your own interests, or pursuing your own affairs; then you shall take delight in the Lord, and I will make you ride upon the heights of the earth; I will feed you with the heritage of your ancestor Jacob, for the mouth of the Lord has spoken.

Ezekiel 20:13 (NRSV) But the house of Israel rebelled against me in the wilderness; they did not observe my statutes but rejected my ordinances, by whose observance everyone shall live; and my sabbaths they greatly profaned. Then I thought I would pour out my wrath upon them in the wilderness, to make an end of them.

Add to this the consideration that the Sabbath predated the tithe and actually does go back to the garden of Eden! Yet it pointed to Christ.

In a previous chapter, we quoted Colossians chapter 2 in response to the claim that the tithe is an *"eternal moral principle"* and not law. Consider what Colossians says soon after warning against being taken captive according to the *"basic principles of this world"* and not according to Christ:

Colossians 2:16-17 (NRSV) Therefore do not let anyone condemn you in matters of food and drink or of observing festivals, new moons, or sabbaths. These are only a shadow of what is to come, but the substance belongs to Christ.

Colossians is clear about Sabbaths. The early church celebrated on Sunday, just as most of us do today, rather than on the Jewish Sabbath.

But more than that, Colossians clearly gives the New Testament position on matters of food, drink, and festivals. The tithe under Jewish law was always food and drink, and it was also a festival.

Deuteronomy 14:23-29 (NRSV) In the presence of the LORD your God, in the place that he will choose as a dwelling for his name, you shall eat the tithe of your grain, your wine, and your oil, as well as the firstlings of your herd and flock, so that you may learn to fear the LORD your God always. But if, when the LORD your God has blessed you, the distance is so great that you are unable to transport it, because the place where the LORD your God will choose to set his name is too far away from you, then you may turn it into money. With the money secure in hand, go to the place that the LORD your God will choose; spend the money for whatever you wish—oxen, sheep, wine, strong drink, or whatever you desire. And you shall eat there in the presence of the LORD your God, you and your

household rejoicing together. As for the Levites resident in your towns, do not neglect them, because they have no allotment or inheritance with you.

Every third year you shall bring out the full tithe of your produce for that year, and store it within your towns; the Levites, because they have no allotment or inheritance with you, as well as the resident aliens, the orphans, and the widows in your towns, may come and eat their fill so that the LORD your God may bless you in all the work that you undertake."

2nd Layer - The Tithe Pointed to Jesus and Is Fulfilled in the New Covenant

A few years ago, I came across a book called *"Jesus is the Tithe,"* by Bertie Brits. Even though I hadn't believed in the modern tithe tradition for some time, my first reaction was *"What?"* It sounded a little out there. But wait! Colossians does say the festivals pointed to Christ, and tithing as instructed in Deuteronomy 14 was a festival. So, I decided to check the book out.

Bertie points to the story in Exodus in which God commanded the Israelites to gather an omer of manna, which is a tithe of an ephah, each day for every man. Then they were to put an omer of manna in the Ark of the Covenant as a perpetual reminder of how God provided for them.[115]

The manna was a tithe? I had never noticed that before. And it pointed to Jesus!

John 6:30-35 (NRSV) So they said to him, "What sign are you going to give us then, so that we may see it and believe you? What work are you performing? Our ancestors ate the manna in the wilderness; as it is written, 'He gave them bread from heaven to eat.'" Then Jesus said to them, "Very truly, I tell

---

[115] Exodus 16:16-18, 32-36

you, it was not Moses who gave you the bread from heaven, but it is my Father who gives you the true bread from heaven. For the bread of God is that which comes down from heaven and gives life to the world." They said to him, "Sir, give us this bread always."

Jesus said to them, "I am the bread of life. Whoever comes to me will never be hungry, and whoever believes in me will never be thirsty."

Bertie did a little study and found that one of the meanings of the root word for *"omer"* is *"figuratively, to chastise."* In the Septuagint, the meaning of an omer is *"Golgotha!"* The manna was a chastised portion, a tithe of an ephah, and it pointed to the true bread from heaven, Jesus, who was chastised for our transgressions, killed at Golgotha, and gave us his body as the bread of life!

As in Deuteronomy 14, the tithe was not about what we gave God, but about what he gave us! And just as the Israelites shared the tithe on the third year with the poor, Jesus gave his body as the bread of life on the third year to those who could never, by their own works, feed themselves! [116]

Isaiah 55:1-2 (NRSV) Ho, everyone who thirsts, come to the waters; and you that have no money, come, buy and eat! Come, buy wine and milk without money and without price. Why do you spend your money for that which is not bread, and your labor for that which does not satisfy? Listen carefully to me, and eat what is good, and delight yourselves in rich food.

Aside from those points by Bertie Brits, Dr. David Croteau points out that there are three aspects to the fulfillment of the Levitical tithe. The first was the fulfilment of the priesthood, the second was

---

[116] Brits, Bertie. *Jesus Is the Tithe: the Message of God.* South Africa: Bertie Brits, 2019. Kindle Location 2205-2315

the fulfilment of the inheritance, and the third, the fulfilment of the temple. Each of these three aspects was clearly fulfilled in the New Covenant.[117] I recommend his book for anybody who wants to study the matter in greater detail.

3rd Layer – Nobody Is Tithing As Malachi Commanded

Some people continue to argue that we are under the law, or under part of it. It's too much to spend more time in this book refuting those arguments, but one of the major themes of the Epistles is that we are not under the law. We referenced plenty of those scriptures in an earlier chapter. Still, arguing that we are under the law only brings up more serious problems for those who teach that Malachi applies to us. They have just put themselves under a curse, for none of them are tithing as the law commanded.

Galatians 3:10 For all who rely on the works of the law are under a curse, as it is written: "Cursed is everyone who does not continue to do everything written in the Book of the Law."

Malachi refers to the tithe under the Mosaic law. If Malachi is speaking to you about tithing, you must observe the tithe according to the law Malachi refers to. Let's consider some points about how the law of Moses commanded Israelites to tithe:

- *If you were going to redeem your tithe with money instead of giving the livestock or agricultural products, you had to add a 5th to it. Money given to redeem your tithe was 12% of the value of your increase in agricultural products and livestock, not 10%.[118]*

---

[117] Croteau, David A. *You Mean I Dont Have to Tithe?: a Deconstruction of Tithing and a Reconstruction of Post-Tithe Giving.* Eugene, Or.: Pickwick Publications, 2010. Kindle Location 6459
[118] Leviticus 27:31

115

- *Hired hands who received monetary wages, as well as tradesmen, were not required to tithe. The Babylonian tithe applied to manufactured goods, but the Mosaic tithe did not.*

- *You had to travel to Jerusalem, the place God chose, to eat your tithe. If you eat it anywhere else, you are in disobedience.[119]*

- *You had to share your tithe with the orphan, widow, and foreigner. If you're under the tithe and aren't doing so, you're being disobedient and missing one of the most basic principles behind the tithe.*

- *According to Jewish tradition and to many scholars' interpretation of scripture, ancient Jews had to give two or three tithes, not one. If you hold to the two or three tithe position, one tithe doesn't measure up. However, if you hold to the position that there was only one tithe with three uses, Malachi is only referring to the tithe of the third year, called in scripture the "year of tithing,"[120] not the tithe of the first and second year which you yourself ate in celebration to God. People also dispute whether the "third year" means the year of tithing was every three years, or was the third year out of the seven-year cycle.*

- *The Levites didn't have their own land inheritance as the other tribes did, but instead had tithes as their inheritance.[121]*

We could go into much more detail, but nobody today tithes as the statutes to which Malachi refers required. I've never heard a modern tithe-teaching which even loosely follows the principles of the statutes Malachi refers to.

Many teach from Malachi, written about the Jewish law to people under the Jewish law, to support tithing. Yet they then say

---

[119] Deuteronomy 14:23, 26
[120] Deuteronomy 26:12, Amos 4:4
[121] Numbers 18:20-21

"The tithe is an eternal moral principle, not law," because they don't want to, and cannot, fulfil the law Malachi refers to! Their reasoning is totally inconsistent. If we don't have to fulfil the law Malachi refers to because the tithe is not law, then how is Malachi relevant and why are they using it to teach tithing?

Jewish tithes were always food from the land or livestock, and never food from the sea, money, or manufactured goods. This is not only a scriptural observation but a well-established historical one. Unlike Babylonian tithes, the Jewish tithe came from what God increased and not from what man created by his labor. In fact, the Encyclopedia Britannica describes how after finally succeeding in collecting tithes, early church leaders worked to change the tithes from agricultural products to money. Even when early church leaders first succeeded in collecting tithes, the tithes were still food!

If anyone does not give tithes of all fruits, of oxen, sheep, goats, after being thrice admonished, he is to be anathematized. -Synod of Rowen (Probably 879 AD)[122]

The process of master minding the conversion of the food tithe to money continued with Constantine's successor, Charlemagne. Around A.D. 250 Cyprian tried to impose tithing in Carthage, North Africa, but his ideas of tithing were never adopted. In A.D. 585 the local church Council of Macon in France, also tried to enforce tithing on its members, but they were unsuccessful in their endeavors. It wasn't until A.D. 777 that Charlemagne legally allowed the church to collect tithes.

When you examine the historical record of tithes in Christendom, the earliest authentic example of anything like a law of the state enforcing payment appears to occur in the

---

[122] Hefele, Karl Joseph von. *A History of the Councils of the Church*. Edinburgh: Clark, 1972. Volume 4. Pg. 468

capitularies (ecclesiasticals) of Charlemagne at the end of the 8th or beginning of the 9th century. Tithes were by that enactment to be applied to the maintenance of the bishop, clergy, the poor, and the fabric of the church.

In the course of time the principle of payment of tithes was extended far beyond its original intention. Thus they became transferable to laymen and saleable like ordinary property, in spite of the injunctions of the third Lateran Council; and they became payable out of sources of income (not just farming and herding, but other trades and occupations and salaries paid in the form of money) not originally titheable.[123]

4th Layer - The "Offerings" Malachi Referred to Included Animal Sacrifices and Other Mandatory Gifts

Malachi refers to tithe and offering statutes in the Mosaic law, yet most people interpret it as if referring to the very different practices of churches thousands of years later. The Young's Literal Translation of Malachi 3:8 reflects the Hebrew text which says *"heave-offerings."* If you examine the other places scripture mentions *"heave-offerings,"* you'll find they included several different kinds of offerings, both voluntary and mandatory, including animal sacrifices as in Exodus 29:7.

Malachi refers to tithes of crops and animals that could only be *"redeemed"* with money by adding 20%. It refers to other mandatory offerings including animal sacrifices, which were partly burned in the fire on an altar. It's not talking about money in the offering plate.

If *"you have robbed me in tithes and heave-offerings"* is directed to us today, and not only to people in Israel, we must reinstate a whole lot more from the books of the law then just

---

[123] Encyclopedia Britannica 1963, volume 2, page 253, tithes

tithes, including animal sacrifices! How can anyone argue that we are robbing God by not bringing the tithe of Malachi 3:8 and avoid the obvious implication that heave-offerings must also be obligatory?

5th *Layer - The Tithe Was Israel's Income Tax*

The tithe commands of the Mosaic law were to the nation of Israel with its unique government, and on produce from within the land of Israel. They were never directed to the other nations, even though gentiles have always been morally accountable to God. The other nations had their own tax systems.

A small portion of the tithe went to the priests, who were national leaders.[124] Much more went to the Levites. Scripture tells us what their roles were. Among other functions, Levites' roles included temple construction and maintenance and acting as guards, teachers, officials, treasurers, and judges.[125] Those functions are typically paid out of a nation's income taxes.

The tithe was also shared with the orphan, the foreigner, and the widow on the third year. It was a part of the Israelite's welfare system.

We've often heard that if they gave 10% in the Old Testament, we should give at least as much under the New Covenant. First, it's far from accurate to say they gave 10% in the Old Testament. Jewish tradition and most scholars agree that there were multiple tithes and many other mandatory offerings and sacrifices. Second, most of us pay a significant portion of our income in taxes to the modern nations we belong to, funding many of the same functions that the Jewish tithe did. Many people are already equaling or surpassing the ancient tithe by the taxes they pay, which likewise fund social security and public servants.

This context makes it quite problematic to use Malachi as an argument for giving a 10th of your money to the local church.

---

[124] Numbers 18:26
[125] 1 Chronicles 23:4-5, 26:19-20, 26:29-32

Malachi refers to ancient Israel's income tax. Nobody reading this book lives in ancient Israel, but the tax code of the country you do live in probably already covers social security and the salaries of municipal workers, police, teachers, judges, and other government officials.

6th Layer - The Probable Context of Malachi Was the Priests Stealing the Levite's Portion of the Tithes

Nehemiah and Malachi were written around the same time period, and many people believe that the context of Malachi chapter 3 is found in Nehemiah chapter 13. Let's consider what the issue was here.

Nehemiah 13:4-13 Before this, Eliashib the priest had been put in charge of the storerooms of the house of our God. He was closely associated with Tobiah, and he had provided him with a large room formerly used to store the grain offerings and incense and temple articles, and also the tithes of grain, new wine and olive oil prescribed for the Levites, musicians and gatekeepers, as well as the contributions for the priests.

But while all this was going on, I was not in Jerusalem, for in the thirty-second year of Artaxerxes king of Babylon I had returned to the king. Some time later I asked his permission and came back to Jerusalem. Here I learned about the evil thing Eliashib had done in providing Tobiah a room in the courts of the house of God. I was greatly displeased and threw all Tobiah's household goods out of the room. I gave orders to purify the rooms, and then I put back into them the equipment of the house of God, with the grain offerings and the incense.

I also learned that the portions assigned to the Levites had not been given to them, and that all the Levites and musicians

responsible for the service had gone back to their own fields. So I rebuked the officials and asked them, 'Why is the house of God neglected?' Then I called them together and stationed them at their posts.

All Judah brought the tithes of grain, new wine and olive oil into the storerooms. I put Shelemiah the priest, Zadok the scribe, and a Levite named Pedaiah in charge of the storerooms and made Hanan son of Zakkur, the son of Mattaniah, their assistant, because they were considered trustworthy. They were made responsible for distributing the supplies to their fellow Levites.

The Levitical tithes were originally to go to the Levites' cities[126] and then the Levites gave a tenth of the tithe to the priests,[127] bringing them to storerooms in the temple. However, a tenth of the Levites, 284, were chosen to live in Jerusalem,[128] and other Levites also worked for two weeks out of a year at the temple in Jerusalem.[129] This explains why the storehouse also contained a tithe portion belonging to Levites.

What happened to the tithes that were in the room for the Levites before Eliashib the priest brought Tobiah to live in the storehouse? The text doesn't expressly say what happened, but it hints at it. Nehemiah brought some offerings and temple articles back into the storehouse again after expelling Tobiah from the room used to store the tithes belonging to the Levites. But it doesn't say he brought the tithes back! And he learned that the Levites had been neglected. What happened to their portion of the tithes?

What seems to have happened is that the priests stole the Levite's portion of the tithe, removing it from the storehouse, when

---

126 Nehemiah 10:37,
127 Numbers 18:25-28, Nehemiah 10:38
128 Nehemiah 11:1, 18
129 1 Chronicles 23 and 24

Eliashib brought Tobias to live in the storehouse. If Nehemiah is the context of Malachi's rebuke, the rebuke is not even about the people failing to pay their tithes, but the priests stealing the portion of the tithe that belonged to the Levites when they removed it from the storehouse.[130] Nehemiah, who feared God, then had the people replace the Levite's stolen portion of the tithe and took care of the Levites so they could do God's work.

As I was considering Dr. Russ Kelly's comments on Nehemiah as the context for Malachi, with the rebuke of Malachi 3 addressed to the priests, it seemed problematic because some translations sound like Malachi is addressing the whole nation for robbing God. But several people pointed out that *the passage is easily read not as addressing the whole nation, but as a rebuke for robbing the whole nation as well as robbing God!* This reading strongly supports Dr. Russ Kelly's belief that Malachi's context is found in Nehemiah.

Malachi 3:9 (NKJV) You are cursed with a curse, For you have robbed Me, Even this whole nation.

A word order which more closely reflects the original language can be read as *"You have robbed me, robbed even this whole nation."* That makes perfect sense if the context of Malachi is found in Nehemiah. The end of Nehemiah 12 tells us that the people did bring the portions of the Levites (tithes). If Malachi is referring to those events in Nehemiah, God was not rebuking the people for failing to tithe. Eliashib and any other priests who removed the tithe robbed the whole nation by taking the tithes they had given for the Levites to serve them, so that Nehemiah had to ask the people to replenish what was taken as seen in Nehemiah 13. They also may have robbed other priests of their portions of the offerings.

---

[130] Kelly, Russell Earl. *Should the Church Teach Tithing?: a Theologians Conclusions about a Taboo Doctrine*. New York: Writers Club Press, 2007. *Chapter 13 Malachi: Ministers Who Robbed God* Dr. Russ Kelley argues that Malachi never stopped talking to the priests. Also online: http://www.tithing-russkelly.com/id10.html

The Young's Literal translation seems to indicate that God was not even promising to bless them and rebuke the devourer if they brought the tithe, but rather exhorting them by reminding them of what he had already done for their nation! It bothered Young that many Bible translations didn't accurately reflect the tense of the original language, so he produced one of the most literal Bible translations that we have. As you read, also consider that the original language does not have punctuation.

Malachi 3:8-12 (YLT) Doth man deceive God? but ye are deceiving Me, And ye have said: "In what have we deceived Thee?" The tithe and the heave-offering!

With a curse ye are cursed! And Me ye are deceiving -- this nation -- all of it. Bring in all the tithe unto the treasure-house, And there is food in My house; When ye have tried Me, now, with this, Said Jehovah of Hosts, Do not I open to you the windows of heaven? Yea, I have emptied on you a blessing till there is no space.

And I have pushed for you against the consumer, And He doth not destroy to you the fruit of the ground, Nor miscarry to you doth the vine in the field, Said Jehovah of Hosts.

And declared you happy have all the nations, For ye are a delightful land, said Jehovah of Hosts.

I can't tell you how many times I've heard it taught *"The local church is the storehouse, and the pastors are the priests. You obey Malachi by giving a tenth of your gross income to the local church."*

Consider what an enormous problem scripture presents for the position that the priests of that day correspond to the pastors of today. Even if Nehemiah 13 isn't the context of Malachi 3, and Malachi is not only addressing the priests, the undeniable fact remains that the Levites received the tithe first and gave a tenth of their tithe to the priests. ***The priests only received 1% at the very most!***

In Nehemiah 13, who did most of the tithe go to? Doorkeepers and singers. 1 Chronicles 23:29-30 says that the Levites were not only dedicated to giving praise and thanks, but they took care of the bread. Think communion elements today. If the priests of that day correspond to the pastors of today, then most certainly the doorkeepers, singers, and those who took care of the bread, who received 9/10ths of the tithe, correspond to the deacons, ushers, and worship leaders of today. What's more, if the deacons, ushers, Sunday school teachers, and worship leaders aren't receiving their 9/10ths of the tithe, the pastor is robbing God and is cursed with a curse, just as the priests of Nehemiah's day who stole the Levite's portion of the tithe!

Don't forget those who prophesy! 1 Chronicles 25:1 says the duty of some of the Levites was to prophesy with musical instruments. ***If pastors today correspond to the priests of old, then surely 9/10ths of the tithe today should go to those who fulfill similar roles as those belonging to the Levites, including helps ministries and Sunday school teachers!***

This is a strong point against the notion that we are following an *"eternal moral principle"* by enforcing the modern tithe, because our modern tithe is contradicting even the principle of the Jewish tithe. ***How can we teach that the tithe applies to the church today and then just make up our own rules for it?***

Creating a doctrine based on interpreting a few select verses totally out of context is an error. Malachi 3:5 comes right before where most preachers start reading, and it rebukes those who oppress the orphan, the widow, and the sojourner. These three groups were included in the Biblical instructions for the distribution of the tithe. ***To teach Christians to tithe according to Malachi without giving a significant portion of those tithes directly to the orphan, the widow, and the sojourner is to rob and oppress them by stealing their portion of the tithe.***

Deuteronomy 26:12-13 When you have finished setting aside a tenth of all your produce in the third year, the year of the tithe, you shall give it to the Levite, the foreigner, the fatherless and the widow, so that they may eat in your towns and be satisfied. Then say to the Lord your God: "I have removed from my house the sacred portion and have given it to the Levite, the foreigner, the fatherless and the widow, according to all you commanded. I have not turned aside from your commands nor have I forgotten any of them."

7th Layer - Very Little of the Tithe Went to Priests

Much tithing doctrine is based on attempting to equate pastors of today with the priests of old, despite scripture's clear teaching about the priesthood of all believers. Yet the priest only received a tenth of the tithe, at the very most.

There are various positions about how many tithes God intended, with people interpreting the scriptures to point to 1, 2, 3, or 4 tithes. The most common position is 3 tithes, one of them only taken every three years. Jewish tradition also has three tithes with different names in Hebrew.

However, the teachers of the law had a tendency to conflate their interpretation and add a lot more than the scriptures actually said. The *Encyclopedia Judaica* says there was one tithe divided to be used for different purposes.

The rabbis... interpreted them as two different tributes: one to be given to the Levite, "the first tithe"; and the other to be brought to Jerusalem and consumed there, "the second tithe." Theoretically, this was an excellent solution. However, from the practical point of view the implementation of these laws was almost impossible. The excise of 20% of the yield was too high...[131]

---

[131] Skolnik, Fred, and Michael Berenbaum. *Encyclopaedia Judaica*. Detroit: Thomson Gale, 2007. Page 739

Pastor Graeme Carlé holds to this position, pointing out the small number of Levites in the Biblical censuses and showing that if they only received the tithe every third year, it would be an equitable amount, but if there was a separate tithe they received every year, they would end up with way more than other people's share. He explains that since the Israelites came into their inheritance at different times, the third year of Deuteronomy 14 would be different for different people, thus giving a constant supply of tithes to help the orphan, foreigner, widow, and Levite.

Graeme has a good point, as the **Levites also didn't depend exclusively on tithes but worked for most of the year, and tithes were only a small portion of the priests' income**. If you hold the position that the Hebrew scriptures only point to one tithe, you must conclude that the Levites only received a third of the tithe, and priests only received a tenth of one third of the tithe, or 1/3 of one percent total. If you interpret the *"third year"* as year three in the seven-year cycle and also hold the single tithe position, that amounts to the priests only receiving 1/6th of a percent or less. (As they would not tithe crops on the Sabbath year.)

I tend towards the position that scripture describes a single tithe with three different uses. The rabbis probably conflated the tithe to mean much more than what God actually said, adding their own rules, as they did with other commands like the Sabbath.

Edersheim, an expert on Judaism, tells us that priests received income from 24 different sources and tithes were one of the least of them.[132] If Israel's priesthood is to be the model for ministerial support today, we must reinstate animal sacrifices and many other mandatory offerings besides just the tithe!

---

[132] Edersheim, Alfred. *The Temple: Its Ministry and Services as They Were at the Time of Jesus Christ.* London: Religious Tract Society, 1900. Pg. 102-103.

8th Layer - Most of the Tithe Wasn't Originally Supposed To Go to the Storehouse, and Did Not Maintain the Temple

As we already mentioned, the Levites received 9/10ths of a tithe at the most, and around the time Malachi was written 9/10ths of the Levites lived outside of Jerusalem.[133] *The people were to bring the tithe to the Levites, and then it was the Levites who brought a tithe of the tithe to the priests. Most of the tithe didn't go to the storehouse.*

Nehemiah 10:37-38 And we will bring a tithe of our crops to the Levites, for it is the Levites who collect the tithes in all the towns where we work. A priest descended from Aaron is to accompany the Levites when they receive the tithes, and the Levites are to bring a tenth of the tithes up to the house of our God, to the storerooms of the treasury.

This fact creates a big problem for the teaching that the storehouse of Malachi is the local church of today, because most of the tithe didn't go to the storehouse of Malachi! When Malachi says *"bring the whole tithe into the storehouse,"* it's referring to the whole tithe that was removed from the storehouse, the Levite's tithe on the tithe they received (1%), as well as the portion of the 284 Levites who lived in Jerusalem.

Nehemiah 10:38 also seriously calls into question the interpretation that Malachi's words are directed to the original tithers. They were not the ones who brought the tithe into the storehouse.

Furthermore, *none of the tithe went to fund building maintenance or expenses*. It was all given as food for Levites and Priests, and to allocate it otherwise would have been robbing them.

---

[133] Nehemiah 11:1, 18

We cannot say the tithe of Malachi applies to us yet then refuse to allocate it in the way scripture prescribes.

In the book of Nehemiah, the people agreed to a temple tax, separate from the tithe.

Nehemiah 10:32 We assume the responsibility for carrying out the commands to give a third of a shekel each year for the service of the house of our God: for the bread set out on the table; for the regular grain offerings and burnt offerings; for the offerings on the Sabbaths, at the New Moon feasts and at the appointed festivals; for the holy offerings; for sin offerings to make atonement for Israel; and for all the duties of the house of our God.

Throughout the Old Testament, we always see the building and maintenance of a temple or tabernacle funded with a tax or freewill offerings, never by a tithe. And Jesus said that he and his followers were exempt from the temple tax! He paid it anyways, not of obligation, but to not offend them![134]

9th Layer-People Are God's Temple Now and Not a Building

The book of Acts says in two separate places that God does not live in temples built by human hands.[135] But the New Testament clearly teaches that God's people are a temple.[136]

Religious buildings are neither forbidden nor required for the church to exist. Many of the fastest growing church planting movements in the world forego them because of high overhead, increased complexity, rapid growth, or persecution. However, if we do have buildings, they are not our temples. Their purpose must be to serve people, who are the true temple of God.

---

[134] Matthew 17:24-27
[135] Acts 7:48, Acts 17:24
[136] 1 Peter 2:5, 1 Corinthians 6:19

Malachi says to bring the tithe so that there may be *"food in my house."* This is so often interpreted as *"so we can pay the electric bill."* In fact, in Spanish and Portuguese speaking cultures, it's *"so we can take care of the temple."* Yet even in the Old Testament, none of the tithe went to care for a temple but all of it was food for people! God's heart was the same then, and the temple of old was only a shadow of better things to come.

The Jewish Christians of the early church met in the Jewish temple, as well as house to house, because they continued to be Jews and follow Jewish precepts. Even Paul, who argued vehemently against enforcing Jewish law on gentile Christians, went through the Jewish ritual purification rites with an offering[137] made for him before entering the temple when he was among his own people.[138] Yet that didn't last long. Jesus prophesied the destruction of that same temple along with the final remnants of the Old Covenant.

I'm not saying we can't have a building to meet in. But the purpose must be to serve people. Accessories like a church building are part of our cultural expression of Christianity, not of Christianity at its roots or foundation. It's unacceptable to make up a doctrine (the modern tithe, based on the Babylonian tithe) and try to mold scripture to conform to that doctrine because we want to support our particular cultural expression of Christianity. If buildings actually were God's temples, they would be a better reason to argue for the reinstatement of the temple tax than for the tithe!

---

[137] Possibly the animal sacrifice recorded in Numbers 6:14-16
[138] Acts 21:26

Chapter 7
The History of Tithing

A large volume could easily be written on this topic alone. You can easily find more information with a little research. If you'd like to learn more, a good place is Dr. Russel Kelly's book *"Should the Church Teach Tithing?* or his website tithing-russkelly.com. Dr. Kelly did his doctoral thesis on tithing. Dr. David Croteau also has a really great chapter on the history of tithing in his thesis *"You Mean I Don't Have to Tithe?"*[139] Both have great compilations of quotes from famous Christian figures, from early church history all the way up to modern theologians, regarding the tithe.

I'd like to give a brief overview of how strong the historical case is against tithing as a component of original apostolic Christianity. We'll also consider churches today which do not teach tithing.

Did Jesus, Paul, or the Early Apostles Receive a Tithe?

Not only does scripture never mention Jesus receiving a tithe, but it's nearly unimaginable that he could have when we consider the context he lived in! Scripture does tell us clearly how Jesus and the twelve received their support:

Luke 8:1-3 After this, Jesus travelled about from one town and village to another, proclaiming the good news of the

---

[139] Croteau, David A. *You Mean I Dont Have to Tithe?: a Deconstruction of Tithing and a Reconstruction of Post-Tithe Giving.* Eugene, Or.: Pickwick Publications, 2010.

kingdom of God. The Twelve were with him, and also some women who had been cured of evil spirits and diseases: Mary (called Magdalene) from whom seven demons had come out; Joanna the wife of Chuza, the manager of Herod's household; Susanna; and many others. These women were helping to support them out of their own means.

Jesus talked about money a lot, but for all his teaching about money, scripture doesn't record him ever preaching a sermon to raise money for his own ministry. Yet he received financial support for himself and his disciples in the form of free-will gifts.

Scripture never records Jesus or the apostles taking up an offering for their own ministries! Every offering scripture records them taking up was for the poor. I'm not arguing that it's wrong to ever pass the basket or take up an offering for the preacher. I'm just pointing out the primary emphasis on giving to the poor, which church historians also highlight.

Jesus's own instructions when he sent the apostles out made no mention of a tithe, but only of enjoying hospitality from the people who received them. Two of his commands seem contradictory, on a surface level.

Matthew 10:7-10 As you go, proclaim this message: "The kingdom of heaven has come near." Heal the sick, raise the dead, cleanse those who have leprosy, drive out demons. Freely you have received; freely give. Do not get any gold or silver or copper to take with you in your belts— no bag for the journey or extra shirt or sandals or a staff, for the worker is worth his keep.

Jesus told them to give freely, yet he also said the worker is worth his keep. They were never to put a price on the gospel, yet it was proper for them to receive hospitality and support as they went. One seminary textbook gives a little background on the world at the time of Christ:

> Among the Jews professional life was limited. The one widely extensive profession was that of rabbi, if profession it might be called, for most rabbis followed some trade or secular pursuit for a livelihood, while devoting all the time possible to the study and teaching of the law. . . Every Jewish boy was expected to learn some trade. Rabbinic tradition declared that "whoever does not teach his son a trade is as if he brought him up to be a robber'"[140]

> The prevalent use of tents [by travelers] made the tent-making trade a lucrative occupation. One belonging to the same trade-guild, religious cult, or having any other personal relationship to any resident of the locality could nearly always find welcome more or less genuine in a private home... This was the prevailing manner in which the first Christian missionaries were provided for, though likely the entertainment was tendered them without cost (cf. 2 John 10-11; 3 John 5-8)[141]

The primary form of giving to ministers in the early church was free hospitality, and that was the support Jesus taught his disciples to receive on a missionary journey. That's a far cry from receiving 10% of the income of the people you minister too. Remember, even the priests in the Old Covenant only received 1/6th of a percent to 1% of livestock and agricultural products when the tithe was collected!

There is no indication Jesus or his disciples ever received a tithe. The only support Scriptures tells us they received was hospitality and free-will gifts. They gave freely, never charging a price for ministry, but receiving hospitality and the generosity of benefactors.

Those who imagine that Jesus could have received a tithe should remember that he was born under the law, kept the law, and

---

[140] Dana, H. E. *The New Testament World* 3rd. ed., Nashville: Broadman, 1937. Pg. 149
[141] Dana, H. E. *The New Testament World* 3rd. ed., Nashville: Broadman, 1937. Pg. 217, 221

had no right under the law to receive a tithe. He was not a Levite. He was a rabbi, and rabbis did not receive tithes. The Jewish leaders tried hard to find fault with Jesus and accused him of breaking the Sabbath. Can you imagine the dispute that would break out if they learned that Jesus and his disciples, being non-Levites, were receiving tithes?

It's most likely that Jesus's disciples continued receiving support in the same way they did before Jesus's death—by freewill offerings. The early church in Jerusalem continued to follow Hebrew law, so the leaders could not have possibly received tithes. Not being priests or Levites, it was unlawful to do so.

Furthermore, Jesus and the disciples would not have paid tithes on the incomes from their professions under Jewish law. When I point out that the Mosaic tithe was only on agricultural produce and livestock, thus tradespeople, hired laborers, and fisherman did not tithe, some people imagine I'm making this up, in spite of the scriptural references. Yet these are well-established historical facts which are easy to verify, with rabbinical tradition and experts on Judaism agreeing.

Paul was clear about the fact that he never demanded money, much less a tithe, from those he preached the gospel to. He received hospitality and free-will offerings.

Philippians 4:15 Moreover, as you Philippians know, in the early days of your acquaintance with the gospel, when I set out from Macedonia, not one church shared with me in the matter of giving and receiving, except you only.

2 Corinthians 12:13-15 How were you inferior to the other churches, except that I was never a burden to you? Forgive me this wrong! Now I am ready to visit you for the third time, and I will not be a burden to you, because what I want is not your possessions but you. After all, children should not have to save up for their parents, but parents for their children. So

I will very gladly spend for you everything I have and expend myself as well.

Acts 20:17+18, 20, 27, 33-35 From Miletus, Paul sent to Ephesus for the elders of the church. When they arrived he said to them… "You know that I have not hesitated to preach anything that would be helpful to you but have taught you publicly and from house to house… For I have not hesitated to proclaim to you the whole will of God… I have not coveted anyone's silver or gold or clothing. You yourselves know that these hands of mine have supplied my own needs and the needs of my companions. In everything I did, I showed you that by this kind of hard work we must help the weak, remembering the words the Lord Jesus himself said: 'It is more blessed to give than to receive.'"

I remember hearing our pastor say *"We rob the churches if we don't teach them about tithing."* Consider the absurdity of such a statement in the light of Paul's words to the Ephesians in Acts 20. The church in Ephesus was composed of primarily gentile Christians. If tithing was of any importance whatsoever, Paul would have had to teach it to them. He didn't hesitate to proclaim the whole will of God or anything that would have been helpful to them, and there is no mention or even allusion to a tithe. He clearly did not teach them to give him tithes, even outside of the Epistle to the Ephesians, because he says he himself supplied his own needs and the needs of his companions. If tithing to him was of any spiritual benefit to the Ephesians, Paul would have taught them to give him tithes.

Paul's sermon in Acts 20 was specifically to elders, or local church leaders. Instead of instructing those church leaders to receive tithes from the congregations, he did the very opposite! He encouraged them to follow his example by working hard to supply not only their own needs but also the needs of others.

The First Generations of the Church Clearly Did Not Practice Tithing

Did the early church practice tithing or require a tithe? As we've already pointed out, to do so they would have had to add an additional tithe to the one (or ones) they already paid under Mosaic law, since the Jewish Christians continued to observe Mosaic law until the temple was destroyed and non-Levite church leaders did not qualify to receive the Mosaic tithe.

Some say the silence of the New Testament epistles on tithing is due to it being universally accepted so nobody needed to say anything about it. That argument is absurd. The silence of the epistles on the issue is a much stronger argument against tithing. If it were such a foundational issue as many churches today treat it to be, Paul would have certainly had to teach it to all the gentile believers and it surely would have needed to be mentioned in Acts 15 as one of the essentials that gentile Christians needed to observe!

Consider the matters for which Paul rebuked and exhorted the churches. The Corinthian church had carnal infighting and sexual immorality to the point that a man slept with his stepmother. Can you honestly imagine that Paul wrote nothing to them about tithing because he had taught it to them in person and had no need to mention it again in his epistles because they were completely faithful with tithes, in spite of their unfaithfulness in so many matters of much greater importance? The idea is preposterous! If tithing were required, failure to tithe would be one of the first signs of unfaithfulness.

Furthermore, the Jewish believers would have needed significant instruction in order to justify giving the tithe to non-Levite church leaders rather than to the Levites and Priests, or to establish an additional tithe on top of the ones the law already exacted. Dr. Kelly states what is evident in Acts 15 and 21: The early Jewish believers continued following Jewish law and tithing to the priests and Levites, not to the church.

Almost every denomination's historians of early church history agree that, until A.D. 70 the Jewish Christians in Jerusalem faithfully attended the temple in obedience to Jewish law and, as faithful Jews, supported the Jewish temple with tithes and offerings in addition to their church support.[142]

The church eventually collected a tithe modeled after the Babylonian tithe rather than the Mosaic tithe. Tithing was introduced to the Christian church partly through the influence of Roman and Greek culture rather than as a *"moral principle"* carried on directly from Judaism. In fact, the Encyclopedia Britannica points out that the Eastern Orthodox churches never accepted the idea of tithes, and Orthodox church members have never paid them.[143]

There is no biblical or historical evidence that the early church used tithing to pay its bills until it was legalized in the late 8th century. This can be documented by almost every notable church historian from any major denomination. Cyprian's attempt in the middle of the third century was not adopted by the Church. Neither was Chrysostom's nor Augustine's attempts in the 5th century. Two local church attempts in the 6th century also failed. Study "tithe" in any major reference work for validation of this history.[144]-Dr. Russel Earl Kelly

Hasting's Dictionary of the Apostolic Church, *"tithe; tithing"*

———

It is admitted universally that the payment of tithes or the

[142] Kelly, Russell Earl. *Should the Church Teach Tithing?: a Theologians Conclusions about a Taboo Doctrine.* New York: Writers Club Press, 2007. Pg. 249
[143] *Encyclopedia Britannica.* Chicago: Encyclopedia Britannica, Inc., 1974. *Tithe.* Online: https://www.britannica.com/topic/tithe Accessed December 3rd, 2019
[144] Kelly, Russel Earl *If We Don't Preach Tithing, How Do We Pay The Church Bills?* Online: http://www.tithing-russkelly.com/id158.html Accessed January 1st, 2020

tenths of possessions, for sacred purposes did not find a place within the Christian Church during the age covered by the apostles and their immediate successors.[145]

A large body of evidence, including historical and scriptural commentary, agrees with this. Major Encyclopedias agree that tithing came into practice only after hundreds of years into church history. Justin Martyr's description of worship and giving in the early church, from around 150 AD, makes it clear that they did not follow a tithe model of giving:

And they who are well to do, and willing, give what each thinks fit; and what is collected is deposited with the president, who succors the orphans and widows and those who, through sickness or any other cause, are in want, and those who are in bonds and the strangers sojourning among us, and in a word takes care of all who are in need.[146]

Where is tithing in this description? People gave what they thought fit? Rather than everybody being obligated to bring tithes, those who were *"well to do"* and *"willing"* gave? Justin Martyr's description of early church giving could not possibly describe the giving of any church today that teaches tithing. But if Justin Martyr's description of early church giving isn't clear enough for you, Tertullian's is even more so:

The tried men of our elders preside over us, obtaining that honour not by purchase, but by established character. There is no buying and selling of any sort in the things of God. Though we have our treasure-chest, it is not made up of purchase-money, as of a religion that has its price.

---

[145] Hastings, James. *Dictionary of the Apostolic Church.* Edinburgh: Clark, 1915. *Tithes* Online: https://www.studylight.org/dictionaries/hdn/t/tithes.html Accessed November 29th, 2019

[146] Chapter LXVII of Justin Martyr's Second Apology, *Weekly Worship of the Christians.* Online: http://www.ccel.org/ccel/schaff/anf01.viii.ii.lxvii.html Accessed November 29th, 2019

On the monthly day, if he likes, each puts in a small donation; but only if it be his pleasure, and only if he be able: for there is no compulsion; all is voluntary. These gifts are, as it were, piety's deposit fund. For they are not taken thence and spent on feasts, and drinking-bouts, and eating-houses, but to support and bury poor people, to supply the wants of boys and girls destitute of means and parents, and of old persons confined now to the house; such, too, as have suffered shipwreck; and if there happen to be any in the mines, or banished to the islands, or shut up in the prisons, for nothing but their fidelity to the cause of God's Church, they become the nurslings of their confession....[147]

Tertullian despised the idea of Christianity having a monetary price, or of there being any buying or selling in the things of God. What is purchase money? It is an obligatory sum that you pay to receive something. The tithe as taught today is purchase money.

Those who teach tithing promote a *"religion that has its price."* Even if the church will accept non-tithers into fellowship, it will usually not accept them as full-fledged members of the body of Christ, allowed to minister as Christ enables them.

Tertullian was crystal clear about the fact that there was no compulsion. His description of early church giving sharply contrasts with what many of us are accustomed to. Each person put in a small donation only if he was able and only if he wanted to!

---

[147] Excerpt from chapter 39 of Tertullian's Apology. Online: http://www.earlychristianwritings.com/text/tertullian01.html?fbclid=IwAR1a11CWFurum2 Chlt6d9xlnEbIyckcNZOSEbrNuSb32RWZECJXYps_8-Kg Accessed November 29th, 2019

Contrasting the Christian Love Feasts to the Pagan Feasts and the Tithe of Hercules

A little while later in the same chapter of his apology, Tertullian contrasted the Christian feasts that supplied the needs of the poor with the self-indulgent pagan feasts:

> **What wonder if that great love of Christians towards one another is desecrated by you! For you abuse also our humble feasts, on the ground that they are extravagant as well as infamously wicked. To us, it seems, applies the saying of Diogenes: "The people of Megara feast as though they were going to die on the morrow; they build as though they were never to die!" But one sees more readily the mote in another's eye than the beam in his own. Why, the very air is soured with the eructations of so many tribes, and curioe, and decurioe. The Salii cannot have their feast without going into debt; you must get the accountants to tell you what the tenths of Hercules and the sacrificial banquets cost; the choicest cook is appointed for the Apaturia, the Dionysia, the Attic mysteries; the smoke from the banquet of Serapis will call out the firemen. Yet about the modest supper-room of the Christians alone a great ado is made. Our feast explains itself by its name The Greeks call it agape, i.e., affection. Whatever it costs, our outlay in the name of piety is gain, since with the good things of the feast we benefit the needy; not as it is with you...[148]**

Tertullian mentioned the accountants keeping track of the tithe of Hercules. That reminds me of many churches today that keep tithe records! It stood in sharp contrast to the practice of the Christians. Tithes were part and parcel of pagan worship and law in many cultures. Many Romans practiced giving a tithe of the spoils of war

---

[148] Excerpt from chapter 39 of Tertullian's Apology. Online:
http://www.earlychristianwritings.com/text/tertullian01.html?fbclid=IwAR1a11CWFurum2Chlt6d9xlnEblyekeNZOSEbrNuSb32RWZECJXYps_8-Kg Accessed November 29th, 2019

to Hercules,[149] similar to Abraham's spoils-of-war tithe given to Melchizedek. Pagan tithes stood in contrast to the Mosaic tithe which blessed the poor.

Although Tertullian is clear that all contributions were strictly voluntary, his description of feasts early Christians shared with the poor reminds me of the Mosaic tithe feast of Deuteronomy 14. It was eaten by the tither and shared with the poor. God's heart of care for the poor stood in contrast to the spirit of the pagan tithes and feasts.

In the Old Testament, we see many common practices of Ancient Near East cultures that God modified as to reflect his heart. That shows us that God was willing to meet people where they were at, in their culture, and reveal himself. The Mosaic Law and the Babylonian Code of Hammurabi have a lot in common, but the Mosaic Law contains compassion and justice that the Code of Hammurabi often lacks.

What Did the Church Fathers Say About Tithes?

We can find quotes from early church leaders both in favour of and against teaching tithing, but it is clear that it was not the early church's practice for several hundred years. The earliest church fathers were generally silent or ambiguous about it. Early church leaders emphasized giving all of their possessions to the poor, not tithing. Irenaeus said:

And for this reason did the Lord, instead of that [commandment], "Thou shalt not commit adultery," forbid even concupiscence; and instead of that which runs thus,

---

[149] I. B. Antela-Bernardez & T. Naco del Hoyo (eds.), *Transforming Historical Landscapes in the Ancient Empires.* (BAR Int. Series 1986). Oxford 2009, 83-97 'Hercules and the triumphal feast for the Roman people' Online:
https://www.academia.edu/241113/Hercules_and_the_triumphal_feast_for_the_Roman_peo ple_in_I._B._Antela-
Bernardez_and_T._Naco_del_Hoyo_eds._Transforming_Historical_Landscapes_in_the_Anc ient_Empires._BAR_Int._Series_1986_._Oxford_2009_83-
97?fbclid=IwAR0FHAxNzRn2EVWwG9H6ZQ3vtGgGZbtSG-
uyZaH01f1CpK7oy_sRNKdiP08 Accessed November 29th, 2019

"Thou shalt not kill," He prohibited anger; and instead of the law enjoining the giving of tithes, [He told us] to share all our possessions with the poor…[150]

Another early Christian writing, the *Didascalia Apostolorum*, clearly stated that tithes are not binding on Christians. It put the tithe in the same category as burnt offerings and other rituals:

The Lord, by the gift of His grace, has set you loose and given you rest…that you should no more be bound with sacrifices and oblations, and with sin offerings, and purifications, and vows, and gifts, and holocausts, and burnt offerings, and [Sabbath] idlings, and shewbread, and the observing of purifications; nor yet with tithes and firstfruits, and part-offerings, and gifts and oblations – for it was laid upon them [Jews] to give all these things as of necessity, but you are not bound by these things…[151]

Some people falsely claim that certain church fathers such as Tertullian taught tithing, though nothing on record shows they did. Trying to create support for their position, they often interpret statements as *"He was saying Christians should tithe"* when that was not actually what was said. Tertullian's description of early church giving strongly contrasts with a tithe paradigm.

Even some quotes from those who wanted to implement a tithe show it was not the practice of the churches at the time. If you've heard that Clement of Alexandria thought Christians should tithe, it's true. But keep that in the context of him also wanting Christians to keep Sabbatical years and the year of Jubilee!

The earliest tithe proponents were ascetics who advocated denying themselves and giving as much as possible of the tithe to

---

[150] *Against Heresies*, Book IV, Chap XIII, Para 3. Online: www.ccel.org/ccel/schaff/anf01.ix.vi.xiv.html, Accessed November 17th, 2019
[151] *Didascalia Apostolorum*, IX, ii. 35, translated by R. Hugh Connolly, Oxford; Clarendon Press, 1929. Online: www.earlychristianwritings.com/text/didascalia.html Accessed November 17th, 2019

the poor. Their view strongly contrasted with how most churches use the tithe today.

When you hear that someone in the early church taught or didn't teach tithing, it's a good idea to consider the commentary on both sides. Some very clearly did teach for or against tithing, but many were ambiguous or seemed to contradict themselves.

The early church fathers were sometimes prone to error and often disagreed with each other. Studying their writings gives us insight into how they interpreted the scriptures, but their teachings are not the definite word on a subject and mean little if they contradict scripture. Several church fathers promoted antisemitism and other ideas that most of us would disagree with or consider harmful. Jerome said *"Woman is the root of all evil,"*[152] and some other church fathers also held an extremely negative view of women. Even the apostles who walked with Christ missed the mark sometimes, as Peter did on the circumcision issue.

Tertullian and Justin Martyr were describing the churches' practice concerning giving, and not just opinions on the matter. As the years passed, some tried unsuccessfully to implement tithing, such as Cyprian in 250 AD and the Council of Macon in France, in 585 AD. Charlemagne legally allowed the church to collect tithes in 777 AD.[153] Unsuccessful attempts to collect tithes, and the complaints of tithing proponents that the churches didn't practice tithing, show how unpopular tithing was.

Lest anybody accuse those non-tithing early Christians of lacking commitment, remember that many of them faced severe persecution and were martyred for their faith.

---

[152] Phelips, Vivian. *The Churches and Modern Thought: an Inquiry into the Grounds of Unbelief and an Appeal for Candour.* London: Watts, 1934. p284
[153] *Encyclopedia Britannica.* Chicago: Encyclopedia Britannica, Inc., 1974. *Tithe*

What Else Accompanied the Increased Emphasis on Tithing?

Emphasis on tithing increased after Constantine united the church and state in 325 AD. Dr. Croteau comments that it becomes increasingly difficult to know if references to tithing were talking about a religious duty or a government tax.[154]

Tithing became a church law with the joining of church and state, and it became state law in 779 as Europe entered the dark ages.[155] However, influential Christians remained throughout those times who disagreed about the New Covenant requiring tithing, including Epiphanius, the Waldenses, Thomas Aquinas,[156] John Wycliff, and John Huss. Quoting Dr. David Croteau:

> **Therefore, the church has not had a unanimous opinion on tithing throughout its history. Instead, the doctrine of the tithe has developed throughout church history from being nearly nonexistent in early church history, to an exhortation to voluntarily tithe, to tithing becoming part of the ecclesiastical law, and finally to it being made state law...Opposition to tithing grew in the fourteenth and fifteen centuries. However, this opposition was not as widespread as it would be in the following centuries.[157]**

> **For the most part (with few exceptions), those who held to the 'two swords' view of Christianity also believed that tithes were binding on Christians; those who denied this view of the**

---

[154] Croteau, David A. *You Mean I Dont Have to Tithe?: a Deconstruction of Tithing and a Reconstruction of Post-Tithe Giving.* Eugene, Or.: Pickwick Publications, 2010. Position 506

[155] Croteau, David A. *You Mean I Dont Have to Tithe?: a Deconstruction of Tithing and a Reconstruction of Post-Tithe Giving.* Eugene, Or.: Pickwick Publications, 2010. Position 563-564

[156] For the sake of accuracy I should note that although Thomas Aquinas did not believe the New Covenant mandated tithes, he believed that Christians should follow one of the three Jewish tithes because of his view of ecclesiology and the authority of the Roman Catholic church.

[157] Croteau, David A. *You Mean I Dont Have to Tithe?: a Deconstruction of Tithing and a Reconstruction of Post-Tithe Giving.* Eugene, Or.: Pickwick Publications, 2010. Position 641-648

church and state appear to have abrogated the tithe laws. Their view on 'Christian sacralism' seems to have driven their view on tithing.[158]

The Protestant Reformation and Opposition to Tithes

Martin Luther said of the tithe:

But the other commandments of Moses, which are not by nature, the Gentiles do not hold. Nor do these pertain to the Gentiles, such as the tithe and others equally fine which I wish we had too.[159]

Luther liked the idea of a tithe as a civil tax, since it would be a much lighter burden than the taxes of his day. However, he said the tithe didn't pertain to the Gentiles and was not a part of natural law. Zwingli entered the Reformation over the issue of tithing, but later seemed to backpedal.[160] The Anabaptists reacted radically against tithing and called for its abolition.[161,162] Calvin's position was unclear and confusing.[163] John Smyth, often credited as being the first Baptist, said that Christ abolished tithes.[164] John Robinson, the pastor of the *"Pilgrim Fathers"* [165] before they left on the Mayflower, wrote that tithing was abolished[166] and ministers should be maintained with voluntary contributions.[167]

---

[158] Croteau, David A. *You Mean I Dont Have to Tithe?: a Deconstruction of Tithing and a Reconstruction of Post-Tithe Giving.* Eugene, Or.: Pickwick Publications, 2010. Position 648
[159] Luther, Martin. How Christians Should Regard Moses. Pg. 168
[160] Croteau, David A. *You Mean I Dont Have to Tithe?: a Deconstruction of Tithing and a Reconstruction of Post-Tithe Giving.* Eugene, Or.: Pickwick Publications, 2010. Position 695
[161] Bax, Ernest Belfort. *Rise and Fall of the Anabaptists.* London: s.n., 1903. Pg. 12, 37
[162] Croteau, David A. *You Mean I Dont Have to Tithe?: a Deconstruction of Tithing and a Reconstruction of Post-Tithe Giving.* Eugene, Or.: Pickwick Publications, 2010. Position 719
[163] Croteau, David A. *You Mean I Dont Have to Tithe?: a Deconstruction of Tithing and a Reconstruction of Post-Tithe Giving.* Eugene, Or.: Pickwick Publications, 2010. Position 734-774
[164] Smyth, John. Parallels, Censures, Observations. Pg. 120-121
[165] Croteau, David A. *You Mean I Dont Have to Tithe?: a Deconstruction of Tithing and a Reconstruction of Post-Tithe Giving.* Eugene, Or.: Pickwick Publications, 2010. Position 788.
[166] Robinson, John. Works. Volume 2, Pg. 467
[167] Robinson, John. Works. Volume 2, Pg. 466-467

The English Baptists and Quakers also opposed tithing, with particularly fierce resistance coming from the Quakers. Quakers said they were not bound to obey the civil authorities when they gave commands in contradiction to scripture.[168] Quakers were imprisoned, beaten, heavily fined, and had their goods seized for refusing to tithe.[169,170] Any Quaker who did tithe was threatened with expulsion from the group.[171]

Many English Baptist groups continued paying the tithe as obedience to a civil law, but not because they believed scripture mandated it. One said that tithing *"over throws the priesthood of Christ."* They concluded that a minister who accepted tithes should be dealt with according to Matthew 18:15-17, be put on church discipline, and excommunicated if they didn't repent.[172]

John Bunyan was the author of Pilgrim's Progress, known as the best-selling Christian book in history next to the Bible. He was imprisoned for his faith. He said the tithe was ceremonial, passing away with the ending of the Levitical priesthood.[173]

Again, quoting Dr. David Croteau:

Contrary to the conclusions of most, the Reformation period closed with no (major) reformer explicitly advocating tithing.

---

[168] Gough, John. *Tracts on Tithes. I. Brief and Serious Reasons Why the People Called Quakers Do Not Pay Tithes. ... II. Plain Reasons Why the People Called Quakers May in Conscience, and Ought in Duty, to Pay Tithes. ... Said to Be Written by a Prelate of This Kingdom. III. A Vindication of the Brief and Serious Reasons, in Reply to the Last. By. J.G. One of the Said People.* Dublin: Printed by Robert Jackson, 1786. Pg. 26, 48, 51, 60, 70, 73

[169] Besse, Joseph. *A Collection of the Sufferings of the People Called Quakers, for the Testimony of a Good Conscience: from the Time of Their Being First Distinguished by That Name in the Year 1650, to the Time of the Act, Commonly Called the Act of Toleration, Granted to Protestant Dissenters in the First Year of the Reign of King William the Third and Queen Mary, in the Year 1689.* London: Printed and sold by Luke Hinde ..., 1753. Pg. 85 and 85

[170] Online: http://www.midessexquakers.org.uk/history-persecution.php Also Online: http://banburyeveshamquakers.org.uk/ettington/6-history Accessed December 17th, 2019.

[171] Murray, Stuart. *Beyond Tithing.* Eugene, Or.: Wipf & Stock Publishers, 2012. Pg. 170

[172] Croteau, David A. *You Mean I Don't Have to Tithe?: a Deconstruction of Tithing and a Reconstruction of Post-Tithe Giving.* Eugene, Or.: Pickwick Publications, 2010. Dr. Croteau discusses the English Baptists from position 878-897. Although he cites original sources for these statements about the English Baptists, I was unable to find them.

[173] Bunyan, John. *Bunyans Searching Works.* Philadelphia: American Baptist Publication Society, 1851. Pg. 24

Their hesitancy to support tithing was based largely on scriptural arguments, not as a reaction to Catholic abuses of the tithe system.[174]

Up to the Present Time

I've left out many names and quotes of historical Christian figures who did not believe in tithing. As we continue in history, the number of famous Christians and Bible commentators teaching that tithing ended with the old covenant becomes overwhelming. I recommend reading the works of Dr. David Croteau and Dr. Russ Kelly if you'd like to go into more detail.

Charles Noble wrote an open letter to C.H. Spurgeon's church in July, 1918. He complained about certain changes in the church since the death of Spurgeon:

Many other offensive changes were allowed—amongst them Tithes. Tithes were demanded and money grabbed in every way… Then later Tithes were introduced, and the Law was hooked on to the Gospel. "But we are not under the law, but under grace," which you so soon forgot. It was Paul speaking by the Holy Ghost, who said that "Christ had abolished in His flesh the enmity, even the law of commandments"; and James, speaking to the Church at Jerusalem, of the Gentiles, said, "we will lay on them no other burden than that they abstain from fornication and from things offered to idols and from blood." Tithes were not named, nor called for in the early Church for hundreds of years. Only when she became corrupt were they called for, and then by a greedy, extravagant, pocket-picking priesthood. Tithes caused trouble enough in this country, and yet you allowed Dr. Dixon to preach sermon after sermon on our duty to pay tithes.[175]

---

[174] Croteau, David A. *You Mean I Don't Have to Tithe?: a Deconstruction of Tithing and a Reconstruction of Post-Tithe Giving.* Eugene, Or.: Pickwick Publications, 2010. **Position 807**
[175] Murray, Iain H. *The Forgotten Spurgeon.* Edinburgh: Banner of Truth Trust, 2009. Pg. 242, 243-234

G. Campbell Morgan, a renowned preacher and pastor of Westminster Chapel, said the following in a sermon called *"The Grace of Giving."*:

> **I hear a great deal about the tithing of incomes. I have no sympathy with the movement at all. A tenth in the case of one man is meanness, and in the case of another man is dishonesty. I know men today who are Christian men in city churches and village chapels, who have no business to give a tenth of their income to the work of God. They cannot afford it. I know other men who are giving one-tenth, and the nine-tenths they keep is doing harm to their souls.**[176]

Tithing was not the norm among churches for several hundred years in the United States, where many persecuted groups such as the Quakers fled. Various other methods of support were practiced, including voluntary contributions, renting or selling pews, and at times taxes. The Baptists continued to oppose tithing for hundreds of years. Then major change began in 1876. Quoting Dr. Russ Kelly and then Dr. David Croteau:

> **Except for state-run churches such as the Anglican Church of England, the Lutheran Church of Germany and the Catholic Church of Spain and Germany, tithing did not appear in other churches in the U.S.A. until the late 1890s. It was not even introduced until the 1870s.**[177]*-Dr. Russel Earl Kelly*

> **The fact that a tithing advocate (i.e. Salstrand) mentions a "rediscovery" of tithing indicates that tithing must not have been very widespread or popular in America in the nineteenth century. Regardless, Kane wrote a pamphlet in 1876 and sent it out to 75 percent of the evangelical pastors in the United**

---

[176] Morgan, George Campbell. *The Westminster Pulpit: the Preaching of G. Campbell Morgan. V. 4.* Marshall Morgan And Scott, 1970. Pg. 40
[177] Kelly, Russell Earl. *If We Don't Preach Tithing, How Do We Pay The Church Bills?* Online: http://www.tithing-russkelly.com/id158.html Accessed January 1st, 2020

States free of charge. For years he distributed his pamphlets free of charge.[178]**-Dr. David Croteau**

Even Kane's own writing to promote tithing testifies that the tithe was virtually nonexistent in the first few hundred years of American Evangelical church history:

The twin laws that the seventh of our time and the tenth of our income shall be devoted in a special sense to God's service have never been repealed or abrogated, although until recent years the law of the tithe was almost universally disobeyed; indeed, comparatively few had any distinct knowledge of its existence.[179]

What Does the History of Tithing Tell Us?

I have only given a very brief history on tithing. Of course, history doesn't establish doctrine. History does show us that the tithing debate isn't new. The lack of tithing in the first generations of the church and in many renewal/reformation movements is cause for serious question. The tithe generally became established in conjunction with other changes that most evangelicals don't view positively. Dr. Russ Kelly's observation hits the nail on the head:

The introduction of tithing emerged in direct proportion to the disintegration of the doctrine of the priesthood of believers and the emergence of the power of the bishop-priests.[180]

In fact, Chapter 17 of an early document advocating tithing, *The Constitutions of the Holy Apostles*, uses the following points as its

---

[178] Croteau, David A. *You Mean I Don't Have to Tithe?: a Deconstruction of Tithing and a Reconstruction of Post-Tithe Giving.* Eugene, Or.: Pickwick Publications, 2010. Position 1115
[179] Brown, George W. *Gems of Thought on Tithing.* Nabu Press, 2010. Pg. 18-19
[180] Kelly, Russell Earl. *Should the Church Teach Tithing?: a Theologians Conclusions about a Taboo Doctrine.* New York: Writers Club Press, 2007. Pg. 247

argument that a bishop should receive tithes and other old-testament offerings that went to the priests and Levites:

> **The bishop, he is the minister of the word, the keeper of knowledge, the mediator between God and you in the several parts of your divine worship. He is the teacher of piety; and, next after God, he is your father, who has begotten you again to the adoption of sons by water and the Spirit. He is your ruler and governor; he is your king and potentate; he is, next after God, your earthly God, who has a right to be honored by you.**[181]

Most evangelical Christians consider such doctrine to be dangerous and even blasphemous, yet it's the ecclesiology that went hand-in-hand with the rise of tithing in church history. Jesus Christ is the one and only mediator between God and man. With the Protestant reformation came increased emphasis on the authority of scripture and the priesthood of all believers. People began to read the Bible for themselves. Along with these changes came a flood of resistance towards the tithe. Here is Dr. Stuart Murray's conclusion:

> **Those who advocated reform of the tithing system or who resisted the tithe itself and proposed alternatives often did so on the basis that tithing—at least as it was currently practiced—was contrary to the gospel or not supported by scripture.**[182]

> **Rather than tithing being viewed as a marker of spiritual renewal, the groups that resisted tithing were groups who advocated spiritual renewal and radical discipleship.**[183]

---

[181] Roberts, Alexander, James Donaldson, and A. Cleveland Coxe. *Ante-Nicene Fathers the Writings of the Fathers down to A.D. 325. Volume 7, Lactantius, Venantius, Asterius, Victorinus, Dionysius, Apostolic Teachings and Constitutions, 2 Clement, Early Liturgies.* Peabody, MA: Hendrickson, 1995. Pg. 410

[182] Murray, Stuart. *Beyond Tithing.* Eugene, Or.: Wipf & Stock Publishers, 2012. Pg. 159

[183] Murray, Stuart. *Beyond Tithing.* Eugene, Or.: Wipf & Stock Publishers, 2012. Pg. 173

My personal observation has been that the more regularly Christians begin living out the priesthood of all believers, the more they become open to reconsidering tithing. It stops making sense. In the last decade, the street-healing movement has paved the way for many people to reconsider what they'd been taught about tithes.

The history of tithing should provide serious food for thought to anybody who assumes that opposition to tithing is rooted in stinginess, half-hearted faith, or lack of Christian commitment; even more so to anybody who believes non-tithers will go to hell. Many who did not practice or even opposed tithing gave their lives for their faith or were imprisoned, even imprisoned specifically for resisting tithing as a matter of conscience.

The Quakers excommunicating anyone who tithed, and the English Baptists subjecting pastors to church discipline if they received tithes, shows that they considered the doctrine a serious affront to the gospel. They lost far more for resisting tithing than it would have cost them to tithe, because they took the matter as seriously as the circumcision issue which Paul addressed in Galatians.

Many other renowned preachers and theologians have disagreed with tithing. I've named only a very few. It's difficult to find any motive for preachers such as G. Campbell Morgan to disagree with tithing other than love for the truth.

The United States was a refuge for those seeking religious freedom, including the Quakers and Anabaptists who radically opposed tithing, and other groups which did not practice it. Therefore, there is little history of tithing in the United States until the late 1800s. Mormonism has a much stronger history of tithing than American Evangelicalism does.

Even today, many major Bible reference works, large seminaries (such as Moody Bible Institute and Dallas Theological Seminary), and influential teachers and theologians, conclude that the tithe ceased with the Old Covenant. Both Dr. Russ Kelley and Dr. David Croteau have compiled lists with some of these. It seems absurd to me that tithing would so often be treated as if it were a fundamental of the Christian faith.

Chapter 8

You Break God's Commandments for the Sake of Your Tithing Tradition

Human Religious Tradition

Churches teaching that Christians must tithe break God's commands regularly for the sake of this tradition, even if they claim to teach *"grace tithing."* Their tradition, rooted in pagan tithing practices, misrepresents how God relates to his people. It differs vastly in both principle and practice from the tithe practiced under Mosaic law.

Leviticus 27, Numbers 18, and Deuteronomy 12, 14, and 26 describe the tithe Malachi refers to. Nobody who teaches tithing from Malachi observes the tithe Malachi refers to.

Those who teach that 10% is a standard for everyone are either making things up or passing on the traditions they have heard. Even under the Mosaic law, 10% was never a standard for everyone. Not everybody tithed under Mosaic law. My personal belief in the modern tithe had entered through human tradition, not through reading scripture. When I promoted it, I was passing on the tradition I'd been taught.

It's also making things up to interpret Abraham's one-time tithe on the spoils of war, never even commanded by God, as a divine command for all time that all Christians tithe regularly on their gross incomes. It's pure human tradition, since even Abraham didn't tithe on his own income or tithe regularly! Let's examine several commands of God that churches regularly break for the sake of their tithe tradition.

Matthew 7:5-13 So the Pharisees and teachers of the law asked Jesus, "Why don't your disciples live according to the tradition of the elders instead of eating their food with defiled hands?" He replied, "Isaiah was right when he prophesied about you hypocrites; as it is written:

'These people honor me with their lips, but their hearts are far from me. They worship me in vain; their teachings are merely human rules.'

You have let go of the commands of God and are holding on to human traditions."

And he continued, "You have a fine way of setting aside the commands of God in order to observe your own traditions! For Moses said, 'Honor your father and mother,' and, 'Anyone who curses their father or mother is to be put to death.' But you say that if anyone declares that what might have been used to help their father or mother is corban (that is, devoted to God)— then you no longer let them do anything for their father or mother. Thus you nullify the word of God by your tradition that you have handed down. And you do many things like that."

Open Your Hands to the Poor and Do Not Oppress Them

If you ever just open your Bible and read it cover to cover, some of the main themes you'll find are justice for the oppressed and compassion for the poor. Check out Compassion International's compilation of scriptures concerning the poor for a few of them.[184]

Scripture talks about the poor more than anything else when discussing giving. The New Testament has extremely harsh words for those who oppress the poor and defraud workers of their wages. God's heart is huge on this matter.

My wife said to some girls at her work *"Let's give our tithe to this girl who makes only 1,000 reais. It's hard for her to live on that."* (About $250 a month) They gave her R$400. She cried and said *"But your tithe belongs to God."* Maybe she didn't know that Jesus said, *"Whatever you do for the least of these, you do for me"*?[185] Giving to the poor is giving to God.

Many churches teach that giving to the poor and giving to missions only come after the tithe. However, **the poor under the Old Covenant received from the tithe rather than paying it.** Even if we were 100% under the law of the Old Covenant, following today's modern tithe tradition would still be breaking God's commandments. Many people claim to teach tithing by grace, yet they tell the poor that they are obligated to tithe rather than sharing the tithe with the poor. Even tithing under the law had more grace in it than that!

The verb *"to decimate"* meant *"to levy a tithe"* in the Middle Ages; as in the phrase *"poor as a decimated Cavalier."*[186] You know what connotations this word continues to have! Consider how this has reflected on people's perception of the gospel message throughout history. Mere human religion has decimated many poor people throughout history, but Jesus didn't come to decimate anybody. He brought good news to the poor!

Instead of helping the poor as the ancient Jewish tithe did, modern tithe traditions tell them they're cursed God-robbers if they don't pay their tithe before anything else including food or rent, and it would be better if they had never been born.[187] Even

---

[184] *What The Bible Says About Poverty* Online: https://www.compassion.com/poverty/what-the-bible-says-about-poverty.htm Accessed November 2nd, 2019
[185] Matthew 25:40
[186] *The Merriam Webster Dictionary.* Dallas, TX: Zane Pub., 1995. *Decimate*
[187] Heward-Mills, Dag. Spiritual Problems of People who Don't Pay Tithes. https://www.youtube.com/watch?v=qdzndumL_P8&t=1863s Retrieved August 26th, 2022

many who supposedly preach *"grace tithing"* continue to teach that *"the original sin was not tithing"* and *"non-tithers are God-robbers."*

People in financial straits stop going to church because they can't afford it. This situation is common. My aging mother-in-law, whose income covers only half her expenses, said one night *"I can't go to church tonight because I don't have my tithe."*

Her pastor is a loving guy, sincere, and he's just teaching the tradition he's been taught and thinks is right. His tradition, like many, treats tithing as a fundamental tenet of the Christian faith. I doubt he would tell her she couldn't go to church without her tithe, although there are pastors who do. In spite of her pastor's good heart and intentions, the message that came across to my elderly mother-in-law as she heard him preach the denomination's position on tithing was *"You're not welcome if you don't come with a tithe."* So, she didn't go when she didn't have one.

I personally know a widow who adopted over 20 orphans and cared for dozens of others as foster children. She was evicted for not paying rent. She was a faithful tither, but under Mosaic Law she would have received help from the tithe. A man in South America was disfellowshipped from his church for not paying a tithe as he cared for five special-needs orphans and paid their expenses out of his own pocket.

When I share such stories, similar ones start coming out of the woodwork. I've received various messages from people sharing their own experiences. These pervasive issues are common even within churches that claim to teach tithing by grace, but people usually only share their stories when they feel safe and don't believe they will be judged.

Even if you believe Christians are under the law (which is the error of the Galatians), knowing that Mosaic law commands that the needy receive the tithe but telling them they must pay the tithe before even their rent or grocery bill, is fraud. Telling them that God will curse them if they do not tithe is extortion. Even if oppressing the poor by extracting money from them with untruths or threats is tolerated by the church, in God's eyes the sin is no less than it would be if the perpetrator had been convicted of fraud or extortion in a criminal court. **Many non-Christians have a sharper moral compass than some religious people do, and can see this clearly!**

Under the tithe law of Israel, those in need received help from the tithe and landowners gave it. I realize that many preachers have taught error as it was passed down to them, believing it sincerely. But the one who is faced with the Scriptural facts and continues teaching error has no excuse. He is knowingly participating in the sins of fraud and extortion. Jesus rebuked the Pharisees for devouring widows' houses right before lamenting how the poor widow put all she had to live on in the offering.[188] The same rebuke applies today.

This reminds me of our experience with being sold a business by fraud. When shown facts like differing financial statements for the same time periods, the franchise owner and representatives were silent. When confronted with proof of their salespeople's lies and of injustices, they became angry. It even seemed like the representative of the franchise whom I corresponded with was honestly convinced that the franchise was in the right.

Many who teach tithing deceive themselves in the same way. When confronted with the fact that the poor received, rather than paid, the ancient tithe, they become angry. When they hear the stories of people they've received money from by fraud or extortion, they are silent. They have deceived themselves and believe what they want to, in spite of facts to the contrary.

Even people who agree with me that tithing is not the New Covenant model, ask *"Why is this such a big deal?"* The first reason is that these teachings are untrue, and we participate in a spirit of fraud when we continue to hold to them and ignore the facts. **Nobody can argue with the fact that the tithe of the Old Covenant helped the poor rather than demanding from them.**

---

[188] Mark 12:38-44

Declaring What Would Have Helped Your Father or Mother Is Dedicated to God

This is the specific example that Jesus gave to the Pharisees of how they nullified God's word for the sake of their tradition. Instead of caring for aging parents, they made a *"gift dedicated to God."*

The teaching that wrongly equates a tithe with the separate Old Testament *"first fruits"* offering, telling people they must tithe before anything else, has resulted in the same injustice. Many people taking this *"first fruits tithe"* teaching seriously have not adequately cared for their families. As a missionary who's seen some of the global church and who corresponds with Christians from many nations, I can say these situations are quite common in third-world countries. Elderly people in many countries often have no retirement savings, get a small amount from the government, and rely primarily on their children to care for them.

There have been reports of African women prostituting themselves to pay tithes.[189] I've personally heard similar stories from African Christians, such as churchgoers throwing their tithes on the coffin of a dead relative so he would go to heaven, or a man tithing on the money he gained in a massive fraud scheme because he thought his tithe brought God's blessing.

1 Timothy 5:8 Anyone who does not provide for their relatives, and especially for their own household, has denied the faith and is worse than an unbeliever.

Romans 13:8 (NRSV) Owe no one anything, except to love one another; for the one who loves another has fulfilled the law.

---

[189] *The Offering As An Act Of Worship* Online:
https://www.academia.edu/2487744/The_offering_as_an_act_of_worship   Accessed
November 15th, 2019

Paying a tithe before caring for your family or paying bills is nullifying God's word for the sake of human tradition. This happens often and tithe teachers don't want to come face-to-face with these situations. Some preachers will say *"Oh, those people are just victims of preachers who abuse the truth of tithing. It doesn't invalidate the principle."* Yet the same situations often exist in their own churches. It's not that someone is *"abusing the teaching."* The teaching itself is abusive.

People have asked *"What should I do? Care for my aging mom or give the tithe?"* Many pastors have insisted that the tithe comes first. Teaching people to give sacrificially yet failing to teach them the scriptural priority of caring for family is lying by omission. It's like Abraham telling Pharaoh that Sarah was his sister (she was his half-sister), and not telling him she was his wife![190]

Many people pay tithes first yet are behind on bills or not paying what is due, and are living in guilt and condemnation. Others are full of self-righteous pride. I heard one man speaking boastfully of his tithe, saying *"The tithe is grace, and really, it's only a starting point for generous giving"* and then upbraiding other people for their supposed *"stinginess."*

What many people didn't know is that that guy owed one of his workers seven months of unpaid wages. He eventually paid, but not before his tithe! The irony is that that man qualified as an elder in the local church for paying his tithes, yet the one who would pay the worker first rather than tithing would be disqualified for leadership!

Let No Debt Remain Outstanding Except for the Continual Debt To Love One Another

Dr. David Croteau relates the story of meeting a seminary student who testified of God's overwhelming faithfulness to meet his needs. He was deeply in debt and had purchased a house he

---

[190] Genesis 12:10-20

couldn't afford, yet he was faithfully tithing and, in fact, giving 16% of his income to the local church.

David inquired as to how the Lord had delivered him from the pressing financial situation, and the young man explained that the Lord had allowed him to file for bankruptcy![191]

I couldn't stop laughing at the thought of how that young man imagined that God's deliverance in response to his faithful tithing was a bankruptcy filing. However, this story reminded me of one of the primary issues that I wrestled with when I stopped tithing. As the accountant told me he was working on the case and he thought we could win, the amount the IRS was charging me doubled due to penalties and interest. I had never held any outstanding credit card debt before that. At that point, I wanted to get out of that situation as soon as possible in order to focus on missions and serving the Lord.

Romans 13:8 Let no debt remain outstanding, except the continuing debt to love one another, for whoever loves others has fulfilled the law.

Proverbs 22:7 The rich rule over the poor, and the borrower is slave to the lender.

1 Corinthians 7:21-23 Were you a slave when you were called? Don't let it trouble you—although if you can gain your freedom, do so. For the one who was a slave when called to faith in the Lord is the Lord's freed person; similarly, the one who was free when called is Christ's slave. You were bought at a price; do not become slaves of human beings.

In biblical times they did not have modern bankruptcy laws and people could literally be enslaved for not paying debts. I would not conclude that the Bible absolutely prohibits Christians from ever

---

[191] Croteau, David A. *You Mean I Dont Have to Tithe?: a Deconstruction of Tithing and a Reconstruction of Post-Tithe Giving.* Eugene, Or.: Pickwick Publications, 2010. **Position 4037**

getting a mortgage or using credit. Lenders today evaluate risk and charge interest accordingly, and we have modern bankruptcy laws. However, when people are in debt and paying large amounts of interest, in a sense they are still slaves to the one they are paying interest to. Paying a tithe while paying large amounts of interest is not the best stewardship.

Deciding whether to take on debt, or how much, needs to be left up to the individual Christian's conscience. Remember that scripture says *"Whatever is not of faith is sin."*[192] It is wrong to compel a believer to violate their conscience for the sake of the human tradition of tithing. If a believer's conscience says *"Prioritize getting out of debt,"* we must not interfere, as every individual believer must give an account of himself to God.

A couple from the local church is quite adamant about the importance of tithing, yet they still owe me money for something they promised to reimburse me for over a year ago. I've mostly forgotten about it, and I think they have too! I don't hold the money against them, but I wouldn't want to be in a business partnership with them!

In many similar situations, the person the tither owes money to is an unbeliever. The tither self-righteously deceives himself to think he is acting with integrity, and is commended by the religious for putting the tithe first. But to God and to the unbeliever he still hasn't paid, such a person is untrustworthy and isn't acting with integrity at all!

Don't Test the Lord Your God

In Acts, the early church determined that trying to compel Gentile Christians to be bound by Jewish law was testing God.

Acts 15:10 (NRSV) Now then, why do you try to test God by putting on the necks of Gentiles a yoke that neither we nor our ancestors have been able to bear?

---

[192] Romans 14:23

> **Matthew 4:7 (NRSV) Jesus answered him, It is also written: "Do not put the Lord your God to the test."**

In Matthew 23, Jesus upbraided the Pharisees for their self-righteous boasting in their money and for laying heavy burdens on people and locking them out of the kingdom of heaven. His rebuke is just as applicable to those who test God today by putting the yoke of the law on Christians.

Don't Cause Any of These Little Ones To Stumble

> **Matthew 18:6-7 If anyone causes one of these little ones—those who believe in me—to stumble, it would be better for them to have a large millstone hung around their neck and to be drowned in the depths of the sea. Woe to the world because of the things that cause people to stumble! Such things must come, but woe to the person through whom they come!**

I've talked to many unchurched people about Christ. So many of them avoid church precisely because they believe the church cares about what they have, not about them. This stumbling block does great harm to the cause of the gospel. On the contrary, the apostle Paul said, *"We want not what is yours, but you."*[193]

Jesus himself is a stumbling block.[194] Yet in Matthew 18, Jesus talks about causing little ones who believe to stumble by wronging them or causing unnecessary offence. A significant group of people were once in fellowship but got burned out on tithe and give-to-get messages and now want nothing to do with the church. Some want nothing to do with Jesus. Many were single mothers and others who would have received part of the tithe under Jewish law, but they were compelled to give one under today's religious tradition.

Tithing traditions are also a stumbling block to hinder unbelievers from coming to Christ. One father shared about his 24-

---

[193] 2 Corinthians 12:14
[194] 1 Corinthians 1:23

year-old daughter, who was a single mother with two children, tithing $200 a week. Yet many times he, the grandfather, would get diapers and formula because she hadn't bought them. He said, *"I don't understand how she puts god first before her children."*[195]

I don't know if he is a believer, but I noticed that he wrote *"god"* with a lower-case *"g."* I have personally seen and heard of similar situations multiple times. Some are young people tithing and relying on unbelieving parents, or elderly parents tithing yet relying on unbelieving children for support.

Those who attempt to dress up tithing as *"grace"* should consider this: whether the young woman was tithing because she was afraid of a curse, or she was just doing so-called *"grace tithing,"* her father would still wonder why she was *"putting god before her children,"* as if her children weren't a priority to God!

One brother recently shared that he advised a man in his congregation to stop tithing. This father of four, whose wife was not currently working, was faithfully tithing yet relying on his unbelieving parents to give him gas money to get to work by the middle of each week.

1 Corinthians 9:12,15 If others have this right of support from you, shouldn't we have it all the more? But we did not use this right. On the contrary, we put up with anything rather than hinder the gospel of Christ... But I have not used any of these rights. And I am not writing this in the hope that you will do such things for me, for I would rather die than allow anyone to deprive me of this boast.

1 Corinthians 10:32 Do not cause anyone to stumble, whether Jews, Greeks or the church of God— even as I try to please everyone in every way. For I am not seeking my own good but the good of many, so that they may be saved.

---

[195] A comment from "Rob" on this article online: https://seedtime.com/tithing-in-the-new-testament/?fbclid=IwAR3ocPTlZltgD0ssh_-0GSLEfwyECopRvcE0H0YC8N14PRRyNTxzNfXkv-w Accessed November 27th, 2019

Here, Paul is not talking about the necessary offence that comes with the gospel, but about adding offence unnecessarily. Paul chose not to take support that was proper for him to receive, which was the expected food and lodging given to a traveling minister, in order to not hinder the gospel. How is it that now we're willing to demand tithes even from people the old covenant tithe would have helped?

So many people are bitter against the church for various reasons and say *"The church just wants my money."* Many have projected that bitterness onto God, whom the church has misrepresented. The message that has come across to them is anything but what Paul said to the Corinthians: *"...what I want is not your possessions but you. After all, children should not have to save up for their parents, but parents for their children. So, I will very gladly spend for you everything I have and expend myself as well."*[196]

Churches have sometimes confronted a person for failing to tithe with full knowledge that their spouse is an unbeliever and disagrees with tithing on their income. What kind of witness is it for the church to cause marital strife between the believer and the unbelieving spouse?

Other people have totally rejected the faith or left Christian fellowship after asking questions nobody could answer and coming to the same conclusions many leading theologians and scholars have reached. **The level of vitriol that has come against many people for simply asking questions about tithing and coming to honest conclusions is astounding.**

People have found themselves shunned, losing long-term friendships and relationships, treated as traitors against God and the church, simply for saying in good conscience *"Tithing is indefensible as a doctrine for the church today."* One friend related to me how his dad went into a years-long depression after the church cut ties with him. Dr. David Croteau shares how he contacted a scholar who had written a book on the tithe. He

---

[196] 2 Corinthians 12:14+15

learned that every church had ostracized that man for his view and he couldn't get a job, so that he lost hope of ever working in ministry and instead pursued another education and career. When Dr. Croteau talked to him, the man was no longer in fellowship with a church.[197]

One author shares that when he studied tithing and learned how inaccurate the tithe tradition was which he had believed for so long, it triggered a crisis of faith and he considered embracing agnosticism.[198] The kickback against him was so intense that his oldest son, who grew up in church, **feared his father's life might be in danger** and asked him not to write the book for the sake of his physical safety.[199]

I've interacted with several people who lost long-time friendships and were shunned by churches because they dared to state their own honest conclusions after studying tithing biblically and historically. A significant group are not in a Christian fellowship and are still extremely angry and bitter over their experience.

About ten years ago, several of my Facebook friends began to realize the glaring problems with the tithe dogma they had been taught. A root of bitterness sprang up in some of their hearts, worsened by the vitriol directed at them from many Christians. I grieved as I saw some of them continue to reject nearly everything the church had ever taught them and soon reject orthodox Christianity.

Although others have had much worse experiences, I still felt my stomach twist when my pastor said *"We can no longer support your ministry."* I lost so much trust in the integrity of leaders I respected when I saw how this subject was a taboo and we couldn't ask certain questions because they couldn't answer them. If my

---

[197] Croteau, David A. *You Mean I Dont Have to Tithe?: a Deconstruction of Tithing and a Reconstruction of Post-Tithe Giving.* Eugene, Or.: Pickwick Publications, 2010. Position 62
[198] Chase, Frank. *Kleptomaniac Who's Really Robbing God Anyway?* Fc Pub Llc, 2016. Position 256-266, 515
[199] Chase, Frank. *Kleptomaniac Who's Really Robbing God Anyway?* Fc Pub Llc, 2016. Position 547

faith had been built on those leaders and not firmly on Christ, I would no longer be a Christian.

I have at times encountered downright hatred from *"Christians"* over questioning tithes, but fortunately not from the ones I was in close fellowship with. I've seen enough that I'm not so surprised to hear of a son's concern that his father's life was in danger over the issue.

Hearing of that level of hatred may be shocking to those who have never seen it, but we soon find out if we question tithing! Creflo Dollar said he was joking about lining up non-tithers to shoot them down and throw them into a mass grave, but Jesus said that what comes out of the mouth is the overflow of the heart and is what defiles a man.[200]

I can only write now without a twinge of bitterness because God imparted such a supernatural love to me for the church. Rather than holding resentment, my heart is soft towards the people Jesus died for and I weep for them. I grieve when I see so many Christians who have been blinded to truth, especially those who even state that nobody will make it into heaven without a tithe.

Give in Secret

> **Matthew 6:3-4 (NRSV) But when you give alms, do not let your left hand know what your right hand is doing, so that your alms may be done in secret; and your Father who sees in secret will reward you.**

Many people simply take this scripture at face value. Others say Jesus is addressing the heart issue and it's all right to talk about our giving sometimes. No matter what an individual's conviction is about this scripture, they must follow their conviction because whatever is not of faith is sin,[201] and each of us must give an

---

[200] Matthew 15:18
[201] Romans 14:23

account of himself to God. [202] Churches that check their member's tithe records and ministries that ask if people are tithers are not allowing them to give in secret to be seen only by God. Jesus rebuked the Pharisees who gained honor by doing their deeds to be seen by men.[203] It's completely reasonable that some Christians, as a matter of conscience, want to give in secret.

In Galatians, Paul said certain people were spying on their freedom in Christ and he didn't put up with it for a moment! Anyone who demands to know how much you're giving is spying on your freedom in Christ. They are no better than Judaizers wanting to peek and see who's circumcised!

> **Galatians 2:3-5 Yet not even Titus, who was with me, was compelled to be circumcised, even though he was a Greek. This matter arose because some false believers had infiltrated our ranks to spy on the freedom we have in Christ Jesus and to make us slaves. We did not give in to them for a moment, so that the truth of the gospel might be preserved for you.**

I've often heard tithers self-righteously boasting of their giving and speaking disparagingly of people they consider stingy. Jesus spoke directly to that situation and His words are no less applicable today than they have ever been.

> **Luke 18: 9-14 (NRSV) He also told this parable to some who trusted in themselves that they were righteous and regarded others with contempt "Two men went up to the temple to pray, one a Pharisee and the other a tax collector. The Pharisee, standing by himself, was praying thus, 'God, I thank you that I am not like other people: thieves, rogues, adulterers, or even like this tax collector. I fast twice a week; I give a tenth of all my income.'**

---

[202] Romans 14:12
[203] Matthew 23:5-7

But the tax collector, standing far off, would not even look up to heaven, but was beating his breast and saying, 'God, be merciful to me, a sinner!' I tell you, this man went down to his home justified rather than the other; for all who exalt themselves will be humbled, but all who humble themselves will be exalted."

Let Giving Be As Each Decides in His Heart, Not Under Compulsion

2 Corinthians 9:7 (NRSV) Each of you must give as you have made up your mind, not reluctantly or under compulsion, for God loves a cheerful giver.

Teaching Christians tithing clearly violates Paul's New Testament instructions for giving. Giving must not be by external compulsion but rather must flow internally from communion with the Holy Spirit. We teach people to walk in communion with God.

The free will giving of the early church helped the same people whom the tithe law of the Old Covenant helped. But by controlling giving instead of letting it flow out of a heart in communion with the Holy Spirit, the tithe supplants giving to missions and helping the needy.

Do you remember Edgar's story? Our giving to a church didn't amount to 10% when we cared for him. The Baptist church that helped us with a bed for him has never taught tithing or used any form of compulsion in giving, yet we've seen them do far more to help the needy than many churches ten times their size. In fact, when I posted on Facebook that I was writing about how much the tithe doctrine has harmed the church, I got a *"like"* from the profile of that Baptist church.

Many of my friends don't believe in tithing. In my experience, which Christians are less likely to believe in tithing? Christians involved in missions to people who never heard the gospel, laypeople ministering supernaturally in daily life, and those caring for others in need. Some of my friends who want nothing to do with tithing are taking in hundreds of street kids or helping broken people get off the streets and away from prostitution and drug addiction.

A friend shared her story in the comments of our blog post *"Tithing and Injustice."* She wasn't supposed to be on the worship team if she wasn't tithing. She was struggling to make ends meet and trusting God for food and clothing, but upon joining the worship team, she had signed her name that she would agree to tithe to the church. Then one day she felt the Holy Spirit guiding her to give $50 (more than her tithe would have been) to a lady in the church. She argued with God but he said firmly *"She is my church!"* So, she obeyed. The lady cried because that $50 was grocery money for her and her two kids that week.

My friend disobeyed the tithe tradition of men, but she obeyed God. She would have disobeyed God for the sake of a human tradition if she had given a tithe that week.

Welcome One Another As Christ Has Welcomed You

Romans 15:7 (NRSV) Welcome one another, therefore, just as Christ has welcomed you, for the glory of God.

Many churches make it clear that non-tithers aren't welcome as functional, participating members of the Body of Christ, or even as church members at all. To doom anyone who gives less than 10% to spectator status is not accepting them as Christ has. Even many so-called *"grace-tithing"* churches do this. You aren't allowed to minister with the grace God has given you if you're unable to commit to a tithe. On what basis did Christ welcome us into his body? On that of a tithe?

Many claim *"We don't teach you are accepted by tithing. You are already accepted in Christ."* Yet their practice is not so! If they teach that non-tithers are *"God-robbers,"* it brings cognitive dissonance. It's hard to keep this scripture out of people's minds:

1 Corinthians 5:12 Expel the wicked person from among you.

Since their human tradition says that non-tithers are God-robbers, they shun those who don't come with a tithe!

Do Not Show Favoritism

James 2:1-6 (NRSV) My brothers and sisters, do you with your acts of favoritism really believe in our glorious Lord Jesus Christ? For if a person with gold rings and in fine clothes comes into your assembly, and if a poor person in dirty clothes also comes in, and if you take notice of the one wearing the fine clothes and say, "Have a seat here, please," while to the one who is poor you say, "Stand there," or, "Sit at my feet," have you not made distinctions among yourselves, and become judges with evil thoughts? Listen, my beloved brothers and sisters. Has not God chosen the poor in the world to be rich in faith and to be heirs of the kingdom that he has promised to those who love him? But you have dishonored the poor. Is it not the rich who oppress you?

In many churches, being in leadership is out of the question if one is not a tither, although it is not one of the qualifications for leaders set forth in 1 Timothy 3:1-7 or Titus 1:6-9. We often see extreme leniency in applying the scriptural qualifications for elders, yet a person who does meet those scriptural qualifications but has the integrity to pay bills first would never be considered if they don't give at least a tithe. Some leaders say openly that the amount people contribute to the church is one of the main factors when they choose elders.

The command to *"not show favoritism"* also applies to practices like calling all the tithers up front to receive a *"special blessing."* I've seen many miracles ministering to people on the streets, in churches, and in their homes. The thought of giving someone a *"special blessing"* for giving money is abhorrent to me.

170

It's contrary to everything I want to communicate to people about God's nature and grace.

Don't Judge by Mere Appearances, but Judge With Righteous Judgment

John 7:2 Stop judging by mere appearances, but instead judge correctly.

1 Samuel 16:7 But the Lord said to Samuel, "Do not consider his appearance or his height, for I have rejected him. The *Lord* does not look at the things people look at. People look at the outward appearance, but the *Lord* looks at the heart."

This is why appointing elders based on how much they give is problematic. If mammon is our measure of a person's faith, devotion to Christ, or favor with God, we are deceived. Focusing on the outward appearance destroys discernment. Nobody's heart before God can be measured by a percentage or a dollar amount.

I agree with John Wesley's teaching that as we live for Christ 100% of our money is holy, and what we spend to care for our own needs and those of our families is just as holy as the rest. Wesley taught to first care for your own needs, then the needs of your family, then the world.[204] There is no guilt trip in that view of giving.

Sometimes people who are overflowing with God's life don't have a lot of money at the moment. When I was in that crisis situation and decided it wouldn't honor God to tithe but not pay my electric bill, I was living on fire for Jesus and trying sincerely to be a good steward of my money before God.

Weekly, I saw people weeping as God touched them. I sometimes saw more people healed in a day than I had seen

---

[204] Wesley, John. *Sermons on Several Occasions: in Two Volumes.* London: Published and sold by J. Kershaw, 14, City-Road, and 66, Paternoster-Row, 1825. Volume 1. Sermon *The Use Of Money.* Pg. 633

previously in years of church attendance. I often started weeping as I walked down the street because of Christ's compassion. My motivation wasn't wanting a position in church or wanting to be seen. I just wanted to see people meet Jesus. For part of that time, I had homeless people living in my house. I often spent about twenty hours a week praying for people everywhere I went and talking about Jesus. When I met somebody who needed to be healed, it felt like time stopped and ministering to the person in front of me was the most important thing in the world. Yet I was in financial distress.

Some friends seemed to think I was backslidden or being stingy since I wasn't tithing. The pastor said they could no longer endorse my ministry, and I didn't know a church that would. I didn't know who would stand behind me as a missionary. I was often more welcome to minister in the houses of unbelievers and idol-worshippers than in churches.

Twenty or more hours of pouring out my heart in love for people that week and ministering healing was more of a sacrifice for me than the four hours it took another person to earn their week's tithe money! Not to mention the trips to minister in small churches where the small offering, if there was one, didn't always cover my travel expenses. (I'm not saying this begrudgingly. It was my privilege to see what God did in every place I visited and I am thankful for whatever the people could give.)

What about my mission trip to Russia and Ukraine, which cost as much as a year of tithes and was a financial sacrifice? I went with tears because love compelled me. I could barely afford the trip, but I felt God's love for the people turn into a current like electricity flowing through my whole body from head to foot and I had to go. What if there was more risk and sacrifice in sheltering a homeless couple and their baby in my home than there was for another person who gave the full 10% of their income to the church that week? As I write these last paragraphs, I feel uncomfortable, thinking, *"Why should I even need to talk like this?"*

2 Corinthians 10:7,12,17-18 You are judging by appearances...We do not dare to classify or compare ourselves with some who commend themselves. When they measure themselves by themselves and compare themselves with themselves, they are not wise...But, "Let the one who boasts boast in the Lord." For it is not the one who commends himself who is approved, but the one whom the Lord commends.

Paul went on to say in the next chapter that he was boasting like a fool, but he did so to cut the ground out from under those who boasted and compared themselves to others based on outward things. Likewise, I speak to cut the ground out from under those who see a percentage or dollar amount as the measure of a person's heart. No, I didn't pay a tithe that year, but I gave much more than a tithe!

If we fail to judge with right judgment, we will reject Jesus himself coming to us. Jesus didn't come with anything in his outward appearance that people should desire him,[205] and he continues to come humble and riding on a donkey. When leaders determine by outward appearance with whom to entrust God's flock, they end up appointing those who will divide and devour rather than build up and care for God's people. There are many poor who are rich in faith, as scripture says. We should not fail to honor their faith if they make their first priority caring for a mother or father rather than dedicating *"A gift offered to God."*

---

[205] Isaiah 53:2

Chapter 9
"But Tithing Works!"
"Just Try It!"

Many of us have heard testimony after testimony of people who started tithing and their financial situations turned around. For example, I talked to a friend who agreed with my perspective about tithing. Her spouse had become disillusioned with Christianity and disagreed with tithing, but the church confronted them about it. This friend said *"I agree with you. But why does it seem like it works for so many people?"*

Some people revert to the argument *"It just works and I believe in it"* when the insufficiency of the biblical foundation for tithing is exposed. I'd like to bring those tithing testimonies into perspective—a perspective that will seriously challenge anybody who says *"I believe in tithing because it works."* I'm no skeptic when it comes to miracles or supernatural provision. But I don't believe tithing is the key to experiencing God's provision.

Confirmation Bias

One thing we need to consider is *confirmation bias*. In a culture that promotes tithing, people are encouraged to tell their positive stories related to tithing, but not negative stories such as being evicted for not paying rent after they *"tested God"* with their tithe. People often risk being ostracized if they share those negative stories. Other Christians turn the blame back on them, saying that if tithing didn't work, they must have not been doing it in faith or with a cheerful heart.

Many Christians who believe tithing is totally irrelevant have amazing testimonies of God's miraculous provision. Michael Van Vlymen doesn't follow tithe teachings because he believes handing over your money and letting someone else distribute it is poor stewardship. He's experienced many financial miracles, even to the point of cold hard cash just appearing![206] Reinhard Hirtler believes tithing is irrelevant for Christians, regularly believes the Lord for large sums of money, and doesn't ask people for funds. Bertie Brits rejects both tithing and common *"sowing and reaping"* teachings, and has remarkable testimonies of financial provision. Somebody even came to him and said *"I want to buy you a house!"*[207]

I felt like there were holes in my pockets when I was tithing but the *"windows of heaven"* opened when I stopped! Yes, some tithers have testimonies of provision. Yet for every prosperity story there are also stories of people going broke and not paying bills or not eating so they can tithe. Others have lost their apartments or had their utilities shut off yet they were tithing. Some got so frustrated tithing that they now want nothing to do with God, church, or Christians!

People usually only share those stories if they feel it's safe or have already rejected the faith. I rarely heard of negative tithing experiences until I spoke up about my own experience. When I did, then other people shared their stories.

Some Miracle Provision Testimonies Are Made up!

2 Peter 2:1-3 But there were also false prophets among the people, just as there will be false teachers among you. They

---

[206] Vlymen, Michael Van. *Supernatural Provision Book One*. Michael Van Vlymen, 2017. Position 121
[207] Brits, Bertie *Healing For The Financially Abused (Tithing Will Kill You)* starting 1 hour, 21 minutes, and 56 seconds into the video. Online: https://www.youtube.com/watch?v=VcyYnrQp7YA&t=4651s

will secretly introduce destructive heresies, even denying the sovereign Lord who bought them-bringing swift destruction on themselves. Many will follow their shameful ways and bring the way of truth into disrepute. In their greed these teachers will exploit you with stories they have made up.

I don't doubt miraculous provision testimonies just because they are supernatural or wild. I know four people who have had cash appear or handed to them by angels,[208] and I have no doubt as to the veracity of their testimonies. But when somebody tells a story to manipulate people's giving, I often wonder if the story is made up. We shouldn't discount that possibility, since 2nd Peter warns of teachers who make up stories to exploit people.

Their teachings bring the way of truth into disrepute. They introduced them *"secretly,"* meaning the teachings sounded good and the error came in a subtle way. What do you think these *"destructive heresies"* of greedy teachers are today?

Are People Who Tithe More Likely To Be Rich or Poor?

A quick Google search on giving statistics gave me multiple results. All agreed. *The lower a person's income is, the more likely they are to give more than 10% of their income.* It's easy to cherry-pick a few stories, but tithing does not make people rich.

The 2000 Social Capital Community Benchmark Survey shows that households with incomes below $20,000 gave 4.6% to charity, higher than any other income group.[209]

---

[208] Stuart Morrison, Reinhard Hirtler, Michael Van Vlymen, who we mentioned, and Pete Cabrera Jr. Pete's testimony is online here: https://www.youtube.com/watch?v=yp5mC6M_k8g Accessed August 6th, 2019
[209] Online: https://www.financialsamurai.com/the-average-percent-of-income-donated-to-charity/ Accessed November 19th, 2019

> **According to a 2015 Sharefaith article, people with a salary of less than $20,000 are eight times more likely to give than someone who makes $75,000.**[210]

Many rich people are actually tightwads, which is why scripture encourages them to also be rich in good deeds. Of course, some rich people are extremely generous and give away large portions of their incomes.

Poorer people, on average, give a larger portion of their incomes than rich people do. They are more likely to be tithers. That throws a big wrench in the *"gain is godliness"* mentality that poor people must be poor because they don't give generously.

You may have heard statistics such as *"tithers are much less likely to be overdue on credit card payments."* However, correlation doesn't equal cause. Those overdue on credit card payments are less likely to keep tithing, rather than tithing being the reason they aren't overdue! That's just common sense.

What's the Goal of Our Faith?

I recently heard a famous *"grace preacher"* relying heavily on stories of rich people who tithed to argue the importance of tithing. He said it's *"not the law"* but that it's a *"principle"* and a secret to wealth. He mentioned figures like Henry Ford and Thomas Edison who tithed and became extremely rich.

I thought it strange that he would use Ford and Edison as role models, as if the end goal of our faith were becoming rich. Ford promoted anti-Semitism, influencing the development of Nazism. He wrote a four-volume work entitled *"The International Jew, the World's Foremost Problem,"* which Hitler read and which converted the leader of the Hitler Youth to anti-Semitism. Heinrich Himmler called Ford *"one of our most valuable, important, and witty fighters,"* and he was the only American

---

[210] Online https://pushpay.com/blog/church-giving-statistics/ Accessed November 19th, 2019

mentioned favorably in *Mein Kampf*. Hitler said he regarded Ford as *"my inspiration."*[211]

Edison was a deist who thought it doubtful that the soul lived on after death.[212] He reportedly backed out of paying Tesla $50,000.[213] The people this preacher held up as examples of *"rich tithers"* weren't the best role models. Let's not get caught up in the mentality that *"gain is godliness."*

1 Timothy 6:3-11, 17-19 If anyone teaches otherwise and does not agree to the sound instruction of our Lord Jesus Christ and to godly teaching, they are conceited and understand nothing. They have an unhealthy interest in controversies and quarrels about words that result in envy, strife, malicious talk, evil suspicions and constant friction between people of corrupt mind, who have been robbed of the truth and who think that godliness is a means to financial gain.

But godliness with contentment is great gain. For we brought nothing into the world, and we can take nothing out of it. But if we have food and clothing, we will be content with that. Those who want to get rich fall into temptation and a trap and into many foolish and harmful desires that plunge people into ruin and destruction. For the love of money is a root of all kinds of evil. Some people, eager for money, have wandered from the faith and pierced themselves with many griefs. But you, man of God, flee from all this, and pursue righteousness, godliness, faith, love, endurance and gentleness...

Command those who are rich in this present world not to be arrogant nor to put their hope in wealth, which is so

---

[211] Online: https://en.wikipedia.org/wiki/Henry_Ford Accessed December 2nd, 2019
[212] Online: https://en.wikipedia.org/wiki/Thomas_Edison Accessed December 2nd, 2019
[213] Online: https://listverse.com/2012/06/07/10-ways-edison-treated-tesla-like-a-jerk/ Accessed December 2nd, 2019

uncertain, but to put their hope in God, who richly provides us with everything for our enjoyment. Command them to do good, to be rich in good deeds, and to be generous and willing to share. In this way they will lay up treasure for themselves as a firm foundation for the coming age, so that they may take hold of the life that is truly life.

If Edison, Ford, or any of the other *"rich tithers"* this preacher referred to never ended up taking hold of the life that is truly life, what's the point of saying *"they tithed and became rich?"* This highlights a serious problem with many tithe theologies. The *"gain is godliness"* mindset insidiously creeps in through those teachings. It slips in subtly so that many Christians who say *"Oh no, I don't believe gain is godliness"* are actually manifesting that very belief in their words and actions. It's rooted in the teaching that faithful tithing brings prosperity.

I have no problem with Christians becoming rich. I'm in favor of it, especially as God gives us seed to sow in order to bring about a harvest of righteousness. Bertie Brits points out that where it says *"Godliness with contentment is great gain,"* the word *"gain"* is the same as is often used of financial gain.[214] I'm all for Christians prospering out of a place of contentment and seeking God's kingdom first. However, becoming financially wealthy is neither the end goal of our faith nor the standard by which we measure faith! Our goal is love springing from a pure conscience and sincere faith.[215] Scripture clearly speaks of poor people who are rich in faith and rich people who are spiritually impoverished.

James 2:1-9 My brothers and sisters, believers in our glorious Lord Jesus Christ must not show favoritism. Suppose a man comes into your meeting wearing a gold ring and fine clothes, and a poor man in filthy old clothes also comes in. If you

---

[214] Brits, Bertie. *Jesus Is the Tithe: the Message of God.* South Africa: Bertie Brits, 2019. Kindle Locations 1595-1603
[215] 1 Timothy 1:5

show special attention to the man wearing fine clothes and say, "Here's a good seat for you," but say to the poor man, "You stand there" or "Sit on the floor by my feet," have you not discriminated among yourselves and become judges with evil thoughts?

Listen, my dear brothers and sisters: Has not God chosen those who are poor in the eyes of the world to be rich in faith and to inherit the kingdom he promised those who love him? But you have dishonored the poor. Is it not the rich who are exploiting you? Are they not the ones who are dragging you into court? Are they not the ones who are blaspheming the noble name of him to whom you belong?

If you really keep the royal law found in Scripture, "Love your neighbor as yourself," you are doing right. But if you show favoritism, you sin and are convicted by the law as lawbreakers.

Revelation 3:17 You say, "I am rich; I have acquired wealth and do not need a thing." But you do not realize that you are wretched, pitiful, poor, blind and naked.

James's writings and Jesus's parables flew in the face of the Jewish *"gain is godliness"* mentality. Many Jews of that day thought the poor were cursed by God but riches showed God's blessing. That mindset has crept in through popular tithe teachings. What does it matter if spiritually impoverished people like Henry Ford tithed?

Preachers have honored unscrupulous people as if their money made them role models. The deception has so blinded people that some are committing fraud and stealing yet believe they are blessed by God and their victims are cursed non-tithers!

I was giving away God's riches and regularly seeing many healing miracles, but Christians with the *"gain is godliness"* mentality despised me because of my financial situation. I could sure relate to the apostle Paul!

> **2 Corinthians 6:8, 10 (NRSV) We are treated … as poor, yet making many rich; as having nothing, and yet possessing everything.**

The one who is genuinely rich knows how to rejoice and continually give God's life to others whether they are abased or abounding at the moment.[216] The apostle Paul was rich, and he knew it. Yet he was often abased.

> **1 Corinthians 4:11 (NRSV) To the present hour we are hungry and thirsty, we are poorly clothed and beaten and homeless.**

> **2 Corinthians 11:29 (NRSV) …in toil and hardship, through many a sleepless night, hungry and thirsty, often without food, cold and naked.**

Why do some Christians disregard the fact that Paul sometimes lacked food and clothing? Was it because of his insufficient faith or failure to tithe faithfully? Would you have asked the apostle Paul if he was tithing or sowing enough? All too often, that's the only solution that the church presents to people in need!

Seeking Life Through "Spiritual Principles" Apart From Christ Is Witchcraft!

An ex-Satanist friend remarked that when he first read the Mosaic law, he was surprised at how close it was to the magic rituals he had learned. They even sacrificed animals!

I was talking about Macumba (a Brazilian form of witchcraft) with my wife. She remarked about how closely *"Macumbeiros"*

---

[216] Philippians 4:12

adhere to the Old Testament. Several other forms of witchcraft also use the Old Testament.

The Old Testament is full of wonderful teaching and promises. It points to Jesus. Yet the Old Covenant and the Jewish law were fulfilled in Christ. Animal sacrifices, the temple, and many other things were shadows of Christ. The book of Hebrews says they were imperfect and could never actually deal with sin. Jesus is the only perfect sacrifice!

Hebrews 10:1 (NRSV) Since the law has only a shadow of the good things to come and not the true form of these realities, it can never, by the same sacrifices that are continually offered year after year, make perfect those who approach.

When we separate Old Covenant practices and principles from the Christ they pointed to, we connect with ungodly spirits. Can anybody offer an animal sacrifice for sin today as they did in the Old Covenant without being guilty of witchcraft? Any trust we put in that old system is misplaced and obscures our revelation of Jesus, the only way of perfect redemption.

Paul said to the Galatians who were relying on the law *"Who has bewitched you?"*[217] Now that Jesus has come, those who continue to sacrifice animals are no longer sacrificing them to God, but to demons. Are you still not convinced? Look at what Paul said in 2nd Corinthians, related to his debate with the Judaizers. Those who relied on circumcision and the law were *"receiving a spirit"* that wasn't from God!

2 Corinthians 11:4 For if someone comes to you and preaches a Jesus other than the Jesus we preached, or if you receive a different spirit from the Spirit you received, or a different gospel from the one you accepted, you put up with it easily enough.

---

[217] Colossians 3:1

Colossians warns about being taking captive according to the *"elemental spirits of the universe"* or *"basic principles of this world"*[218]and not according to Christ. Some Bible scholars understand this phrase as referring to the Old Covenant law. The Old Covenant law, like various spiritualistic and New-Age practices, operated according to the basic principles of this world. It was far inferior to Christ. When we read the Mosaic law we must see the more perfect realities it points to, found in Christ.

> **Titus 1:10-14 For there are many rebellious people, full of meaningless talk and deception, especially those of the circumcision group. They must be silenced, because they are disrupting whole households by teaching things they ought not to teach—and that for the sake of dishonest gain. One of Crete's own prophets has said it: "Cretans are always liars, evil brutes, lazy gluttons." This saying is true. Therefore rebuke them sharply, so that they will be sound in the faith and will pay no attention to Jewish myths or to the merely human commands of those who reject the truth.**

"Rebellious people" were disrupting whole households by teaching what they ought not to. Their teaching about money undermined the Cretans' faith in Christ and was ruining whole congregations. Making money out to be the mediator and covenant connector between God and man is rebellion against the gospel.

1 Samuel 15:23 says rebellion is as the sin of witchcraft. Teaching merely human commands to bring in the money is witchcraft. Paul tells Titus to rebuke the Cretans sharply so they will not participate in the sins of rebellion and witchcraft by paying attention to such commands.

Balaam fell into the sin of divination because of greed. 2 Peter 2:15 and Jude 11 warn against false teachers who rush into Balaam's error motivated by bringing in the money. They are *"waterless springs"* (2 Peter 2:17) and *"clouds without rain."* (Jude

---

[218] Colossians 2:20

12) These images speak of empty promises that never materialize. If you've ever kept *"paying your tithe first"* and *"sowing your best seed"* in expectation of some miracle that never happened, you know what Peter and Jude were talking about!

Chicken Blood

When a Santeria priest slaughters a chicken and pours its blood on somebody, it's an affront to the perfect sacrifice of Jesus. When Christians try to attain what Jesus's sacrifice provides for by some other means, they do no better than sacrificing a chicken and pouring out its blood.

Do people get supernatural results by sacrificing chickens? Sometimes. We've heard of healings happening by such practices, and I don't doubt it. Yet even if witchcraft gets short-term results, it eventually leads to greater bondage and brings the practitioner under the influence of a curse. Many spiritual practices are anti-Christ in that they obscure the revelation of Christ by causing people to misplace their trust.

Likewise, relying on the works of the law brings a curse. Jesus bought forgiveness, deliverance, healing, freedom, peace, and wholeness through his blood. He is the only way. When we try to attain those things through other means, we subject ourselves to the curse of the law.

Galatians 3:10 (NRSV) For all who rely on the works of the law are under a curse; for it is written, "Cursed is everyone who does not observe and obey all the things written in the book of the law."

I've often heard it suggested that people might be able to attain their healing, freedom, salvation of a loved one, or something else by *"sowing a seed,"* or *"tithing?"* Is that really much different than giving money to a witch doctor so he can slaughter a chicken and pour its blood over your head?

I recently heard a pastor in Brazil teaching that we must *"sacrifice"* so God's presence comes and fills the temple. He was referring to the church building. His teaching isn't much better than that of the Spiritists, practitioners of Reiki, or shamans. Why? Like all of them, his teaching obscures the truth and thus is in opposition to the gospel. The truth is that our bodies are God's temple and they can be filled with the presence of God because of the sacrifice of Jesus. God doesn't live in temples made by human hands, but he lives in us.

Most of us have never sacrificed a chicken. However, many of us have heard subtle suggestions in church that we can relate to God through some way other than Jesus. They come by insinuating we must do something more to continue in our salvation and in God's blessing than what we did to first receive salvation. If we aren't approaching God through Jesus but are trying to access him in some other way, are we really doing much better than slaughtering chickens?

People can get results by receiving *"another spirit"* and operating according to the *"basic principles of this world."* I'm no stranger to the supernatural. We've heard reports of people levitating, shape-shifting, and performing wild feats through witchcraft. I have no reason to doubt those reports. I once saw a spirit manifest as blue and red light in the air as a practitioner summoned it. However, I don't care if some ritual results in *"miracles"* or supernatural signs if it doesn't point people to Jesus! I'm totally unimpressed. If it obscures the work and person of Christ, it brings a curse! Lying signs and wonders are those which lead people away from relating to God through Christ.

Moses got results when he disobeyed God and struck the rock so water would pour fourth, instead of trusting the provision in God's voice and speaking to the rock. However, God called it rebellion and he was not allowed to enter the promised land because of it.[219] You can act on spiritual principles, get results, and still be guilty of rebellion and witchcraft.

When Christians Have The Same Mindsets as Idol Worshippers

I live in Brazil. I've encountered plenty of people who worship idols. I came across a slaughtered chicken and various sacrifices to demons on the street corners near our house in Rio. People would offer food, alcohol, cigarettes, perfume, cash, and all kinds of other things to various deities.

Several wealthy and famous Brazilians made pacts with those spirits, giving them expensive gifts. Seeing their wealth and fame, others devoted to spirits say *"It worked!"* But I don't care if it worked if it's not Jesus! In the end it's a curse!

Large groups of people dressed in white go to the beach at certain times to send out their offerings to the sea goddess, Iemanjá. They send boats out on the sea with thousands of dollars in perfumes, soaps, money, and other gifts.

Brazilian billionaire Eike Batista was once the seventh richest man in the world. Two seers advised him to make peace with the sea goddess and give an offering because he had to return something in thanksgiving for all he had taken from the sea. (Oil) He sent out a boat with an offering of flowers, imported perfumes, expensive champagnes, and 700 gold coins. Each coin was worth about R$1,000, or several hundred dollars. The seer prophesied that he would return to being the richest man in Brazil again in a matter of months.

Eike believed that the *"gods"* had helped him before in return for his devotion, and he thought his gift to Iemanjá would regain the billions he had lost in the recession. Instead, he soon went to jail on corruption charges.

Spiritism and idolatry are widespread in Brazil. Many evangelical Christians have a background in spiritism and some who attend evangelical churches continue sacrificing to African

---

[219] Numbers 20:2-12, 24

entities in secret. Many Catholics also mix their religion with African religions. I've prayed for and ministered healing to Catholics, Protestants, Spiritists and *"Macumbeiros."* I often recognize mental strongholds as I talk to people about Christ.

I often hear Evangelical Christians respond as I would expect from a Spiritist or a Macumbeiro. Many may have rejected idolatry but continue to relate to God as they did to an entity like Iemanjá. One lady wanted to give me a gift when I prayed and all the pain left her body. I felt uncomfortable because it felt like she was making a connection between the gift and receiving healing. I told her the story of Naaman's healing and how Elisha didn't receive a gift from him.

Mental strongholds hinder people who aren't rooted in the gospel from resting in Jesus's redemptive work. We mention manifestations of the Holy Spirit and they respond with, *"I hope that one day I might be good enough to receive that."* Or when Jesus heals someone, they say *"They deserved it."*

I visited a hospital in Brazil and people were being healed. It was wonderful. A lady began crying as she saw the miracles, and then evil spirits were leaving a young man. An onlooker took me aside to talk. He was a pastor in a poor slum. The man being delivered from evil spirits went to his church. He said they wanted healing and deliverance in his church, and asked me how much I would charge to come and bring it!

My heart burned to share the gospel with these people and watch Jesus heal them one after another. I pay to go on mission trips and see Jesus touch people. It broke my heart that they wanted healing and deliverance but were worried whether they could afford it! Why should anyone be afraid they cannot afford Jesus? I'm happy to receive free-will offerings. But how could I ever put a dollar amount on bringing people what Jesus already paid such a high price for them to have? Jesus deserves what he paid for!

If I'm sharing the gospel with someone who worships the sea goddess and just sent a thanksgiving offering of money and perfume to escape her curse and gain her blessing, will I now teach

"Give God a tithe in thanksgiving for what you've received, and in return he will bless and not curse you?" Doing so would misrepresent Almighty God's nature as if he were like their gods. How do you think I feel about sending a new Christian to a church that teaches that? I'm trying to bring them out of the mindset of idolatry and teach them to relate to God through Jesus, not through their gifts!

Do you understand my struggle over sending a new convert to a church? I did find a small Baptist church in which the pastor never mentioned a tithe and only asked people to give *"as you are able and as you are willing,"* which is what 2 Corinthians teaches. Although the church had little understanding of God's power and healing, they were open. They had sincere love for people. The message of relating to God through Jesus stood in contrast to the mindset of the Macumbeiros.

The claim that *"tithing works"* to resolve anybody's financial troubles is highly questionable. But even if it would work, I don't care! Witchcraft sometimes *"works"* too, with certain short-term results, but it's deceptive and brings a curse in the end. I don't want something that *"works"* if it is relating to God by any way other than through Christ.

Chapter 10
Tithing Undermines Spirit-Led Giving
Buzz Words and Propaganda Techniques

Assigning new or double meanings to common words and charging those buzz words and phrases with emotion was a common propaganda technique used by communists and Nazis to manipulate people's thinking. Joseph Goebbels, the Nazi minister of propaganda, said *"If you tell a lie big enough and continue to repeat it, people will eventually come to believe it."*

A more recent example of this propaganda technique is cloaking abortion in nice but deceptive words like *"women's rights"* and *"healthcare."* It makes out people who oppose abortion to be anti-woman's rights and anti-healthcare! Yet they would never use a term like *"killing a baby."* *"Terminating the fetus"* sounds so much better!

Similarly, several buzz words have developed around tithing. I doubt that it was planned intentionally; nevertheless, Christians often use these buzz words and phrases without thinking. They are often used to demonize anybody who questions the tithe doctrine, accusing them of being *"against giving,"* *"a traitor to God's kingdom,"* a *"God robber,"* or something similar, to avoid rational thinking. Other language is used to cloak the facts that demanding a tithe is using compulsion to bring in the money, charging a *"kingdom of heaven tax,"* and putting a price tag on God's blessings.

One example is irrationally applying the word *"obedience"* to the tithe, as if that word ended all arguments. God never commanded tithing as practiced today, not even to those under the old covenant! The Mosaic tithing statutes differed vastly from the modern tithe tradition. Neither was Abraham commanded to tithe.

Buzz words charged with emotion to describe non-tithers include *"God-robbers"* and *"crooks."* Manipulating people with curses and accusation is witchcraft. Tithing advocates say *"Tithing is a principle"* to cloak the legalism just as abortion advocates say *"It's a blob of tissue"* to help you forget that it's a baby. This *"principle"* is incompatible with the gospel!

Some people's entire argument for tithing revolves around the word *"honor."* Yet the modern tithe tradition dishonors the poor in the church and even demands a tithe from those who would have received from the Jewish tithe! That dishonors Christ himself, for he said *"Whatever you do for the least of these my brothers, you do for me."*[220] Human tithing traditions dishonor Jesus's sacrifice and the price he paid for us by teaching that the blessing or curse hinges on tithes and that tithing can open the heavens or deliver us from the curse of Adam's sin. These tithe traditions dishonor the Spirit of Truth because they are based on one falsehood after another.

Tithing was a way of showing honor in the ancient cultures, just as sacrificing animals was a way of honoring God. Yet tithing is no more a way of honoring God today than animal sacrifices are! Most of Malachi chapter 1 is a rebuke for not honoring God with animal sacrifices, yet who uses Malachi to argue that Christians today must sacrifice animals to *"honor"* God? Sacrificing an animal today would dishonor Christ! God revealed that it was never sacrifices and offerings that he desired, and he had no pleasure in them.[221] Similarly, what God wants from us is not a percentage of our crops but is our hearts!

The principle of honoring God remains, but how we honor God in the New Covenant is different. Spirit-led giving flowing

---

[220] Matthew 25:40
[221] Psalm 51:16, Hebrews 10:8

from God's love in our hearts honors him. As soon as it's about a magic percentage, we've missed it.

Tithing Is Paying, Not Giving

I tried to explain to one pastor that rejecting tithing is not rejecting giving. He responded most emphatically *"tithing is giving!"* I was dumbfounded over his inability to understand that a person can be generous and believe tithing is irrelevant.

Giving is free-will by definition. Nothing that is obligatory can rightly be called *"giving."* Spirit-led giving is neither motivated by fear of a curse nor by desire for selfish gain. It is motivated and defined by love and can never be defined by a percentage. Nobody calls paying taxes *"giving,"* and nobody says a farmer sowing his field to reap a harvest is *"giving."* Exchanging money to gain favor with someone powerful is called bribery or *"buttering them up!"* Exchanging money for a good is paying. Exchanging it for intimacy is prostitution. What we do can only be called Spirit-led giving when it is selflessly motivated by God's love and the benefit of the receiver.

Equating tithing with giving is especially ironic when we consider the oft-repeated teaching that *"Giving only starts after you pay your tithe."* Many teach that our *"offerings"* are only what we give over and above the tithe. They say the tithe isn't really giving but obedience, paying God his due. In fact, I just heard a sermon saying your giving is worth nothing if you don't pay a tithe first. Yet if anybody questions tithing, the same teachers accuse them of being against giving. Their definitions suddenly change.

I know people who oppose tithing and give far more than most tithers do. Dr. Kelly had accusations hurled at him as being stingy for teaching that tithing isn't biblical, and he responded *"I probably give more than most tithers. I'm just honest enough not to call it a tithe."*[222]

---

[222] Online: http://www.tithing-russkelly.com/id234.html

Let's get our definitions straight. If you owe or are obligated to pay something, it is paying, not giving. If tithing is obligatory and defined by a percentage, it is a tax. Giving is only truly giving when it is free-will. Consider C.H. Spurgeon's thoughts:

It is also noteworthy that, with regard to Christian liberality, there are no rules laid down in the Word of God. I remember hearing somebody say, "I should like to know exactly what I ought to give." Yes, dear Friend, no doubt you would; but you are not under a system similar to that by which the Jews were obliged to pay tithes to the priests. If there were any such rule laid down in the gospel, it would destroy the beauty of spontaneous giving, and take away all the bloom from the fruit of your liberality.[223]

The idea of our being priests, or Levites, in order to get compulsory tithes, would be too abhorrent to be entertained for a moment.[224]

The tithe is law. Yet scripture speaks of giving as grace.[225] Could it be that the old law of tithing distances people from walking in the grace of giving? I believe so! As Spurgeon said, tithing destroys the beauty of spontaneous giving.

Bertie Brits says tithing and *"give-to-get"* teachings destroyed the joy of giving for him. Many of us share his experience. Yet we must leave that place of hurt in order to begin giving freely out of fellowship with the Father. I love the gentle way Bertie encourages people to leave the hurt behind so it no longer defines them.

The grace that empowers Spirit-led giving is in God's voice. God's empowering grace isn't in today's tithe tradition because it is rote and human tradition, not our Heavenly Father's voice.

---

[223] Spurgeon, Charles H. *The Metropolitan Tabernacle Pulpit.* Pasadena, TX: Pilgrim Publications. Volume 47 Page 97

[224] Spurgeon, Charles H. *The Metropolitan Tabernacle Pulpit.* Pasadena, TX: Pilgrim Publications, 1977. Volume 28 Pg. 694

[225] 2 Corinthians 8:7

There Is No Kingdom-of-Heaven Tax!

Matthew 17:24-2 After Jesus and his disciples arrived in Capernaum, the collectors of the two-drachma temple tax came to Peter and asked, "Doesn't your teacher pay the temple tax?"

"Yes, he does," he replied.

When Peter came into the house, Jesus was the first to speak. "What do you think, Simon?" he asked. "From whom do the kings of the earth collect duty and taxes—from their own children or from others?" "'From others," Peter answered. "Then the children are exempt," Jesus said to him. "But so that we may not cause offense, go to the lake and throw out your line. Take the first fish you catch; open its mouth and you will find a four-drachma coin. Take it and give it to them for my tax and yours."

Jesus made it clear that there is no *"kingdom-of-heaven tax."* Today's tithe usually has more to do with the temple tax of Jesus's day than it does with the Mosaic tithe law. The Mosaic tithe was always food for people and was never money designated for the construction or maintenance of a building.

In his book, *"Jesus Is the Tithe,"* Bertie Brits appeals to family logic as a framework for understanding the New Covenant. Notably, Jesus used family logic in Matthew 17. Children don't owe their father taxes! Jesus taught a broad principle: God is not collecting duty or taxes from his own children!

Slaves and subjects owe. Scripture says those under the law are in slavery like Hagar,[226] but God has not given us the spirit of slavery but of sonship which cries *"Abba, Father!"*[227] Jesus said, *"I*

---

[226] Galatians 4:21-31

no longer call you servants, but I call you friends."[228] No matter how much you attempt to dress tithing as grace, it does not reflect the family logic of the New Covenant. It misrepresents how God is relating to us!

A certain preacher, who has made a tremendous positive impact on my life and on Christian churches around the world, calls the tithe our *"rent"* for living on God's land. As much as I appreciate him, I couldn't disagree more about tithes! Notice how contrary his statement is to the logic Jesus used talking about sons' relation to the Father in Matthew 17. And can you imagine a wife paying her husband rent?

Family logic doesn't say *"You owe the Father 10%."* Neither does it say *"You owe the Father everything."* Rather, the Father in Jesus's parable said *"All that I have is yours."*[229] Scripture uses the husband-and-wife relationship as representative of Christ and the church. The wife does not owe the husband. The principle is *"All I have is yours, and all you have is mine."* [230]

Everything I have belongs to Jesus. Jesus himself said *"Those of you who do not give up everything you have cannot be my disciples."*[231] But also, all he has is mine! If the Father did not withhold his only Son, but gave him up for me, he will also with him freely give me all things![232]

After Ananias and Sapphira sold their land, Peter said, *"Didn't it belong to you before it was sold? And after it was sold, wasn't the money at your disposal?"* Another version says *"You could have used the money as you wished."*[233] Notice that Peter didn't say *"All but the tithe belonged to you, and you could have used 9/10ths any way you wished after removing the tithe."*

---

[227] Galatians 4:6, Romans 8:15
[228] John 15:15
[229] Luke 15:31
[230] John 17:10, Romans 8:32
[231] Luke 14:33
[232] Romans 8:32
[233] Acts 5:4 (NIRV)

God didn't give his one and only Son for us because he owed, but because he loved! Likewise, to give from a New Covenant position of having been joined to the Lord in spirit,[234] we must give as God gives, not out of indebtedness but out of love. My debt has been paid! Jesus's reward for giving his life was the joy set before him,[235] which was our salvation! To give out of communion with the Spirit of Christ, the reward we seek must be the joy of blessing people and glorifying God.

100% Is God's!

All I have is at my Heavenly Father's disposal for the sake of his Kingdom, but all that He has is also mine! 100% is holy, not 10%. Neither does 10% sanctify the rest. We would only need a tithe to sanctify or redeem anything if Jesus's redemptive work were insufficient to do so!

John Wesley's sermon *"On the Use of Money,"* gives us insight into what it looks like to give all our money to God:

Do not stint yourself, like a Jew rather than a Christian, to this or that proportion. Render unto God, not a tenth, not a third, not half, but all that is God's, be it more or less.[236]

Wesley taught that Christians should first use their money to meet their own needs, then the needs of their families, then the needs of the household of faith (poor Christians), and then the needs of the world.[237] His teaching was in line with the Biblical emphasis on caring for your family first. It contradicted *"your tithe comes first."*

I like that Wesley said the money you spend on your own needs and your family's needs is just as holy as the money you

---

[234] 1 Corinthians 6:17
[235] Hebrews 12:2
[236] Wesley, John. *Sermons on Several Occasions: in Two Volumes.* London: Published and sold by J. Kershaw, 14, City-Road, and 66, Paternoster-Row, 1825. Volume 1. Sermon *The Use Of Money.* Pg. 634
[237] Wesley, John. *Sermons on Several Occasions: in Two Volumes.* London: Published and sold by J. Kershaw, 14, City-Road, and 66, Paternoster-Row, 1825. Volume 1. Sermon *The Use Of Money.* Pg. 633

spend on the needs of the household of faith or the world.[238] 100% is holy. 100% is God's.

How did Wesley practice that? He emphasized living frugally so as to be able to give. He said, *"Earn all you can, save all you can, give all you can."*[239] That reminds me of the scriptural exhortation to work hard with our hands so as to have something to share with those in need.[240]

Wesley's support has been claimed by both advocates and opponents of tithing. However, his practice shows how his beliefs differed from today's tithe tradition. As he preached, he lived frugally and cared first for his own needs and those of his family. He figured that he needed 28 pounds to live on, and gave the rest away, which was two pounds.[241] As his income increased, his giving increased but his standard of living stayed the same, until he was giving away about 98% of his income and living on about 2%.

Wesley began giving at about 7%, less than a tithe. According to his own teaching the 93% he lived on was just as holy as the 7% he gave. God blessed him despite his failure to tithe! His income grew rapidly. When he was giving away 98% of his money, the 2% he lived on continued to be as holy as the rest.

Those who prioritize paying their bills and caring for their families first should never feel guilty as if they aren't giving enough. The money spent on their own needs is just as holy as the rest. We aim to work hard so as to have something to share with those in need, to use our money wisely, and to advance Christ's kingdom in every way possible. We know we will all give an account of ourselves to God.[242]

---

[238] Wesley, John. *Sermons on Several Occasions: in Two Volumes.* London: Published and sold by J. Kershaw, 14, City-Road, and 66, Paternoster-Row, 1825. Volume 1. Sermon *The Use Of Money. Pg. 633*

[239] Wesley, John. *Sermons on Several Occasions: in Two Volumes.* London: Published and sold by J. Kershaw, 14, City-Road, and 66, Paternoster-Row, 1825. Volume 1. Sermon *The Use Of Money.* Pg. 626-633

[240] Ephesians 4:28

[241] Harshman, Charles W. *Christian Giving.* New York: Eaton and Mains, 1905. Pg. 79

[242] Romans 14:12

When Wesley said *"save all you can,"* he wasn't talking about putting money in a bank, but rather of refraining from spending on anything unnecessary. He didn't seem to have any place in his mindset for saving, investment, or leaving an inheritance. I don't fully agree with Wesley's view on that, and I imagine that few of you do either. There is a Biblical place for saving, investment, and leaving an inheritance to your children. For example, Proverbs says *"A good man leaves an inheritance for his children's children."*[243] Joseph saved grain and prepared for a famine because of the wisdom and revelation God gave him. Even vacations are Biblical, as Graeme Carlé pointed out in his book that the tithe was a kind of vacation and shows us the importance of rest.

I like Wesley's emphasis on 100% of our money being holy. However, I think we must add to his paradigm a place for saving, investment, and leisure. The emphasis is on loving the Lord with all our heart, soul, and mind,[244] seeking to use our money in the best way possible as we walk in close fellowship with the Lord, our hearts moved by what moves his heart. We also emphasize caring for the poor as scripture does and as Wesley did.

This paradigm will not always result in giving as much as a tenth, since many Christians in the world today barely have their own basic needs met, and paying for one's own basic needs and caring for one's own family come before giving to other causes. But living by this paradigm also leads many people to give away far more than a tithe, some over 90% of their income. It also leads to a higher emphasis on giving to the poor and to missions.

You Are Responsible for Where You Give!

One of my Facebook friends, Michael Van Vlymen, wrote a book called *Supernatural Provision.* Michael has many amazing testimonies of giving bountifully as lead by the Holy Spirit and receiving miracles of supernatural provision, even angels literally

---

[243] Proverbs 13:22 (NKJV)
[244] Matthew 22:37

putting physical money in his hand and money multiplying.[245] He teaches readers how to ask the Holy Spirit for seed to sow in order to meet needs. I like Michael's book because it teaches about how to exercise faith in giving and finances without the legalism or ulterior motives.

Michael strongly believes we are responsible for where we give. He believes many Christians are not walking in abundance because they give not as led by God or scripture, or even an *"inner witness"* that it's the right thing to do, but because *"this is what I know, and this is the way we have always done it."*[246] He encourages readers to hear God's voice about where to give rather than following human traditions like tithing or giving in response to pressure, which he says is poor stewardship. He often gives to individuals who have needs as the Lord leads him, such as to a single mother. Calling the tithe a *"rule of men,"*[247] Michael points out:

It is hard for people to go against tradition. For most, it would be easier to go against the Word of God.[248]

Our modern tithe is based on human tradition and not even on the Mosaic tithe, yet the Church has broken many of God's commands for the sake of this tradition. Michael continues:

Is God more impressed if we send that $100.00 to the guy on TV with the nice clothes and big organization than He would be if we gave the money to one of our kids who wants to make sandwiches for homeless people? Would that money given to our kids even count with God?[249]

---

[245] Vlymen, Michael Van. *Supernatural Provision Book One*. Michael Van Vlymen, 2017. Position 121

[246] Vlymen, Michael Van. *Supernatural Provision Book One*. Michael Van Vlymen, 2017. Position 200

[247] Vlymen, Michael Van. *Supernatural Provision Book One*. Michael Van Vlymen, 2017. Position 372

[248] Vlymen, Michael Van. *Supernatural Provision Book One*. Michael Van Vlymen, 2017. Position 358

[249] Vlymen, Michael Van. *Supernatural Provision Book One*. Michael Van Vlymen, 2017.

Michael also believes we are not under obligation to give 10%, but everything we have belongs to God.[250] He points out that sometimes we miss God's best purposes for our money by giving just because it was *"time to give,"* but without hearing the Lord.[251]

One of the main things I gleaned from Michael's book is that it's not OK to give without thought of what the Master's money yields, or shift the responsibility for it onto someone else.[252] That would be like the wicked and lazy servant in Jesus's parable of the talents.[253]

In contrast to Michael's teaching on good stewardship and Spirit-led giving, a tithing proponent repeats what I have heard so often, writing about his struggle over how a particular pastor was using tithes:

> **But as I wrestled with that, God showed me that when I give to the church, I am giving to God. Not to man. So, it doesn't matter if he is stealing from the Church. It doesn't matter if he is using the funds wisely. That is between him and God, but my job is to give and give in faith to God.**[254]

Most modern tithe traditions give leaders control of where the money goes, and it's never according to the instructions in the Mosaic law for distributing tithes. We can't just say a Mosaic ordinance applies but refuse to accept the whole package. If we must tithe according to Malachi, we must distribute it according to the ordinance Malachi refers to. The notion that our money must go through a leader who uses it as he wishes rather than giving

Position 472
[250] Vlymen, Michael Van. *Supernatural Provision Book One*. Michael Van Vlymen, 2017. Position 520
[251] Vlymen, Michael Van. *Supernatural Provision Book One*. Michael Van Vlymen, 2017. Position 760
[252] Vlymen, Michael Van. *Supernatural Provision Book One*. Michael Van Vlymen, 2017. Position 833
[253] Matthew 25:14-29
[254]*Tithing In The New Testament* Online: https://seedtime.com/tithing-in-the-new-testament/?fbclid=IwAR3ocPTlZ1tgD0ssh_-0GSLEfwyECopRveE0H0YC8N14PRRyNTxzNfXkv-w Accessed November 23rd, 2019

directly is wholly unscriptural, bad stewardship, and based on erroneous ecclesiology.

How the Tithe Supplants Spirit-Led Giving

God has given individual Christians responsibility for how we use our money to bring a return for his kingdom. We will individually give account to God for our stewardship. Modern tithe traditions supplant giving as truly led by the Holy Spirit. Instead of giving from communion with the Holy Spirit as they decide in their hearts, many people hand over the tithe and say, *"I did my part. I'm not responsible for what happens from here on with the money."*

We see this in how current giving trends contrast with the scriptural and early church emphasis on where to give. Biblical texts on giving overwhelmingly emphasize helping the poor. The Mosaic tithe helped the poor. The second most-common context of New Testament giving passages is apostolic ministry: supporting traveling ministers who take the gospel to the unreached. In contrast to this, most tithe teachers say helping the poor or supporting missions can only come after your tithe.

Although it's hard to find statistics on how much of church giving goes to help the poor, *Empty Tomb Incorporated*[255] concluded that 85% goes to internal operations, and 15% goes to outreach. I was unable to find how much of that 15% goes to the poor, but I don't think it's very much!

How much goes to missions? In 1920, the percentage of giving to missions from the total offering was 10.09 percent, just over a dime out of every dollar. In 2003, conservative and evangelical denominations gave 2.6 percent (about three cents per dollar), with the liberals giving only 0.9 percent (one cent). The combined average for overseas work is about two pennies per dollar.[256]

---

[255] *The State of Church Giving through 2016: What Do Denominational Leaders Want to Do with $368 Billion More a Year?* 28th edition. Empty Tomb Publications. 2018. Order online: http://www.emptytomb.org/pubs.html Accessed November 23rd, 2019
[256] *The State of Church Giving through 2003*. Empty Tomb Publications. Order online: http://www.emptytomb.org/pubs.html Accessed November 23rd, 2019

How much of this goes towards reaching people who've never heard the gospel? According to 2001 statistics from thetravellingteam.org, in 2001 only 1% of giving to *"Missions"* went to unreached people.[257] One writer concluded, *"For every $100,000 that Christians make, they give $1 to the unreached."*[258] (If you want to give towards reaching people who've never heard the gospel, you might consider globalfronteirmissions.org and pioneers.org.)

From 1920 until now, as emphasis on tithing has increased, the percentage of churches' giving to missions has drastically decreased. With increased emphasis on tithing, today's churches are now giving only about a fifth, percentage-wise, of what churches gave to missions in the 1920s! Even overall giving seems to have decreased with increased emphasis on the tithe. The average Christian is giving 2.5 percent of his income today. During the Great Depression it was 3.3%.[259] (Consistent with what would have gone to the Levites and the poor under Mosaic law according to the single tithe view.)

Teaching tithing has not made people more generous. The extremely small amount of money churches receive that goes to helping the poor and frontline missions is surely inconsistent with the emphasis of scripture on helping the poor and reaching the unreached.

Mike Holmes wrote an article in Relevant Magazine about what would happen if all Christians tithed. He points out that it would make $165 billion available which could be used in the following way:

---

[257] *Missions Stats: The Current State Of The World.* Online: http://www.thetravelingteam.org/stats Accessed November 23rd, 2019
[258] *Missions Statistics.* Online: https://messagemissions.com/mission-statistics/ Accessed November 23rd, 2019
[259] *The Ultimate Source Of Charitable Giving Statistics For 2018.* Online: https://nonprofitssource.com/online-giving-statistics/ Accessed November 23rd, 2019

- *$25 billion could relieve global hunger and eliminate deaths from preventable diseases within five years*
- *$15 billion could solve the world's water and sanitation issues—specifically in places where a majority of people live on less than $1 a day*
- *$12 billion could end illiteracy*
- *$1 billion could fully fund all overseas mission work*
- *$100–$110 billion would be left over for additional ministry expansion[260]*

While Mike's theory sounds nice, the history of how churches have used tithe money casts serious doubt on the notion that the tithes would ever be used thus if all Christians started tithing. On the contrary, I'm sure Christian giving to the top four categories would increase if all Christians gave as they decided in their hearts and lead by the Holy Spirit, not by tithes. While some who believe in tithing do teach that Christians decide where to give their tithe, many (and most charismatic churches) teach that the tithe goes to the local church and only after paying the tithe can you give to other causes.

Today's tithe traditions motivate people by external compulsion, being seen by men, shame, fear of a curse, and other selfish considerations rather than love from a pure heart. **Such motivations keep us from being led by the Holy Spirit in our giving.**

Baptist missionary J. Guy Muse wrote an article sharing many stories of seeing the Lord's hand in provision and finances. He notes that money given out of routine or obligation, such as tithe money, never seems to stretch any further than it normally would. Yet he has seen Spirit-led giving multiplied again and again, having a huge impact regardless of the amount. He mentions $200 gifts accomplishing more than $2,000 normally could have,

---

[260] *What Would Happen If The Church Tithed?* Online: https://relevantmagazine.com/love-and-money/what-would-happen-if-church-tithed Accessed November 23rd, 2019

supernatural multiplication of food, small amounts of money somehow covering all a missionary's needs, and a $1,500 dollar evangelism investment that enabled them to reach 3 million people, at a cost of 1/20th of a cent per evangelistic contact. He says:

Remodeling and upgrading the church office will probably cost dollar for dollar what it would cost anywhere else in town. But, say I have only $50 for Bibles for new believers when $500 is what is needed in order for there to be one Bible per family. $50 Kingdom Dollars is enough to buy $500 of the needed Bibles. Believe me![261]

Some say *"We tithe out of a joyful heart, not under compulsion."* Yet they fear that giving would drastically drop if they let go of the 10% figure. If giving would drop, the drop would just show the extent that people were already giving out of compulsion instead of from communion with the Holy Spirit. The very admission of this fear shows that the leader already knows the people are giving under compulsion. Using compulsion to get people to give robs them of the joy of giving and interferes with the Holy Spirit's leading.

To the extent that people are compelled to give by what other people think, shame, *"give to get,"* fear of a curse, or anything but love, they are not giving as led by the Holy Spirit. People who are used to responding to pressure often don't respond when there is no pressure. I've seen *"giving burnout."*

I spoke at one church four hours away from my home and the offering from the congregation was $32.00, not enough for gas money and tolls. I don't share this begrudgingly at all, not even a little, as I share Paul's sentiment *"We want not what is yours, but you."* I would have gladly paid my own way and received nothing but the privilege of participating in the Holy Spirit's work. I treasure the memory of what God did in that congregation. But my impression was that the people were so *"burnt out"* on high-

---

[261] *Kingdom Finances.* Online: http://guymuse.blogspot.com/2010/02/kingdom-finances.html Accessed November 23rd, 2019

pressure offerings that they didn't know how to respond without pressure.

I'm so thankful when people do give. It helps to pay travel expenses and enables me to dedicate more time to edifying the body of Christ. Yet whether I receive a large offering or none, I rejoice. I get my thrills from feeling God's love move through me and seeing the Holy Spirit heal and bless people. I treasure the memories of what God does in every place!

Many of my friends who don't believe in tithing are the quickest to offer hospitality or help a homeless person or single mother. Many tithers won't even respond to such a situation because they think there's nothing in it for them. Rejecting tithing doesn't amount to being a tightwad. Some people who share my view are giving away well over half of their incomes. Others may not be giving 10% of their income to a church but regularly give more than most give to the poor and missions. If you give even a dollar a month supporting missions to the unreached, you are giving a lot more to that high-priority cause than the average Christian does!

My wife and I turned our wedding into a time to pray for people and minister healing. We extended an open invitation; anyone who wanted to come was welcome. People were lying on the floor after receiving prayer, and one guy was baptized in the Holy Spirit. We also asked for prayer as I was about to move as a missionary to Brazil.

At the wedding were several friends who believed tithing was Old-Covenant only, and other friends who believed tithing is for today. One tither gave a very generous gift. Aside from that exception, every wedding gift from someone in the former group was at least twice the amount of any gift from a tither!

I was happy to have everyone even if they gave no gift. But that experience was a great illustration of how those who question a mandatory tithing paradigm are often more generous in unseen ways, when there's nothing in it for themselves, and when the cause might not be considered the most *"spiritual"* thing to give to but directly helps people.

The Difficulty of Getting the Most Generous People on Earth To Tithe!

I read a book by Glenn Schwartz called *When Charity Destroys Dignity*. Glen has extensive experience in foreign missions and made many great points in his excellent book. However, when I got to the part about tithing, I was left scratching my head.

I quote here from Emmanuel Olidapo who at one time served as International Secretary of Scripture Union. He has this to say about generosity in Africa: "It isn't that African people don't know how to give. There are hardly more generous people on earth. They give for festivals and many other special occasions. They give to relatives needing education or to unemployed or orphaned people in their community. However, many simply don't give generously to the church."[262]

Contrary to the common assumption that people who don't practice or believe in tithing are stingy, Schwartz praises the African people's generosity. He laments that in spite of their rich generosity, it is so hard to get them to tithe. He continues:

Dr David Barrett is a missiologist and researcher who provides information for the Christian movement. He has made the statement that if Christians in Africa give just 2% of their income they would be able to pay all of their bills. He says that would be able to support their leadership training, pay their pastors, build their own church building, fund their development projects, and buy computers if they want them -- all on 2% of the income of Christians in Africa!

---

[262] Schwartz, Glenn. *When Charity Destroys Dignity: Overcoming Unhealthy Dependency in the Christian Movement: a Compendium.* Lancaster, PA: World Mission Associates, 2007. Pg. 153

From time to time I try to check this out. Some time ago I asked a church leader in East Africa whether he agreed with Dr. Barrett's observation. His response was as follows: "It's interesting that you say that. We recently calculated that if the members of our church gave only one percent of their income we could pay all the bills at our church. "

Imagine what would happen in a church like that if the members gave ten percent! They would have far more than they needed for local ministry. In fact, if they gave that much, they could give to missions and send their own people elsewhere with the Gospel.[263]

Schwartz continued, saying that if all African Christians tithed, the church would have so much money they wouldn't know what to do with it all! And I thought, *"Why do they need to tithe so their churches have so much money that they don't know what to do with it all? Why not let them continue to be the 'most generous people on earth,' and be led by the Spirit as they continue to help the needy among them?"*

Why didn't Schwartz consider that in Deuteronomy 14 the people ate their tithe in a festival and gave it directly to the poor on the third year, and the early church spent their collections on love feasts shared with the poor? He just finished talking about how the Africans gave to festivals and gave generously directly to the poor. Considering that the heaviest emphasis in scripture is on giving to the poor, it seems like those Africans were already engaging in Spirit-led giving!

As YWAM church planting coach Brian Hogan taught us, those missionaries were trying to impose the *"heavy package"* of our way of doing church on the Africans instead of the *"light*

---

[263] Schwartz, Glenn. *When Charity Destroys Dignity: Overcoming Unhealthy Dependency in the Christian Movement: a Compendium.* Lancaster, PA: World Mission Associates, 2007. Pg. 161

package" of the bare Biblical necessities. The heavy package includes a high-overhead mode of operation. But even with the heavy package, 1 or 2 percent of the Africans' income was enough to pay for everything!

Schwartz's experience in Africa was a few decades ago. His speculation on what would happen if the people tithed has been proven wrong, as have been the hypotheses of many others who've imagined what we would accomplish if everyone tithed. Certain churches in Africa now put extreme emphasis on mandatory tithing. Rather than more money going to the poor and to missions, influential pastors have become rich and the poor have heavy burdens placed on them.

The tithing emphasis has done great harm to the willingness to help a brother in need, which was already built into many of their cultures. We forsake Spirit-led giving to the extent that we embrace compulsion. The mandatory tithing doctrine has hurt Africans' propensity towards Spirit-led generosity. One African brother commented to me that many do tithe but will do nothing to help someone in need. Another lamented seeing tithers fail to care for aging parents. These descriptions of many tithing Africans contrast with Emmanuel Olidapo's description of the *"most generous people on earth."*

The Context of "It's Better To Give Than To Receive"

Acts 20:33-35 I have not coveted anyone's silver or gold or clothing. You yourselves know that these hands of mine have supplied my own needs and the needs of my companions. In everything I did, I showed you that by this kind of hard work we must help the weak, remembering the words the Lord Jesus himself said: "It is more blessed to give than to receive."

Paul quoted Jesus's words *"It is more blessed to give than to receive"* in the context of working hard in ministry at his own expense and setting an example of helping the weak! He was exhorting a group of local church leaders. On the contrary, we most often hear this verse quoted today in the context of the speaker receiving and the ones he is speaking to giving!

I can so relate to the passionate love that Paul had for the churches, expressed in his words *"I will most gladly spend for you everything I have and expend myself as well."* Scripture qualifies money spent and energy expended in ministry as an expression of Jesus's heart, who became poor so that we might become rich.[264] Are we now willing to give all and become poor so that others might become rich?

> **2 Corinthians 12:14-15 Now I am ready to visit you for the third time, and I will not be a burden to you, because what I want is not your possessions but you. After all, children should not have to save up for their parents, but parents for their children. So I will very gladly spend for you everything I have and expend myself as well.**

In the middle of trials God confirmed that I was to go to Russia and Ukraine with a love for the people that turned into a current I physically felt flowing through my whole body from head to foot. I wasn't tithing, but I was spending and being spent in partnership with the Holy Spirit's work. After that was the open door to visit a country where preaching the gospel is illegal and to stay with the family of someone Jesus had already healed.

Consider those situations and consider the figures we saw for the percentage of church giving that goes towards getting the gospel to the unreached. I was in a position few others were in to bring the gospel to those who had never heard it. I wasn't giving a tithe because I had already spent and expended myself in fellowship with the Holy Spirit's work. I had already given my life!

I would have disobeyed God if I'd paid a tithe that year rather than go to Russia. Yet our pastors regarded me as *"disobedient"* with my finances and I could no longer even expect prayer support

---

[264] 2 Corinthians 8:9

from my church as I went. Wasn't there something more important at that moment than the church receiving my tithe? Was it more important that I *"support the local church?"* than bring the gospel to people who had never heard it in a closed nation?

Why Would So Many Church Planters Consider the Tithe a Hindrance to Multiplication?

As I share the perspective of many frontline church planters, I imagine many pastors thinking *"You're saying we need to sell our building and meet in houses!"* I'm not necessarily saying that. However, Western Christian culture does not equate to the kingdom of God. An honest look at the global church may help us to differentiate between the two.

Brian Hogan's church-planting seminar gave me boldness to voice my questions about the tithe. His team partnered with the Holy Spirit to start a rapidly-growing church planting movement in a country that previously had almost no Christians. They were soon sending more missionaries per believer than any other Christian movement in the world. They had to give generously to do so, and Brian said they would have given much less if they were taught tithing!

Many others on the front lines of the gospel oppose tithing and refuse to teach it. Dr. Victor Choudrie leads a church planting movement that has started tens of thousands of churches in 40 nations, with over a million people baptized in a single year. Many of those Christians are poor and face severe persecution. Check out the fourth of his 21 steps on *"How to go from a barren church to become a millionaire of souls"*:

4. Replace Mosaic tithing with Christian sharing, thereby harnessing the enormous, financial resources, hospitality and goodwill available in Christian homes. Believe that God is going to work a work among the nations through you which

will leave you utterly amazed, and also provide resources for it. Deut. 8:17-18; Acts 5:32-34; Hab. 1:5[265]

Ironically, many Christians believe the Church would fall apart without tithing. Yet some of the world's most successful church planters see the tithe tradition as a primary factor which hinders the church from multiplying! It supplants Holy Spirit-led giving by bringing in control.

Movements like the one Dr. Choudrie leads put a more holistic and Biblical emphasis on caring for the poor and apostolic missions. Serving the church and extending hospitality are some of the primary ways of giving. Many of the Christians who agree with me about tithing are involved in frontline church multiplication movements.

Many frontline leaders have come to similar conclusions as Dr. Choudrie has, so a lot of literature on church-multiplication movements reflects this. Our friend Steve Hill has been involved for years in church-multiplication movements targeting unreached people. He says the hindrances to growth are *"buildings, bigshots, and budgets!"*

Those used to the *"heavy package"* say the Church would fall apart without money. The movement Dr. Choudrie leads meets in homes with no paid pastors. The Kingdom of God consists not of mammon, food, or drink, but of righteousness, peace, and joy in the Holy Spirit.[266] I recently read a Baptist church-planter's description of a church meeting in Ecuador in which the offering totaled $5! Yet the whole offering went towards the evangelistic blitz they were planning, and many American congregations could hardly equal the evangelistic fervor of that little church![267]

---

[265] Choudrie, Victor. *How To Go From A Barren Church To A Millionaire Of Souls.* Online: http://guymuse.blogspot.com/2010/11/victor-choudries-21-steps-to-transit.html   Accessed December 12th.

[266] Romans 14:17

[267] Muse, J. Guy *Those Questionable Churches Being Planted Overseas.* Online: http://guymuse.blogspot.com/2006/03/those-questionable-churches-being.html   Accessed December 26, 2019.

Chapter 10

But How Will We Pay for Things?

Most of the rapidly multiplying churches we've been speaking of meet in homes with low overhead. Some Christians are totally against any church meeting in a big building, and many leaders of successful church planting movements consider church buildings a hindrance to growth.

One of my friends founded a missions organization and has been involved for decades in church-multiplication movements. He doesn't seem to see much good in the institutional church. While I respect this friend and agree with him about most issues, I see the Holy Spirit doing a lot in many churches that meet in their own buildings.

Scripture doesn't say you need big facilities, and neither does it prohibit them. Some churches which do have high overhead, big buildings, and lots of infrastructure have made positive contributions to the body of Christ. I often used to visit a particular large charismatic church in Pennsylvania. They miraculously acquired their large facilities after a prophetic word. Their conferences have blessed me.

Many of us like big meetings, conferences, and worship music from churches like *Hillsong*. That's not necessarily wrong, but global Christianity and church history remind us that the high-overhead model is only a certain expression of Christianity, with certain strengths and weaknesses. Many western Christians falsely believe we can't have church in any other way and God's kingdom will fall apart if we don't bring in enough money!

Meeting in school auditoriums or other facilities has worked well for some congregations. I taught a group that met in a school here in Brazil for some time. Graeme Carlé's congregation met in school facilities which they rented for $1.00 per person. Brian Hogan shared that the churches in Mongolia had a large *"celebration"* meeting monthly and met the rest of the time in houses. If they had the large meeting more often than once a month, the churches stopped multiplying.

Should you meet only from house to house, rent facilities from time to time, or have your own facilities? Be led by the Holy Spirit and remember that the purpose of any building must always be to serve people, who are the true temple of God. I don't think it would be right to tell every church that has a building to just sell it and start meeting in houses. Make sure the building is serving the people, and not the people serving the building or imagining it's God's temple!

If you have infrastructure and facilities that are serving people and the Holy Spirit leads you to keep them, how will you pay for them without teaching tithing? If we want our own facilities and a salaried pastor, we should do our part to pitch in. Yet we cannot continue with integrity to teach tithing as the *"kingdom model"* for finances.

When we point out the many problems with teaching tithing, many people have nothing left to say except *"How will we support the church without it?"* Some pastors even agree that it's scripturally indefensible but conclude that even if it's unbiblical, we need tithing to raise money. They're afraid that if they stop teaching tithing, people will stop giving. It's clearly not even about *"What does scripture teach?"* but to *"How will we raise money?"*

Are there churches with a big Sunday meeting in their own facilities that pay for everything by only free-will giving? Yes! Check out Bertie Brits and *Dynamic Love Ministries*, for example. You can find them online. Bertie has some of the best messages I have heard on money, coming from a biblical foundation of contentment. He believes neither in tithing nor in sowing money to reap money. His TV program is funded completely by free-will giving, without a hint of compulsion. He says it's as simple as this: *"We can have a large facility if you want it. If that's for you, please pitch in to pay for it. If you don't like the high overhead, you can also be part of our online church."*

John MacArthur, the notorious anti-charismatic preacher, is quite an opponent of teaching tithing. As much as I disagree with him about some other matters, I agree on this! He leads a megachurch with large facilities and doesn't teach tithing. Andrew Farley of the *Church Without Religion,* in Lubbock, Texas, is another one. Vitor Azevedo leads a megachurch in Brazil that has experienced explosive growth among young people. They do not teach tithing and take a no-compulsion offering. People run to the front eagerly to contribute!

Several major seminaries don't teach tithing. Many churches which are related to those seminaries and have traditional facilities also do not believe in a tithe model. The Baptist church I attended paid rent, never mentioned a tithe and did more to minister to the poor than many larger churches do.

T.B. Joshua's church draws more foreign visitors than any other church in Nigeria. They have a powerful healing and deliverance ministry and reach many people through their channel, *Emmanuel TV.* Although Joshua uses the word *"tithe,"* what he teaches is much closer to the heart of scriptural giving. He tells people NOT to give all their tithes to his church because the church might be tempted to keep the money instead of giving it to the poor.[268] Instead, he encourages Christians to share their tithes directly with the poor. He refunded the tithe a poor man gave to another church and told him to not worry about tithing when in a financially weak situation, but to invest the money to get a business going first. Joshua said *"there are many areas you can render your service to ministry, but financially you are not strong."*[269] Thus this large church and its TV station prosper in a country where many churchgoers have a low income, and they teach people not to give the tithe directly to them. They have plenty to help the needy, and refuse to accept tithes from people the church should be helping.[270]

For a while after moving to Brazil, we invited my wife's friends to our home for prayer and fellowship and I didn't

---

[268] *TB Joshua Replies Daddy Freeze On Tithe* Online: https://www.youtube.com/watch?v=j_QgnZ-zHXw&t=580s Accessed January 7th, 2020
[269] *Touching: Why TB Joshua Returned This Man's Tithes* Online: https://www.youtube.com/watch?v=6O_CY_Cw_2c Accessed January 7th, 2020
[270] *TB Joshua Speaks About Who Should Give Tithes, Emmanuel TV* Online: https://www.youtube.com/watch?v=SqGqc3YqHVw Accessed January 7th, 2020

regularly attend a traditional church. When I got involved with the group meeting at the school, there was no overhead and I was the preacher for over a year. Then they moved on to meet on someone's property in a roofed area outside the house on a different day. There was still no rent.

The Baptist church in Rio de Janeiro started meeting in a school, then on top of somebody's house, and then in an area where they paid rent. I would have been happy to continue meeting rent-free on the housetop, which was concrete with 4-foot-high walls, pillars, and a fiberglass roof above it. Even so, I contributed when they decided to rent a small building.

The pastor emphasized free-will giving motivated by love. He never mentioned a tithe. I suspect he didn't believe in it because the church profile "liked" my Facebook status about how much harm tithe doctrines have caused to the body of Christ. Some people in the congregation did mention a tithe once in a while, and his refusal to use such language was conspicuous. I think he just never talked about it and left the matter up to individual people's convictions. He may have been following his conviction while avoiding conflict in his denomination.

The pastor set the culture of that church, which reflected God's glory in a way that reminded me of the Christian camp I attended as a kid. I could feel pure and sincere love with no ulterior motives. It stood out to me at a time when I was reluctant to send people to a church after I ministered healing and shared the gospel.

In my current city, I've become involved in home meetings which have low overhead. I prefer to direct the bulk of my giving to apostolic ministry and helping the weak.

Islam has a mandatory 2.5% tax, much lower than the tithe, and they have large mosques. Interestingly enough, in spite of all the teaching about tithing, that is the same as the average percentage that American Christians currently give. Gyms charge much less than a tithe for a membership fee and they have both facilities and full-time staff. A friend in Finland told me that tithing is virtually unknown where he lives, his Pentecostal church doesn't push it, and the Lutheran church charges a three percent tax.

I'm not arguing that Christians should give less, except for those who are having trouble meeting their family's needs and paying what is due even while living frugally. Rather, I'm pointing out that the lower we keep our overhead, the more we can give towards the causes which scripture most emphasizes.

I would rather see churches charge an entrance fee for use of facilities, as a gym does, than teach tithing. Although that wouldn't be ideal, it would better than compromising our integrity and distorting scripture to charge a *"kingdom-of-God tax,"* which people pay in order to obtain God's blessing.

What Will Happen to Church Finances if We Stop Teaching Tithing?

I've heard several stories of churches that stopped teaching tithing. Some had a dramatic decrease in giving. For others, little changed. Some saw giving increase. Dr. David Croteau, who concludes in his doctoral thesis that the tithe is not for Christians today, gave lectures on the matter in two churches. Both saw giving increase slightly after the lectures. In both cases, the pastors felt their congregation was prepared for it. Dr. Croteau suggests first phasing out references to the tithe, such as removing the word from the offering envelopes, and then teaching New Testament giving principles as a lead-up to discussing tithing.

In 2017, I spoke at a church in Maryland. The pastor at that time taught tithing, although the couple that invited me were in agreement with my position. Since then, they have become the new pastors of the church and gone from teaching tithing to teaching generous free-will giving as worship. People continue to give, and some have increased giving.

A pastor in modern-day Macedonia began to pray about what to teach the people because he realized that the tithe is not part of the New Covenant. He started with the principle of being generous, and within a year the offerings of the church increased substantially.

On the other hand, another pastor heavily emphasized tithing and used a lot of pressure in taking the offering. Some people in his congregation were troubled by this and were praying about it. One day, the pastor suddenly said *"God has been dealing with me about teaching tithing and using guilt and pressure to get people to give. From now on, we don't want to make people give out of obligation. God loves a cheerful giver."*

Giving plummeted. Within a few weeks, the pastor was back to teaching tithing. He put the pressure on more than ever, threatening people with a curse if they didn't tithe and enticing them with material blessings if they did.

It may be very difficult for some congregations that have a high-overhead expression of church and have relied on tithe teaching and manipulation to bring in money, to suddenly change their position. But this story illustrates a few things:

First, the fact that giving plummeted when the pastor stopped putting on the pressure shows definitively that the people were already giving out of compulsion. It's irrational to say *"Give as you decide in your heart, but it has to be at least 10%,"* then add *"You'll miss out on God's blessing if you don't"* and claim it's free-will giving and not of compulsion or necessity! **The people in the congregation, for the most part, didn't know how to be led by the Holy Spirit in their giving because they had been trained to respond to pressure**.

If they had already been giving as led by the Holy Spirit, as they had decided in their hearts, and not of compulsion, dropping tithing would have made no difference in the giving. How much giving dropped only showed the extent of the problem and revealed that people were burnt out with the pressure and didn't know how to respond without it. If the house is crumbling, it wasn't built on a solid foundation!

Next, **we must not construct a doctrine because it is convenient.** This story shows that the heart of the matter wasn't truth, but was *"How are we going to pay the bills?"*

When people ask *"What would happen to the church if we didn't teach tithing?"* they don't consider that it's not the ecclesia or the kingdom of God that would be threatened if giving would drop. It would only be their particular high-overhead cultural expression of church that would be unsustainable. Yet I ask *"What good is it to have churches if we don't have the gospel?"*

Tithe teachings have hurt the church's witness, misrepresented how God relates to us, and perverted the way Christians attempt to approach the Father. The purity of the gospel message we preach must be high priority, as we see in the book of Galatians! It breaks my heart to talk to aging Christians who have been in church for decades and realize they still think like pagans; they see God as far and unknowable, are afraid of death, have no assurance of forgiveness, and are hoping to *"be good enough"* to someday possibly receive a blessing from God.

Dan Mohler is a pastor who was local to my area in Pennsylvania. He led Todd White to Christ and also impacted my life when I met him around 2006. People have asked him about tithing several times, and of course it's a really loaded question for a guest speaker! Dan shares his conviction that the tithe is Old Covenant, and in the New Covenant we give not because we owe any percentage but because we are participating in God's love. On one occasion, he said, *"Pastors, there's no reason to be threatened by this, because if you understand what I'm saying you'll be such a giver that the tithe will be irrelevant. I'm a giver. A tithe doesn't even come to my mind. But listen, I'm not saying this to condemn anyone. You start where faith is."*

Removing tithing from the equation has caused contributions to drop in some congregations and caused them to increase in others. I've heard several individuals testify that they have been giving more since they dropped the tithe paradigm. Since giving is a manifestation of God's grace and tithing is of the law and therefore is not of grace, it only makes sense that letting go of a tithe could lead to an increase in giving. Yet leaving the tithe behind is only one step towards Spirit-led giving. Those who let go of tithing often need to come out of a place of hurt in order to be able to experience the joy of giving and walking in the Spirit with their finances. Those who do will often end up going far beyond the tithe.

Remember Brian Hogan's testimony that the Mongolian people would have given far less if they had taught them tithing? Brian asked the Lord what was stopping some churches from multiplying, and the Lord showed him two primary hindrances. The first was that that they needed to lighten the load by presenting the basics of biblical church without the heavy package of cultural add-ons. The second was that they were trying to fulfill the role of the Holy Spirit instead of trusting him to do his job! Brian encourages church-planters to go through scripture and study what the Holy Spirit does, and then leave those things up to him!

Motivating Christians to give and guiding them where and how to give is unquestionably the role of the Holy Spirit! We all want Christians to give. **Our role is to teach them to walk in communion with and be led by the Holy Spirit, giving all their lives and not just their money for the cause of Christ!**

Chapter 11

Spirit-Led Giving

Two Widows Who Gave Out of Their Need

The stories of the Widow of Zarephath and the Widow's Mite have been mistaken for parallel lessons, teaching us the same thing. They are actually very different and show truth in tension. We give our lives to the Lord as living sacrifices. However, not all sacrificial giving is Spirit-led giving.

The Widow of Zarephath

First Kings chapter 17 contains a remarkable story of supernatural provision. There was a drought in the whole land and God had sent Elijah to drink from a brook and be fed by ravens. Wow! If that's how God provided for Elijah, how much more can He provide for us?

When the brook dried up, God commanded a widow who thought she was going to starve to feed the prophet Elijah! Notice how Elijah received God's provision. He heard God's voice and obeyed, even when it sounded crazy like *"Ravens are going to feed you"* and *"I've commanded a widow to feed you."*

> **1 Kings 17:8-15 Then the word of the Lord came to him: "Go at once to Zarephath in the region of Sidon and stay there. I have directed a widow there to supply you with food." So he went to Zarephath. When he came to the town gate, a widow was there gathering sticks. He called to her and asked,**

"Would you bring me a little water in a jar so I may have a drink?" As she was going to get it, he called, "And bring me, please, a piece of bread."

"As surely as the Lord your God lives," she replied, "I don't have any bread—only a handful of flour in a jar and a little olive oil in a jug. I am gathering a few sticks to take home and make a meal for myself and my son, that we may eat it—and die."

Elijah said to her, "Don't be afraid. Go home and do as you have said. But first make a small loaf of bread for me from what you have and bring it to me, and then make something for yourself and your son. For this is what the Lord, the God of Israel, says: "The jar of flour will not be used up and the jug of oil will not run dry until the day the Lord sends rain on the land.""

She went away and did as Elijah had told her. So there was food every day for Elijah and for the woman and her family. For the jar of flour was not used up and the jug of oil did not run dry, in keeping with the word of the Lord spoken by Elijah.

God's nature is love. Participating in his nature gets our eyes off of our own problems and struggles. When we have a need, God often leads us to a place of joy by enabling us to meet someone else's need. We also experience supernatural provision for our own needs. Elijah and the widow experienced a daily miracle of supernatural multiplication.

Philippians 2:4 ...not looking to your own interests but each of you to the interests of the others.

The fish and the loaves in the New Testament were multiplied when the disciples gave them to the people. There were plenty of leftovers for their own provision as well. My grandparents saw God multiply food when they were missionaries in Brazil. My grandfather cut up their little can of ham, thanked God, and shared it with about a dozen guests. Everybody had seconds, some people had thirds, and there was enough to make sandwiches for the next day. He experienced provision for his own family as he shared with others.

But before we start telling everyone in need to sow a *"miracle offering,"* let's review the story of the widow's mite.

The Widow's Mite

The story of the widow's mite is often taught to encourage people to give when they have a need of their own, as if it were making the same point as the story of the widow of Zarephath. However, such an interpretation is taking the story way out of context!

The chapters and verses we have in the Bible are helpful for finding things, but they were added long after the Bible was written. The immediate context for the story of the widow's mite is at the end of the previous chapter.

Luke 20:45-47 While all the people were listening, Jesus said to his disciples, "Beware of the teachers of the law. They like to walk around in flowing robes and love to be greeted with respect in the marketplaces and have the most important seats in the synagogues and the places of honor at banquets. They devour widows' houses and for a show make lengthy prayers. These men will be punished most severely."

Luke 21:1-6 As Jesus looked up, he saw the rich putting their gifts into the temple treasury. He also saw a poor widow put in two very small copper coins. "Truly I tell you," he said, "this poor widow has put in more than all the others. All these

people gave their gifts out of their wealth; but she out of her poverty put in all she had to live on.”

Some of his disciples were remarking about how the temple was adorned with beautiful stones and with gifts dedicated to God. But Jesus said, “As for what you see here, the time will come when not one stone will be left on another; every one of them will be thrown down.”

How could we have so easily missed the context of this story? Jesus was not teaching a lesson about giving out of your need in this passage! He was rebuking the teachers for devouring widow's houses and making a show of their religion! He was exposing injustice and oppression by pointing out the widow! Jesus was saying *“This is wrong! It’s all she has to live on!”* not *“This is a great example for others.”*

Are you still unconvinced? If you've never read the Bible from cover to cover, I encourage you to do so. The Old Testament is full of commands for Israel to care for widows and the disadvantaged. Review Deuteronomy 14:22-29 and Deuteronomy 26:12-13 to see God’s instructions on commanding Israelites to share the tithe with the widows. They should have been helping her, not devouring her house by taking all she had to live on!

Sacrificial Giving Is Not Always Spirit-Led Giving

The widow who gave her mite didn’t have a word from God telling her to give all she had to live on to pay for the magnificent temple stones that would soon be torn down. She gave out of compulsion. The widow of Zarephath did have a word from God to give out of her need. She didn’t give to pay for impressive temple stones but to care for another person who also had a need. The Macedonians, likewise, gave out of their own poverty and of their own volition to care for other people who were hungry, not to adorn a temple.

The New Testament also teaches that it's the Church's responsibility to care for widows who have no family members to help them.[271] Every single offering initiated by the apostles in scripture was taken to help people in need.

Instead of caring for the widows, the teachers of the law were interested in a big religious show and a temple adorned with beautiful stones and *"gifts to God."* According to the law, it was their responsibility to take care of the widow. Yet she was giving all she had to live on to adorn their beautiful temple. While Jesus's disciples were admiring the temple, Jesus said *"Do you see this? It's all going to be destroyed in judgment!"*

Acts 7:48 and Acts 17:24 both say that God doesn't dwell in temples made by hands. God desires people for his temple. God doesn't care about a pretty building adorned with beautiful stones. Jesus wasn't impressed with that *"temple"* like his disciples were. He cared about the true temple of God—people.

We have one story where God commanded a widow to give her last bit of food to a prophet, and another story where Jesus rebukes the teachers of the law for devouring widow's houses! This is truth in tension.

Think of a scenario where a person makes $20,000 a year and their family's basic expenses are the same. If we tell them they need to tithe, we are commanding them to give what they have to live on—which is exactly what Jesus rebuked the Pharisees for. We sometimes hear testimonies of people giving out of their need and experiencing supernatural provision. That is fine if a person has a word from God to do so, or desires to do so. However, there is no excuse for telling people who we are supposed to help that the answer to their trouble is giving all they have to live on in the offering, rather than helping them!

---

[271] James 1:27, 1 Timothy 5:3-4

The Macedonians' Giving

The widow of Zarephath gave out of extreme poverty. By doing so, she experienced supernatural provision. Yet Jesus was upset when he saw the widow in the temple give her last mite in the offering. He said the Pharisees would be judged most severely for devouring widow's houses. What was the difference? Let's consider some other people who gave generously out of extreme poverty:

2 Corinthians 8:1-5,9 And now, brothers and sisters, we want you to know about the grace that God has given the Macedonian churches. In the midst of a very severe trial, their overflowing joy and their extreme poverty welled up in rich generosity. For I testify that they gave as much as they were able, and even beyond their ability. Entirely on their own, they urgently pleaded with us for the privilege of sharing in this service to the Lord's people. And they exceeded our expectations: They gave themselves first of all to the Lord, and then by the will of God also to us...For you know the grace of our Lord Jesus Christ, that though he was rich, yet for your sake he became poor, so that you through his poverty might become rich.

Verse nine is one of my favorite verses in the Bible. It shows God's generous heart. Jesus became poor so that through his poverty we might become rich. Notice that the Macedonians gave *"entirely on their own"* and *"pleaded with us for the privilege of sharing in this service to the Lord's people."* They gave because they participated in God's heart. Just as Jesus became poor to make us rich, they were willing to give all they had out of love for others. That is giving in communion with God.

Nobody had to ask them for an offering. There was no coercion. It sounds like Paul was reluctant to accept their gift because they were so poor, which was why they had to beg to be allowed to participate! Some people point to the Macedonians and say *"It should hurt when you give,"* but notice the contrast between this saying and Paul's words. Paul's desire was not that the Macedonians should give until it hurt, but that there would be equality.

> **2 Corinthians 8:12-15 For if the willingness is there, the gift is acceptable according to what one has, not according to what one does not have. Our desire is not that others might be relieved while you are hard pressed, but that there might be equality. At the present time your plenty will supply what they need, so that in turn their plenty will supply what you need. The goal is equality, as it is written: "The one who gathered much did not have too much, and the one who gathered little did not have too little."**

The widow of Zarephath gave out of her need to help another person in need. She had one meal left, but Elijah had nothing left! The context of 2 Corinthians 8 and 9 is collecting an offering to meet the needs of impoverished Judean Christians in a time of famine. People are what God cares about. People are God's temple.

Give To Meet People's Needs

Take Paul's words about *"equality"* and supplying each other's needs and apply them to the story of the widow who fed Elijah. They fit perfectly. Then try applying them to the story of the widow in the New Testament who put the last she had to live on in the offering. They don't fit.

The New Testament widow who gave her last mite didn't give to help anybody in need. Neither did she give *"entirely on her own."* I believe she was shamed into giving by the boasting and large public offerings of the rich. Contributions were a status symbol. Her offering went not to help people, but to adorn a temple that was about to be destroyed. She gave all she had to live on for the cause of the religious leaders' pride. Those leaders loved the seats of honor, but God would not honor them!

I think the widow who gave her last mite felt like she was nothing if she gave nothing! She could never measure up to those rich people who gave great gifts and had the seats of honor, but at least if she gave a little, she wouldn't be *"nothing."*

If you are going to give out of need, give to meet other people's needs! Don't give because you feel your worth depends on it. Don't give as an attempt to *"measure up."* Make caring for your own family priority, lest you end up giving a gift and calling it *"dedicated to God"* rather than honoring your father and mother! Giving out of your need is great if it's done in faith based on a word from God empowering you to do so.

Let's continue to examine Paul's teaching on giving:

2 Corinthians 9:6-12 Remember this: Whoever sows sparingly will also reap sparingly, and whoever sows generously will also reap generously. Each of you should give what you have decided in your heart to give, not reluctantly or under compulsion, for God loves a cheerful giver. And God is able to bless you abundantly, so that in all things at all times, having all that you need, you will abound in every good work. As it is written: "They have freely scattered their gifts to the poor; their righteousness endures forever."

Now he who supplies seed to the sower and bread for food will also supply and increase your store of seed and will enlarge the harvest of your righteousness. You will be enriched in every way so that you can be generous on every occasion, and through us your generosity will result in thanksgiving to God. This service that you perform is not only supplying the needs of the Lord's people but is also overflowing in many expressions of thanks to God.

I think we can't repeat this part enough: *"Each of you should give what you have decided in your heart to give, not reluctantly or under compulsion."*

228

If we are giving because someone told us to, instead of giving according to what we have decided in our hearts, we are violating Paul's New Testament command on giving. This includes where we give. Are you giving what and where you desire (in your born again, God-filled new heart) to give, or according to what someone has told you?

Giving can never be measured in God's kingdom by an amount of money, a number, or a percentage. It can only be measured according to participation with God's generous heart. It's all about sharing God's nature.

God had already commanded the widow of Zarephath to feed Elijah. That's why he could go and ask her for food. Scripture doesn't indicate that the widow who gave her last mite was giving because God told her to. According to the law and scripture, they were actually supposed to be giving to care for her needs. She was giving out of compulsion, and Jesus called it *"devouring widows' houses."*

God wants us to prosper. There are so many needs in this world that we need to prosper in order to be able to help people! God has provision for us, and scripture has wonderful passages about God's blessing prospering us.

We just read some of those promises in 2 Corinthians 9. But remember that the context is taking an offering for the poor and giving freely, not under compulsion. The quote in 2 Corinthians 9 is from Psalm 112. The context is also caring for the poor.

Psalm 112:2-3 ...the generation of the upright will be blessed. Wealth and riches are in their houses, and their righteousness endures forever.

When should you give out of need? Do so when you desire to and you are meeting another person's need, under no compulsion. And do so when responding in faith to a word you've received from God, with an expectation of supernatural provision.

"I Gave Everything and God Provided!"

Have you ever heard a testimony of someone saying *"I had a big need and I gave everything I had left. Then a miracle happened!"* I believe many such testimonies are genuine. But is the answer to your need always to do the same? I don't think so.

The Israelites had a need in Exodus 17. They were thirsty in the desert, so they started grumbling against God. They forgot the miracles he'd done for them before.

Moses cried out to God because the people were about to stone him. God said *"Strike that rock, and water will come out of it for the people to drink."* Moses hit the rock, water came out, and the people drank. That's a pretty cool story of supernatural provision!

It wasn't too long until the Israelites forgot how God provided for them. The story is in Numbers 20. They needed water again. Instead of praying with thanksgiving for God's deliverance in the past, they turned on Moses. This time God told Moses to speak to the rock and water would come out.

Moses didn't speak to the rock. He struck it again, this time twice. Water gushed out. But God wasn't happy about what Moses did.

> **Numbers 20:12 But the Lord said to Moses and Aaron, "Because you did not trust in me enough to honor me as holy in the sight of the Israelites, you will not bring this community into the land I give them."**

Are You Following Principles or Following Christ?

Could it be that Moses was attempting to follow a *"principle"* instead of trusting God and obeying Him? Moses disobeyed God and did *"what worked last time."*

> **Colossians 2:8-10 (NKJV) Beware lest anyone cheat you through philosophy and empty deceit, according to the tradition of men, according to the basic principles of the**

world, and not according to Christ. For in Him dwells all the fullness of the Godhead bodily; and you are complete in Him...

"Principles" aren't always bad. Yet I think some of the *"financial principles"* we've heard taught are *"the basic principles of this world"* and not *"according to Christ."* Life in Christ is not according to the basic principles of this world. It supersedes them.

"The basic principles of this world" in context refers especially to the law. Life in Christ works differently, by grace. Giving, by definition, cannot be mandated with a specific percentage, because if it is, it's not a gift. It's a tax. And there's no such thing as a kingdom of heaven tax.

Reinhard Hirtler is a missionary and a friend I met here in Brazil. I know few people with as many testimonies of supernatural provision as Reinhard. I just listened to several hours of his teaching on kingdom finances. The whole basis for his teaching on radical generosity and supernatural provision is not anything that we do, but is simply the revelation of God's nature as our Father and provider. The teaching is built on the foundation of seeing God as revealed in Christ, not based on principles.

When I've ministered healing, both pagans and Christians have often started talking about spiritual principles and *"the power of faith,"* but I discerned that it was an antichrist spirit distracting them from the revelation of Christ. It has always been about the revelation that *"This is who Jesus is. He has compassion,"* not the impersonal *"power of faith."* Likewise, the tithe doctrine I received used a *"principle"* to obscure the revelation of God through Christ. That is the foundation for true Spirit-led generosity.

Hearing God's Voice

Jesus told his disciples to get a coin from a fish's mouth. 2nd Kings chapter 4 tells the story of a widow who was about to lose her two sons as slaves to a creditor. The prophet Elisha didn't ask for an

231

offering or tell her to "*sow a seed.*" He told her to borrow as many jars as she could, pour oil in them, and sell the oil. The oil multiplied.

If we consider other Bible stories, we also see that provision came through a specific word of God for the situation. We are missing the point if we teach those stories as mere "*principles*" rather than encouragement to have faith in God and live out of trust and relationship with Him. Modern testimonies of supernatural provision are also about trusting God and hearing His voice.

The consistent pattern is that provision is in God's voice, so do what he says! Many other "*principles*" people have tried to draw out of scriptural stories of provision just don't hold true consistently. Life in Christ is about participating in God's nature, the tree of life! It's not about "*Do A and B and C will be the result.*" It's about a relationship with God and hearing his voice.

Sowing and Reaping

Speaking of "*principles,*" let's consider how we've tried to manage our finances by the principle of "*sowing and reaping*" to the point where we've missed God's grace. This teaching has often gone hand-in-hand with tithing, but even many who don't believe in tithing still think that you can "*sow*" money by giving in order to reap money. When we just read what the scripture says, it seems strange that we've interpreted it that way!

2 Corinthians 9:8-11 And God is able to bless you abundantly, so that in all things at all times, having all that you need, you will abound in every good work. As it is written: "They have freely scattered their gifts to the poor; their righteousness endures forever."

Now he who supplies seed to the sower and bread for food will also supply and increase your store of seed and will enlarge

the harvest of your righteousness. You will be enriched in every way so that you can be generous on every occasion, and through us your generosity will result in thanksgiving to God.

What is the harvest 2 Corinthians 9 says we can expect? It says the *"harvest of your righteousness."* How in the world did we ever get the idea that a *"harvest of righteousness"* is money, which Jesus called *"unrighteous mammon?"*[272]

Psalm 112, James 1:27, and other cross-references show us that righteousness manifests in caring for the poor. We receive Christ's righteousness as a free gift, becoming *"trees of righteousness,"*[273] and helping the weak is one of the fruits of righteousness. The harvest is thanksgiving to God that comes from blessing the poor. We reap heavenly rewards, treasure in heaven which moth and rust do not destroy.[274]

Some say *"We receive a harvest in like kind, so if 2 Corinthians is talking about sowing money, it is also talking about reaping money."* However, that logic simply isn't scriptural. In defending his right to receive support, Paul previously said *"If we have sown spiritual seed among you, is it too much if we reap a material harvest from you?"*[275] He was talking about sowing spiritual seed and reaping material things there. Here, he is talking about sowing money and reaping a spiritual harvest.

Read the passage in 2 Corinthians 9 again. It is clearly talking about a blessing of financial prosperity, but it doesn't say that material blessing is the harvest as a result of sowing money. Rather, the material blessing is the provision for sowing so that we can reap a spiritual *"harvest of righteousness."* The passage is talking about giving because God has already blessed us and we are in communion with him, participating in his generous nature.

---

[272] Luke 16:9 (NKJV)
[273] Isaiah 61:3
[274] Matthew 6:19-20
[275] 1 Corinthians 9:11

T.B. Joshua blessed a poor and disabled man who had lost everything, giving him several bags of rice and a significant sum of money from the church. He then asked for someone to give the man a car, saying that with all the people watching, it shouldn't be a problem for someone to give a car. Instead of promising a financial harvest to the giver, Joshua said *"Give him a car, and see whether you will not receive millions of joy."*[276]

As Benny Hinn talked about how he was *"fed up"* with give-to-get gimmicks, he said *"Let's be honest. How many do you know that ever got the 100-fold return?"*[277] Christians sometimes become disillusioned or frustrated with God after being told he promises them 30, 60, or 100 times their money! But if we just look at what scripture says about reaping a harvest not of money but of righteousness, we'll realize that it very well is possible to reap 30, 60, and 100-fold in blessing that comes through our giving!

When I consider testimonies of radical givers experiencing supernatural provision, I realize how easily they could be misinterpreted as *"reaping a harvest of money"* because they sowed by giving. But rather, God was just giving more seed to the sower. Since the individual had entered so much into participation with God's generous nature, God was giving them seed to express that nature with!

If you still think scripture promises a harvest of money for our giving, I'd encourage you to re-read those passages again and consider the context. Several scripture passages are used out-of-context to teach *"give-to-get."* But for now, I'd like to point out two scripture points that are rarely considered when we discuss sowing and reaping.

---

[276] *Touching: Why TB Joshua Returned This Man's Tithes* Online: https://www.youtube.com/watch?v=6O_CY_Cw_2c Accessed January 7th, 2020
[277] *Benny Hinn Renounces The "Prosperity Gospel."* Online: https://www.youtube.com/watch?v=8qUQwmwC7Oc 16 minutes and 53 seconds into the video. Accessed December 20th, 2019

Matthew 6:26 Look at the birds of the air; they do not sow or reap or store away in barns, and yet your heavenly Father feeds them. Are you not much more valuable than they?

Jesus clearly taught his disciples to rely on their heavenly Father's good nature and love for provision. That supersedes principles like sowing and reaping! Jesus's words are so contrary to sayings we hear like *"If you have a need, sow a seed."* Our confidence should be in God our provider, not in a principle of reaping and sowing. Nevertheless, if you want to sow money to reap money, try investing! If you want an abundant spiritual *"harvest of righteousness,"* start partnering with God in Spirit-led giving.

The second point is very simple. On the Sabbaths, Sabbath years, and the year of Jubilee, the people neither reaped nor sowed.[278] Jesus is our Sabbath,[279] and he proclaimed the year of Jubilee at his coming.[280] Furthermore, some have noted that a tithe was not payable on either the Sabbatical years or the year of Jubilee, because they neither reaped nor sowed![281] That fact creates an interesting dilemma for anybody who believes that Jesus is the fulfilment of the Sabbath or the year of Jubilee yet still teaches tithing.

I recently heard the Lord proclaim "There's a greater Seed, and it's the Seed that I've sown! His name is Jesus, and in Him all my promises are yes and amen!" I understood that many people are so caught up in messages about their own seeds that they can't see the Seed that God has sown and what we have in him!

Give To Get?

When it becomes about only *"following principles"* instead of knowing God, we end up giving out of compulsion. Not only do we

---

[278] Leviticus 25:4-12
[279] Colossians 2:16-17, Hebrews 3+4
[280] Luke 4:16-21
[281] For example, this pro-tithing website online: http://www.ccg.org/s/p161.html Accessed November 21st, 2019

violate Paul's New Testament command, but the motivation for *"giving"* becomes totally self-centered. It's no longer *"don't look only to your own interests, but also to the interests of others."*[282] It's *"give so you can get blessed and so God can take care of your needs."* It's no longer grace and mercy, and it's no longer the gospel.

Giving under compulsion often leads us to give towards things that are straw, hay, and stubble, and will be burned up,[283] just as the widow in the New Testament gave her last to adorn a temple that was about to be destroyed.

How do we respond to testimonies of people giving radically and experiencing miracles of provision? Instead of turning them into *"principles"* of how to get our needs met, we can take them as encouragement to trust God, obey his voice, and grow in the grace of giving.

If God provided for Jesus with a coin from a fish's mouth, we can also walk in communion with the Father, hear His voice, and experience supernatural provision.

---

[282] Philippians 2:4
[283] 1 Corinthians 3:10-15

Chapter 12
Corrupted Wisdom and Jesus's Temptation

We've examined multiple arguments for tithing and seen how they use absurd logic that is never applied consistently or to any similar matter. Yet suddenly that logic seems reasonable when applied to tithing. In this chapter we'll examine other arguments for tithing and see how they were invented by reading the Bible with an agenda and searching for what isn't in the text. But first, let's talk about the heart issue behind such *"corrupted wisdom."*

When I heard Bertie Brits talk about this,[284] I thought *"Man! He hit the nail on the head!"* He started with 1 Timothy 6:

1 Timothy 6:3-10 If anyone teaches otherwise and does not agree to the sound instruction of our Lord Jesus Christ and to godly teaching, they are conceited and understand nothing. They have an unhealthy interest in controversies and quarrels about words that result in envy, strife, malicious talk, evil suspicions and constant friction between people of corrupt mind, who have been robbed of the truth and who think that godliness is a means to financial gain.

But godliness with contentment is great gain. For we brought nothing into the world, and we can take nothing out of it. But

---

[284] Brits, Bertie. *Money Crucified: The Tithe Eating Tithe* Online: https://www.youtube.com/watch?v=8mzICkJqltE&t=1072s Accessed December 17th, 2019

if we have food and clothing, we will be content with that. Those who want to get rich fall into temptation and a trap and into many foolish and harmful desires that plunge people into ruin and destruction. For the love of money is a root of all kinds of evil. Some people, eager for money, have wandered from the faith and pierced themselves with many griefs.

The passage literally says, not that the love of money is a root of all kinds of evil, but that it is a root of all the evils:

1 Timothy 6:10a (YLT) for a root of all the evils is the love of money…

Bertie believes that the *"love of money"* is about so much more than just dollars or euros. It is a mentality that always needs more, the opposite of the attitude of contentment that Paul encourages Timothy to foster.

Many leaders say, *"Hey, I'm not in this for myself! I just want to reach the world for Christ."* I get it. I've come across hurting people who think all ministers are in it for the money. It saddens me. Most ministers aren't getting rich off the ministry, and plenty of pastors deeply care for the people they minister to.

But sometimes the constant desire for more can disguise itself in good intentions and we don't even recognize it. You may have little desire to amass and spend great quantities of money. But are you content with where you are now? Are you happy? Are you happy with where your ministry is? Do you *"need"* it to grow?

Bertie isn't against *"big."* You can have a big church, be on TV, and reach lots of people. Bertie is on TV. But it must be built from a foundation of contentment. If it isn't, the constant drive for *"more"* will corrupt our wisdom. We'll read scripture and somehow see something that just isn't in the passage! To explain the connection between this desire for *"more"* and corrupted wisdom, Bertie takes us to Ezekiel 28, which speaks of the King of Tyre as a figure of Satan:

Ezekiel 28:2-5, 14-17 Son of man, say to the ruler of Tyre, 'This is what the Sovereign LORD says: "'In the pride of your heart you say, "I am a god; I sit on the throne of a god in the heart of the seas." But you are a mere mortal and not a god, though you think you are as wise as a god. Are you wiser than Daniel? Is no secret hidden from you? By your wisdom and understanding you have gained wealth for yourself and amassed gold and silver in your treasuries. By your great skill in trading you have increased your wealth, and because of your wealth your heart has grown proud...

You were anointed as a guardian cherub, for so I ordained you. You were on the holy mount of God; you walked among the fiery stones. You were blameless in your ways from the day you were created till wickedness was found in you. Through your widespread trade you were filled with violence, and you sinned. So I drove you in disgrace from the mount of God, and I expelled you, guardian cherub, from among the fiery stones. Your heart became proud on account of your beauty, and you corrupted your wisdom because of your splendor. So I threw you to the earth; I made a spectacle of you before kings.

Pride and the *"love of money"* were at the root of Satan corrupting his wisdom and thus being thrown to earth. His heart grew proud because of his wealth, and he wanted more!

Bertie points out the first part of the word translated *"love of money"* comes from the Greek *"phileo."* This is the word for the friend of the bridegroom who *"seals the deal"* on arranging a marriage. Notice how wealth *"sealed the deal"* for the King of Tyre/Satan in Ezekiel 28 and led to the pride that caused his downfall.

Common tithe teachings claim that money *"seals the deal"* on our redemption from the curse and even on our entrance into heaven! Even most who supposedly teach *"tithing by grace"* still say it seals the deal on your blessing, which according to the full gospel position is part and parcel of salvation!

The Holy Spirit may lead some people to purchase buildings for ministry purposes. However, if we *"need"* the things to support a big, high overhead model of church so much that we corrupt our wisdom in order to support it, we have fallen to the same deception that caused Satan's fall. This reminds me of Jesus's temptation:

Luke 4:5-8 The devil led him up to a high place and showed him in an instant all the kingdoms of the world. And he said to him, "I will give you all their authority and splendor; it has been given to me, and I can give it to anyone I want to. If you worship me, it will all be yours." Jesus answered, "It is written: 'Worship the Lord your God and serve him only.'"

Jesus's inheritance was already the kingdoms of the world. Yet Satan tempted him with an *"end justifies the means"* scenario. Jesus refused. We've been tempted to bow to Satan's systems such as the Babylonian tithe in order to build ministries and reach people, and the gospel has been compromised in the process. No end justifies teaching falsehood.

Let's examine more lies that have been fabricated out of corrupted wisdom. As absurd as some of them are, they aren't fringe teachings but have been taught by some of the leaders who've done the most to promote tithing today.

"Adam's Sin in the Garden of Eden Was Failing To Tithe."

I first heard this listening to Kenneth Copeland on You Tube.[285] Several other popular pastors have taught it. It's astounding how some preachers can interpret any story in the Bible as if it were

---

[285] Online: https://www.youtube.com/watch?v=aOu84V6FGVA Accessed November 30th, 2019

about tithing. Why? It's corrupted wisdom. The text doesn't say a thing about the tithe but they somehow see it in there because they're looking so hard for it.

This teaching says Adam and Eve sinned by eating of God's portion, the tree of the knowledge of good and evil, which was the tithe! Copeland says Adam's first sin was disobedience and his second was thievery, stealing the tithe. He continues, claiming that failure to tithe led Cain into serious crime and saying *"The first murder was over the tithe. The first sin was over the tithe."*

He speaks as if this were a fact, yet his only attempt to support the *"Garden of Eden tithe"* is stating that Adam's sons Abel and Cain knew about the tithe, so God must have taught Adam about it! However, the argument that Cain and Abel knew about the tithe is as absurd as the one that Adam did.

If the tree of the knowledge of good and evil was the tithe, then there must have only been ten trees in the garden!

"Cain Killed Abel Over the Tithe."

Kenneth Copeland continues in the same sermon to claim that Cain killed Abel because Abel gave a tithe and God was pleased with it, but God was not pleased with Cain's offering because Cain failed to tithe. He gives no basis for this, but states it as if it were an uncontestable fact.

I later learned that a book published in 1956 also connected the forbidden tree in the Garden of Eden with the tithe.[286] Another teaching in 1906 also claimed Cain killed Abel over the tithe. At least it made a desperate attempt to back up the claim.

The teaching was based on the Septuagint, the Greek translation of the Hebrew Scriptures. It argued that the Septuagint is more accurate than the available Hebrew texts. The Septuagint, which differs from the Hebrew texts, says that Cain did not *"rightly divide"* his offering. Assuming that *"rightly dividing"* an offering

---

[286] Kauffman, Milo. *The Challenge of Christian Stewardship*. Scottdale, PA: Herald Press, 1956. Pg. 60

must be separating a tithe, the writer concluded that Cain did not pay a tithe.[287]

Yet that wording is not in the Hebrew texts. To have any reason to even speculate about a tithe in the story of Cain and Abel, one has to make the case that a Greek translation of the Old Testament is superior to the Hebrew Old Testament itself! Dr. David Croteau explains how the translators could have easily misinterpreted the Hebrew text by confusing two particular Hebrew words to come to the conclusion that it was talking about Cain failing to rightly divide his sacrifice. The difference in the translations was due to an incorrect understanding of the Hebrew.[288]

It takes corrupted wisdom to go to such lengths in order to find a tithe in the story of Cain and Abel.

"The First Fruits Is the Tithe"

I was shocked as a young person when I found out that many pastors really thought the first fruits and tithe were the same. Having read through the Bible as a child and several times as a teen, I would never have imagined thinking of the tithe and the first fruits offerings as the same thing. They were obviously different and a 7-year-old could understand that! It takes either corrupted wisdom or just blindly accepting human tradition to come to the conclusion that tithes and first fruits are the same. Let's look at the first fruits offering described in Leviticus 23:

Leviticus 23:9-16 The Lord said to Moses, "Speak to the Israelites and say to them: 'When you enter the land I am going to give you and you reap its harvest, bring to the priest a sheaf of the first grain you harvest. He is to wave the sheaf before the Lord so it will be accepted on your behalf; the priest is to wave it on the day after the Sabbath. On the day

---

[287] Lansdell, Henry. *The Sacred Tenth*. Grand Rapids: Baker Book House, 1955. Pages 1-42
[288] Croteau, David A. *You Mean I Dont Have to Tithe?: a Deconstruction of Tithing and a Reconstruction of Post-Tithe Giving*. Eugene, Or.: Pickwick Publications, 2010. Kindle Locations 2715-2731

you wave the sheaf, you must sacrifice as a burnt offering to the Lord a lamb a year old without defect, together with its grain offering of two-tenths of an ephah of the finest flour mixed with olive oil—a food offering presented to the Lord, a pleasing aroma—and its drink offering of a quarter of a hin of wine. You must not eat any bread, or roasted or new grain, until the very day you bring this offering to your God. This is to be a lasting ordinance for the generations to come, wherever you live. From the day after the Sabbath, the day you brought the sheaf of the wave offering, count off seven full weeks. Count off fifty days up to the day after the seventh Sabbath, and then present an offering of new grain to the Lord."

The first fruits offering described is a sheaf, which is a bundle of grain stalks tied together. Unless a farmer only harvested ten sheaves, that is far less than a tithe! A burnt offering, a grain offering, and a drink offering are part of the same ordinance. Even if the first fruits offering were the same as the tithe, how can we separate the part of the ordinance we want from the rest of the same ordinance? What is the standard for deciding that *"This part of the ordinance applies today but the rest doesn't?"* Not to mention changing it from a sheaf of wheat to money.

They brought the first fruits offering directly to the priest, but did not bring tithes directly to the priest. They shared the tithe with the Levites, who then tithed on the tithe they received, giving it to the priests. They brought first fruits during a specific time of the year and they counted from that time until when they would celebrate the festival of weeks. The first fruits offering was on grain while the tithe was not only on agricultural products but also on animals.

Let's examine another description of a first fruits offering in Deuteronomy:

Deuteronomy 26:1-13 When you have entered the land the Lord your God is giving you as an inheritance and have taken possession of it and settled in it, take some of the firstfruits of all that you produce from the soil of the land the Lord your God is giving you and put them in a basket. Then go to the place the Lord your God will choose as a dwelling for his Name and say to the priest in office at the time, "I declare today to the Lord your God that I have come to the land the Lord swore to our ancestors to give us." The priest shall take the basket from your hands and set it down in front of the altar of the Lord your God.

Then you shall declare before the Lord your God: "My father was a wandering Aramean, and he went down into Egypt with a few people and lived there and became a great nation, powerful and numerous. But the Egyptians mistreated us and made us suffer, subjecting us to harsh labor. Then we cried out to the Lord, the God of our ancestors, and the Lord heard our voice and saw our misery, toil and oppression. So the Lord brought us out of Egypt with a mighty hand and an outstretched arm, with great terror and with signs and wonders. He brought us to this place and gave us this land, a land flowing with milk and honey; and now I bring the firstfruits of the soil that you, Lord, have given me." Place the basket before the Lord your God and bow down before him. Then you and the Levites and the foreigners residing among you shall rejoice in all the good things the Lord your God has given to you and your household.

When you have finished setting aside a tenth of all your produce in the third year, the year of the tithe, you shall give it to the Levite, the foreigner, the fatherless and the widow, so that they may eat in your towns and be satisfied.

This account is also clear about the difference between the first fruits and the tithe. God commanded this first fruits offering when the Israelites entered the promised land, but commanded that they share with the Levite, foreigner, fatherless, and widow on the third year, the year of the tithe. The first fruits and tithes were given at different times. There was no specified amount for first fruits, but it was a small enough offering to carry in a basket, obviously much less than a tithe. It was a relatively small thanksgiving offering.

The tithes given to the Levites were not the first part, but the tenth part! They would count the animals and every tenth animal, whether good or bad, was separated for the tithe. We could discuss other scriptures that also show the obvious differences between tithes and first fruits, but we shouldn't need to. Even in modern Judaism, the first fruits celebration is totally different than the tithe.[289]

Equating first fruits with tithes creates another serious logical problem for those who teach tithing. It is an integral part of a feast which Colossians 2:16-17 says has found fulfillment in Christ, and other New Testament scriptures show the fulfillment of first fruits just as animal sacrifices and burnt offerings were also fulfilled.

1 Corinthians 15:20 But Christ has indeed been raised from the dead, the first fruits of those who have fallen asleep.

One pastor argued that there was no clear fulfillment of the tithe in Christ, so tithing must continue while only animal sacrifices and elements which clearly were fulfilled in Christ had ceased. Yet he claimed first fruits and tithes were the same, and I had heard him preach on the New Covenant fulfillment of the first fruits! His beliefs were completely incoherent and contradictory. Even if it were true that first fruits and tithes were the same, that would be a strong argument against tithing because of the New Testament

---

[289] Feast of Shavuot Online: https://www.myjewishlearning.com/article/shavuot-in-modern-times/
Online: https://reformjudaism.org/shavuot-customs-and-rituals Accessed December 7th, 2019.

scriptures teaching the fulfillment of first fruits which was a *"shadow of better things to come."*[290]

How can seminary-trained Bible scholars use such poor reasoning? It's only possible if their wisdom has become corrupted. They look for something so hard that they think they see it everywhere and it's not in the text!

"1 Corinthians 16:2 Is About Tithing"

This passage says nothing about tithing. Yet to those who are looking for it, it somehow seems like proof that Christians should tithe. The context is so obvious to anybody who has read through 1st and 2nd Corinthians that only corrupted wisdom could make us miss it. Let's look at the verse in context in 1st Corinthians, and then the exhortation in 2nd Corinthians:

1 Corinthians 16:1-5 Now about the collection for the Lord's people: Do what I told the Galatian churches to do. On the first day of every week, each one of you should set aside a sum of money in keeping with your income, saving it up, so that when I come no collections will have to be made. Then, when I arrive, I will give letters of introduction to the men you approve and send them with your gift to Jerusalem. If it seems advisable for me to go also, they will accompany me. After I go through Macedonia, I will come to you—for I will be going through Macedonia.

Who is the offering for? It's for *"the Lord's people,"* not for elders' salaries, a building, overhead, or even for Paul. It's an emergency offering being taken up for the Christians in Jerusalem who are suffering a famine.[291] Paul is giving instructions for a specific offering, not for the method by which the Corinthians were to finance a high-overhead church organization. Church historians

---

[290] Hebrews 10:1, Colossians 2:17
[291] Acts 11:28

generally do not believe they had their own buildings to meet in or paid local church leaders at that time. For example, Robert Baker wrote:

The leaders [before A.D. 100] usually worked with their hands for their material needs. There was no artificial distinction between clergy and laity... The earliest bishops or presbyters engaged in secular labor to make their living and performed the duties of their church office when not at work.[292]

Notice Paul's mention of going through Macedonia. Paul did go through Macedonia between the writing of 1st and 2nd Corinthians, and the Macedonian believers contributed generously to help feed the hungry saints in Jerusalem.

2 Corinthians 8:1-4 And now, brothers and sisters, we want you to know about the grace that God has given the Macedonian churches. In the midst of a very severe trial, their overflowing joy and their extreme poverty welled up in rich generosity. For I testify that they gave as much as they were able, and even beyond their ability. Entirely on their own, they urgently pleaded with us for the privilege of sharing in this service to the Lord's people. And they exceeded our expectations: They gave themselves first of all to the Lord, and then by the will of God also to us. So we urged Titus, just as he had earlier made a beginning, to bring also to completion this act of grace on your part. But since you excel in everything— in faith, in speech, in knowledge, in complete earnestness and in the love we have kindled in you—see that you also excel in this grace of giving.

I am not commanding you, but I want to test the sincerity of your love by comparing it with the earnestness of others. For

---

[292] Baker, Robert Andrew., and John M. Landers. *A Summary of Christian History.* Nashville, TN: Broadman & Holman Publishers, 2005. Pg. 11, 43

you know the grace of our Lord Jesus Christ, that though he was rich, yet for your sake he became poor, so that you through his poverty might become rich.

And here is my judgment about what is best for you in this matter. Last year you were the first not only to give but also to have the desire to do so. Now finish the work, so that your eager willingness to do it may be matched by your completion of it, according to your means. For if the willingness is there, the gift is acceptable according to what one has, not according to what one does not have.

Our desire is not that others might be relieved while you are hard pressed, but that there might be equality. At the present time your plenty will supply what they need, so that in turn their plenty will supply what you need. The goal is equality, as it is written: "The one who gathered much did not have too much, and the one who gathered little did not have too little."

2 Corinthians 9:1-5, 12 There is no need for me to write to you about this service to the Lord's people. For I know your eagerness to help, and I have been boasting about it to the Macedonians, telling them that since last year you in Achaia were ready to give; and your enthusiasm has stirred most of them to action. But I am sending the brothers in order that our boasting about you in this matter should not prove hollow, but that you may be ready, as I said you would be. For if any Macedonians come with me and find you unprepared, we—not to say anything about you—would be ashamed of having been so confident. So I thought it necessary to urge the brothers to visit you in advance and finish the arrangements for the generous gift you had promised. Then it will be ready as a generous gift, not as one grudgingly given... This service that you perform is not only supplying the needs of the Lord's people but is also overflowing in many expressions of thanks to God.

Notice a few additional things in the above texts:

- Paul mentions *"last year."* This weekly offering was to be taken over the time of about a year and saved, after which it would be carried to Jerusalem by trustworthy men. Paul's instructions in 1 Corinthians 16:2 were not for all time, but for a limited period of time in a specific situation!

- In 1 Corinthians 16:2, Paul gave instructions about how to handle or coordinate an offering which they had eagerly decided to give of their own volition and which he did not command them to give. In 2 Corinthians, he doesn't command them to give but exhorts them to follow through on what they previously promised.

- The gift was acceptable according to what one had, not what one didn't have. If you had 5% left after you cared for your family's needs, the gift was acceptable.

- Paul's desire was that the Corinthians' *"plenty"* or overflow supply the needs of the saints in Jerusalem. This contradicts tithe teachings which say your tithe is the first thing you pay, never something that comes out only after you pay your bills. *"Plenty"* is abundance you have left over after meeting needs. This gives the context for Paul's instructions in 1 Corinthians 16:2 that they set aside money in keeping with their income. They were setting aside money according to the abundance they had beyond meeting their own needs, not that they should lack but that there should be equality.

- Paul said: *"At the present time your plenty will supply what they need, so that in turn their plenty will supply what you need."* Paul was clear that if the Corinthians were to have a famine in ten years and the saints in Jerusalem prospered,

249

it would be consistent with the spirit of Christ for the saints in Jerusalem to do the same for the Corinthians. Therefore, if the Corinthians were to find themselves in need Paul would have been collecting an offering for them from the churches that were prospering rather than telling them to take up a weekly offering!

Jesus Referred to Tithing When He Said To Give to God What Is God's

This is another statement that I feel like I shouldn't even have to answer, because like many of these other passages, it says nothing about tithes. Yet I have heard so many people state it as a proof text for tithing lately, so let's briefly consider the context:

Matthew 22:17-21 "Tell us then, what is your opinion? Is it right to pay the imperial tax to Caesar or not?" But Jesus, knowing their evil intent, said, "You hypocrites, why are you trying to trap me? Show me the coin used for paying the tax." They brought him a denarius, and he asked them, "Whose image is this? And whose inscription?" "Caesar's," they replied. Then he said to them, "So give back to Caesar what is Caesar's, and to God what is God's."

As Dr. Russel Earl Kelly points out, the context of this was that the Jews were highly opposed to graven images and revolted over the issue several times in history. A coin with Caesar's image could not enter the temple. Rather, Jews changed the money issued from Rome for the temple shekel in order to pay the temple tax. That is what Jesus referred to when he said to give to God what is God's. It was not a tithe given to priests and Levites, but another tax which was used for the maintenance of the temple.[293] As we've pointed

---

[293] Kelly, Russel Earl *Money With Gentile Images Was Banned* Online: http://www.tithing-russkelly.com/id195.html Accessed January 1st, 2020

out, money could not be tithed and could only be used to redeem your tithe if you added a fifth to the value.

Besides that, the point which we have previously made applies, that Jesus was speaking to Jews under the Old Covenant and when the temple was standing. If we are going to use this as a proof text for tithing, we must also apply it to everything else those Jews were required to give—including not only tithes but the separate offering of first fruits, the temple shekel, animal sacrifices, heave offerings, grain offerings, and everything which sustained the priests as their livelihood. Tithing alone as practiced by the Jews only provided a very small part of the priests' sustenance.

Have We Been Reading the Bible With an Agenda?

It is sometimes easy to fall into reading the Bible with an agenda, and especially so when it comes to the subject of money. That bias gets so engrained in tradition that it is often not even our own bias that is influencing us, but is the way we have always heard a scripture interpreted.

We have heard many sermons preached without even a reference to the immediate context. When I realized the obvious and immediate context for the story of the widow's mite was the rebuke for devouring widow's houses right before it, I was stunned. I've never heard a pastor preaching on the widow's mite read the last few verses of the chapter right before it.

A few other scriptures have also been used to argue for a New Testament tithe. More important, however, than refuting every single argument is letting God's word reveal the heart issues that lead to corrupted wisdom, inconsistent logic, and reading things into scripture passages that simply aren't there.

Chapter 13
What About Ministerial Support?

Let's briefly examine how we've read more into scripture than it actually says concerning ministerial support. This won't be an in-depth treatment of the subject, but it should be enough to help us take off the colored glasses.

I've received free-will offerings when ministering at churches and to support missions and ministry work. I'm also currently contributing to the monthly support of some friends doing full-time ministry.

I've been a bit bewildered by the offense of some people towards a particular friend when he's asked for donations. He sometimes gives money to meet people's needs, and he ministers healing freely. I've never seen him promote a *"give to get God's blessing"* message or use any form of manipulation. It seems strange that people would be offended by a simple *"Please consider supporting us monthly."* Yet people who've been financially abused by teachings of *"give to get"* or *"give to avoid a curse"* sometimes become bitter and make blanket judgments against ministers that *"They're all in it for the money!"*

Some embittered people say they want to make all the pastors get *"real jobs."* I disagree with that sentiment. I don't argue that ministerial support is wrong. Rather, I challenge how it's been used as an argument for tithing or other compulsory *"giving"* rather than free-will giving.

The Cultural Background of Jesus's Teachings

Many have interpreted scripture passages about ministerial support as meaning more than they actually say. They think as if those scriptures were in the context of our culture today. Jesus's teachings and practice concerning ministerial support were consistent with the culture of his day. He was not a Levite or a priest who received tithes, but a rabbi. His disciples also became rabbis when he sent them to make disciples, and Paul was a rabbi who had been a disciple of Gamaliel. Consider how rabbis received support:

> ...it was forbidden to charge a fee to teach the Torah, so it was common for rabbis to practice a trade part of the time and teach part of the time. Disciples did the same. Some rabbis were from priestly families, so they would have a stipend from the Temple, but many were manual laborers. There are many reports of teaching sessions held in the evening or on the Sabbath or festival days, so often men worked and studied at the same time. Some could work seasonally and take time off between planting and harvesting, etc. This makes sense with how the Gospel accounts describe the disciples fishing occasionally, even after they had become disciples of Jesus...
>
> Often disciples would travel together with a rabbi, and they would take weeks away to go on a teaching trip. A disciple had to ask his wife's permission to be away from home to study longer than 30 days. When they traveled, rabbis and disciples would pool their money to buy food, etc. Jesus received contributions from wealthy women, and they were known for supporting other rabbis too. When they traveled, the villages they taught in were expected to extend hospitality, giving them food and shelter."[294]

---

[294] Online: https://ourrabbijesus.com/a-question-about-disciples-rabbis/ Accessed December

If this section were a whole book and not just one chapter, we could extensively quote other sources on Jewish and early church history in support of these facts, which are generally accepted by scholars. Not only did Rabbis and their disciples usually work part-time, first-century local church leaders did not receive salaries!

Charging a fee for teaching God's word was forbidden, but Rabbis and their disciples received contributions and there was an expectation that they would receive hospitality. Notice how this is consistent with Jesus and Paul's teachings:

Matthew 10:7-11 As you go, proclaim this message: "The kingdom of heaven has come near." Heal the sick, raise the dead, cleanse those who have leprosy, drive out demons. Freely you have received; freely give. Do not get any gold or silver or copper to take with you in your belts— no bag for the journey or extra shirt or sandals or a staff, for the worker is worth his keep. Whatever town or village you enter, search there for some worthy person and stay at their house until you leave.

2 Corinthians 2:17 Unlike so many, we do not peddle the word of God for profit. On the contrary, in Christ we speak before God with sincerity, as those sent from God.

John 10:12-13 The hired hand is not the shepherd and does not own the sheep. So when he sees the wolf coming, he abandons the sheep and runs away. Then the wolf attacks the flock and scatters it. The man runs away because he is a hired hand and cares nothing for the sheep.

Rather than receiving tithes, Jesus and the apostles received hospitality and free-will offerings. Jesus and his disciples pooled

---

10th. The author of this text states his source: "My reference here is the chapter, 'Education and the Study of Torah' in *The Jewish People in the First Century*, by Safrai & Stern (Van Gorcum, Brill.) Shmuel Safrai spent a lifetime engaging the original rabbinic texts, and distilled the results of his research here. It is the best scholarly source available on the topic."

their money, consistent with historians' descriptions of Jewish Rabbis and their disciples at the time. Although they took significant time off from fishing to go on teaching trips, scripture does mention them fishing a few times.

Jesus's command for them to give freely was consistent with the prohibition on Rabbis charging for their teachings. His statement that the worker deserves his keep was in the context of receiving hospitality. His words about the *"hired hand"* who wouldn't be there if not for the pay were also consistent with the prohibition on Rabbis charging money to teach.

Paul quoted Jesus in 1 Timothy 5:18 when he said that the laborer was worthy of his hire, and Jesus was clearly not speaking of tithes![295] Jesus and Paul both taught ministerial support, but it was not necessarily full-time. Historical context and early church history give strong reasons to doubt that they were mandating full-time support. Paul himself exhorted first century church leaders to work hard with their own hands.[296]

Hospitality was expected, and receiving free-will gifts which enabled them to go on teaching tours was proper. When there were needs beyond what hospitality and gifts supplied, they continued to work. I think Jesus himself and the apostles in Jerusalem eventually received full-time support and no longer had to work in a trade, as the gifts abundantly provided for them to be able to do so. Yet it is unlikely that anybody else in the first-century church did.

Galatians 6:6 Nevertheless, the one who receives instruction in the word should share all good things with their instructor.

---

[295] Matthew 10:10 is about the sending of the 12, and Luke 10:7 is about the sending of the 72. Both are very similar passages, but they use a different word in the Greek to say what the worker is worthy of. Matthew 10:10 in the NIV says "the worker is worthy of his keep," and Luke is translated "The worker deserves his wages." The wording of Luke 10:7 in the Greek is the same as that of 1 Timothy 5:18. See Dr. Kelly's comments a little further down on the Greek "mithros" usually not meaning "salary." The use of the word "trophes" (translated "provisions" or "keep") in the nearly parallel passage of Matthew 10:10 helps us to understand the sense in which Luke used "mithros," and that it was not a "salary" as we think of it today.

[296] Ephesians 20:17-36

This scripture may be an exhortation encouraging free-will giving, but it is not a command that one who teaches must receive a full-time salary for doing so. In fact, scripture encourages us all to teach each other.[297] Some excel in teaching and devote a lot of time to it. Yet the scriptural model of support is simply free-will giving. It's not all-or-nothing.

Jesus's teaching about ministerial support was consistent with the rabbinical support practices of his day and not tithes. Even those who received tithes did not rely completely on them for their needs. Edersheim, an expert on Judaism, explains that priests received income from 24 sources and their tenth of the tithe was one of the least.[298] Scripture is clear that the Levites also did work outside of the temple, such as herding animals. So even those who received tithes were not in *"full-time ministry"* by our standards. According to Dr. Russel Earl Kelly:

> **Most church historians document that even high priests in Jesus's time also had and worked other vocations.[299]**

Apostolic Ministry

In this context, let's consider what Paul was saying to the Corinthians about ministerial support:

> **1 Corinthians 9:3-15 This is my defense to those who sit in judgment on me. Don't we have the right to food and drink? Don't we have the right to take a believing wife along with us, as do the other apostles and the Lord's brothers and Cephas? Or is it only I and Barnabas who lack the right to not work for a living?**
>
> **Who serves as a soldier at his own expense? Who plants a**

---

[297] Colossians 3:16
[298] Edersheim, Alfred. *The Temple: Its Ministry and Services as They Were at the Time of Jesus Christ*. London: Religious Tract Society, 1900. Pg. 102-103.
[299] Kelly, Russel Earl Online: http://www.tithing-russkelly.com/ Accessed January 2nd, 2020

vineyard and does not eat its grapes? Who tends a flock and does not drink the milk? Do I say this merely on human authority? Doesn't the Law say the same thing? For it is written in the Law of Moses: "Do not muzzle an ox while it is treading out the grain." Is it about oxen that God is concerned? Surely, he says this for us, doesn't he? Yes, this was written for us, because whoever plows and threshes should be able to do so in the hope of sharing in the harvest. If we have sown spiritual seed among you, is it too much if we reap a material harvest from you? If others have this right of support from you, shouldn't we have it all the more?

But we did not use this right. On the contrary, we put up with anything rather than hinder the gospel of Christ.

Don't you know that those who serve in the temple get their food from the temple, and that those who serve at the altar share in what is offered on the altar? In the same way, the Lord has commanded that those who preach the gospel should receive their living from the gospel.

But I have not used any of these rights. And I am not writing this in the hope that you will do such things for me, for I would rather die than allow anyone to deprive me of this boast.

"Receive their living by the gospel" is a bit of a paraphrase for *"live by the gospel."* In context, this most likely refers to receiving food and lodging as they go and preach. When Paul said *"The Lord has commanded that those who preach the gospel should receive their living from the gospel,"* what did he mean by *"those who preach the gospel?"* After all, every disciple of Jesus is supposed to preach the gospel!

Paul was referring to Jesus's instructions when he sent out the 12 and the 70 to preach. The context is apostolic, traveling ministry, not local ministry. Not only was traveling extremely dangerous at the time, but not everybody's profession was as mobile as Paul's was. Paul's words are consistent with the expectation of his day that Rabbis should receive hospitality. They are consistent with the free-will financial gifts of benefactors which enabled rabbis and their disciples to go on teaching tours. It was mobile ministry.

Some take Paul's reference to those who serve in the temple getting their food from the temple, and those who serve at the altar sharing in what is offered at the altar, as support for tithing. However, what the priests received from the altar was animal sacrifices and other offerings, and nobody is arguing for reinstating those! Paul is sharing a principle, not laying down Old Covenant law for gentile Christians! When we read this, we must remember that those who served in the temple and often even those who served at the altar had other professions, and only received these things when they were working in the temple! The Levites and most priests were not in what we would call *"full-time ministry."*

Paul was not teaching a right to demand money or to charge a fee for ministry, which was forbidden! He was defending the right to receive hospitality and to accept free-will offerings. Among them, he had paid for his food when it was expected that a traveling rabbi would receive food and lodging. Even so, he wasn't complaining about that. Although he wasn't even receiving support from the Corinthians, some people complained that he was a freeloader for accepting support freely given by other churches! They were trying to *"muzzle"* him.

Is "Double Honor" Double Money?

1 Timothy 5:1, 17-20 Do not rebuke an older man harshly, but exhort him as if he were your father. Treat younger men as brothers, older women as mothers, and younger women as sisters, with absolute purity... The elders who direct the affairs of the church well are worthy of double honor, especially those whose work is preaching and teaching. For Scripture says, "Do not muzzle an ox while it is treading out

the grain," and 'The worker deserves his wages." Do not entertain an accusation against an elder unless it is brought by two or three witnesses. But those elders who are sinning you are to reprove before everyone, so that the others may take warning.

This passage is often taken as a reference to financial compensation. However, I'm not aware of anybody who holds that position applying this scripture accordingly.

Paul quoted Jesus when he said *"the laborer is worthy of his hire."* Jesus was talking about receiving food and lodging, not demanding money. Although extending hospitality is honoring a guest, and honoring your aging father and mother includes caring for their needs, the word *"honor"* is still not a reference to a salary, and *"double honor"* does not mean *"double money."* Jesus himself had said *"freely you have received, freely give."* This is not talking about monetary compensation. In context, Paul instructs us to speak to elders with honor and not treat accusations against them lightly.

Honor is a theme in Paul's writing to Timothy. Right after the above text in chapter five, Paul begins chapter six by saying slaves should honor their masters. He then continues by warning against people who think godliness is a means of financial gain. Paul speaks of being content with having food and clothes. He warns Timothy not to be ensnared in the desire for riches. In Acts 20 Paul encouraged the Ephesian elders to follow his example by working with their own hands so as to help the weak. Considering all this, it seems quite strange to imagine that Paul was saying Timothy or anyone else should receive a double salary!

Dr. Russel Earl Kelly points out that the word *"honor"* can be used once in a while in a certain context to mean *"value"* but is never used in the New Testament to mean *"wage."* Other language in Greek would be more appropriate for that. Furthermore, the Greek word *"kopiao,"* translated *"labor"* in verse 17 does not implicitly mean *"labor for a living."* It differs from the word *"ergazomai"* which is the common verb in Greek meaning *"work to aquire,"* and is used 41 times in the New Testament. The Greek word *"mithros,"* which is translated as *"wages"* in the NIV above, occurs 29 times in the New Testament and could only possibly be translated as *"wages"* or *"salary"* in five of those places. It is used to speak of Paul's *"reward"* in 1 Corinthians 9:17-18 as he works with his hands and does not charge for the gospel, as well as our *"reward"* in heaven. In all, Dr. Kelly lists 19 reasons why 1 Timothy 5 is not talking about a salary or a tithe.[300]

I have always noticed that so many people treat 1 Timothy 5 as a reference to salaries, yet nobody seems to apply it thus. If 1 Timothy 5 were a command to give salaries to elders, then all elders in the church should receive salaries. Few who interpret *"honor"* as *"salary"* actually propose giving salaries to all elders and double salaries to those who do well. If 1 Timothy is mandating salaries for elders, many more people have a right to demand full-time salaries than are currently receiving any compensation. For example, many large churches have dozens or even hundreds of cell-group leaders. If 1 Timothy is talking about salaries for elders, all of those workers should be receiving salaries!

The Ecclesiological Implications of Mandatory Pastoral Salaries

The underlying issues keep going deeper. They're too much to deal with more extensively in this book because they lead us into ecclesiology. The New Testament only uses the noun *"pastor"* in one place referring to any church leader other than Jesus,[301] and it's in the plural. However, the New Testament uses of the verb *"to pastor"* show no distinction between *"pastors"* and *"elders."* The New Testament denotes a plurality of leadership. If scripture

---

[300]Kelly, Russell Earl. *Should the Church Teach Tithing?: a Theologians Conclusions about a Taboo Doctrine.* New York: Writers Club Press, 2007. *Chapter 24 1 Timothy 5:17-20 Worthy of Double Honor* Also online: http://www.tithing-russkelly.com/id35.html
[301] Ephesians 4:11

teaches that *"elders"* have a right to demand a full-time salary, then to be scriptural we should be giving all elders a full-time salary, and a lot more people would be getting a salary from ministry than are currently. The strong passages for ministerial support are in the context of apostolic, mobile ministry, and must be understood in their cultural context.

I discussed ecclesiology in my first book, *"I Am Persuaded."* We examined the enormous pressure on many pastors, as well as high burnout rates caused by overemphasis in our culture on the role of a single pastor. We also examined the tendency for that heavy emphasis on a few leaders to stifle church multiplication. When a few leaders are expected to do so much, many Christians fall into a co-dependent relationship with leaders rather than each person acting as a minister of Christ.

My intention isn't to tell all pastors receiving full-time support that they must *"get a real job"* or start meeting in houses. Yet I point out the pitfalls which many experienced missionary church-planters have noted with pastoral salaries. Many of the world's fastest-growing church-planting movements, including the one Victor Choudrie leads, intentionally have no salaried pastors.

As I sought out literature on church multiplication movements, I read experienced missiologists saying repeatedly that pastoral salaries hinder the church from multiplying. I was surprised when I read a Christianity Today article in which even Heidi Baker said the same![302] Many of us appreciate Heidi and are familiar with the rapidly multiplying church-planting movement in Mozambique and Africa which she and her husband lead. There seems to be a good deal of consensus among the leaders of such movements that pastoral salaries hinder multiplication.

The Holy Spirit is moving in many different models and cultural expressions of church. I'm often overwhelmed with thanksgiving for what he's doing. Some churches which have a

---

[302] Bakery, Heidi *Miracles In Mozambique* Online: http://www.christianitytoday.com/ct/2012/may/miracles-in-mozambique.html?type=prev&number=13&id=96235&start=7 Accessed July 7th, 2019

more institutional expression still have a good deal of participation with many members of Christ's body ministering to each other, and have been experiencing great moves of the Holy Spirit. That is why I've written prayerfully here, not to tear down such movements but to point out that they are a particular cultural expression of church, and not the essential biblical pattern for all churches.

This relates closely to the issue of tithes because many leaders in our culture seem to feel that the kingdom of God would fall apart without a great deal of money. Many of the things that we feel we couldn't do without are the very things that leaders of church-multiplication movements name as hindrances to growth! We must also consider the fact that the earliest local church leaders did not receive salaries. George E. Ladd comments in the Wycliff Bible commentary:

The main objective of giving in the early church was to provide for the needs of the poor brothers rather than to support the preaching of the gospel, as is the case today.[303]

Salaried pastors and buildings are not forbidden and may be helpful in some cases, but if we want them, we must support them by the biblical model of free-will giving. So many feel that they must hold to the human tradition of the modern tithe to support buildings and salaries, and thus the perceived need becomes the reason for teaching tithing, rather than truth. We can no longer continue the tithe tradition when we consider how the tithe is undermining a pure gospel message, the need for integrity with handling scripture, and the many commandments of God which the church has been breaking for the sake of this tradition. The perceived *"need"* doesn't justify corrupting our wisdom and continually seeking support for what simply isn't true.

---

[303] Pfeiffer, Charles F., and Everett Falconer Harrison. *Wycliffe Bible Commentary*. Chicago: Moody P., 1962. Commentary on Acts 20:34

I believe there are some people whom God has called to leave their jobs in order to preach or do other Christian work. Plenty of full-time gospel workers don't rely on tithes for their incomes. We are also in a more prosperous time of history than ever before and can sustain many full-time Christian workers with free-will giving.

Support for Apostolic Workers Intentionally Put Them in Dependency Rather Than in Power!

In his Luke 10 Manual for church planters, Stephen W. Hill explains Jesus's instruction to not take a purse as they went:

Luke 10:4 Do not take a purse or bag or sandals; and do not greet anyone on the road.

As we read down the passage, we find Jesus instructing His disciples to find a person of peace, enter their home and eat and drink with them. His instruction is that they would stay with that person and serve them in their home. If we do that and especially if we begin the journey without money, we are dependent upon that person for our daily living. Thus, the money bag, while literally true, also becomes a metaphor for power in relation to the other and how we handle differences in power. If we take our money with us, we have the power to create a little island of our own preference in the middle of any culture and that is exactly what western missionaries have done all around the world.[304]

Stephen continues, explaining how the one who has the money has the power and how this has been a hindrance to the spread of the gospel. Many modern missiologists concur about the danger of the

---

[304] Hill, Steven W. and Marilyn. *Luke 10 Manual*, Page 35. Available Online: https://www.harvest-now.org/uploads/media/LK10_Manual__26_04_01.pdf Accessed January 1, 2020.

ones with the money imposing their cultural ideals on another culture rather than letting the gospel take root within that culture.

The way Jesus sent his disciples and taught them to receive provision on missionary journeys did not put them in power, but in dependence. Jesus's words *"The laborer is worthy of his hire"* were in that context, yet they have been wrongly interpreted as denoting a right to control the money!

Chapter 14

Good News for the Poor

Those in Humble Circumstances Should Take Pride in Their High Position!

James 1:9-11 Believers in humble circumstances ought to take pride in their high position. But the rich should take pride in their humiliation—since they will pass away like a wild flower. For the sun rises with scorching heat and withers the plant; its blossom falls and its beauty is destroyed. In the same way, the rich will fade away even while they go about their business.

The gospel is good news to the poor, primarily because it proclaims that material wealth doesn't determine your standing with God! This so contrasts with the Jewish cultural mentality that *"gain is godliness."* The Jews saw wealth as a sign that a person was accepted by God, and poverty as a sign that a person was a sinner and not accepted by God.

Do you remember the story of the rich young ruler?[305] Jesus told him to give away all he had if he wanted to gain eternal life. Bertie Brits points out that the Jews of that time thought a poor person was headed to hell. Jesus was not teaching that poverty was desirable or more spiritual than riches. He was dealing with the thing that the rich young ruler was relying on for justification instead of on God's grace![306]

---

[305] Mark 10:17-27

Probably nothing has done more to promote the *"gain is godliness"* mentality in the church today than the modern tithe tradition. It includes promises of gain for the tither and threats of financial disaster for the non-tither. This subtle deception culminates with people judging their standing with God by how much money they have rather than by what Jesus has done.

The gospel exalts everyone who receives it to a high position, even those in humble circumstances! But the rich must take pride in their humble position of dependence on Christ, remembering that money is not true riches and it soon passes away.

Many believers who've followed give-to-get tithe teachings and find themselves in humble circumstances wonder what they are doing wrong. Rather, they should take pride in their high position! These Christians get mired in guilt and condemnation and confused. They wonder if they weren't giving enough on top of their tithe, tithing cheerfully enough, or tithing in faith when they find themselves in humble circumstances. On the other hand, how many tithers have we heard boasting in their current plentiful circumstances and how their tithes *"worked"* for them rather than boasting in Christ?

Yet we do see financial prosperity in scripture as a manifestation of God's blessing. I hold to a full-gospel position. How can I see prosperity as a part of the gospel, yet recognize James' statement that many who are poor are rich in faith? I've wrestled with this question, and I think I can provide some insight on the matter.

Viewing Poverty and Prosperity Primarily in Terms of Relationship Rather Than Money

Although prosperity can manifest financially, the essence of prosperity cannot be defined as *"having lots of money."* According to Jesus, money isn't *"true riches."* Prosperity is having abundance,

---

[306] Brits, Bertie. *Jesus Is the Tithe: the Message of God*. South Africa: Bertie Brits, 2019. Kindle Location 714

much more than only what is required to supply your own need. When I was in financial straits after the IRS put a lien on my house, I still felt like I was rich as I saw surgeries cancelled and people healed. I was distributing an endless supply of heavenly riches! Abundance is so much more than just money. In fact, some people have plenty of money but have anything but abundance.

I recently read a widely-acclaimed book on poverty alleviation, called *"When Helping Hurts."* Chapter two discusses how many of us have defined poverty in material terms. This has actually caused us to harm ourselves and the poor in our efforts to alleviate poverty. The poor themselves tend to describe poverty with much more psychological and social terms.

Poor people typically talk in terms of shame, inferiority, powerlessness, humiliation, fear, hopelessness, depression, social isolation, and voicelessness. North American audiences tend to emphasize a lack of material things…[307]

According to Bryant Myers, God established four fundamental relationships for each person before the fall; a relationship with God, with self, with others, and the rest of creation. We experience the fullness of life as God intended it when these relationships are functioning properly.[308]

Brokenness in any of these areas may manifest in material poverty. For example, many poor people in the third world spend a great deal on sacrifices to idols, trying to mend a broken relationship with God. A broken relationship with oneself hinders confidence to overcome obstacles and manifests in choices that bring poor economic outcomes. Broken relationships with others include divorce, which brings many to poverty. They lead to injustice in society. Broken relationship with the creation includes

---

[307] Corbett, Steve, Brian Fikkert, John Perkins, and David Platt. *When Helping Hurts How to Alleviate Poverty Without Hurting the Poor … and Yourself.* Chicago: Moody Publishers, 2014.Page 51

[308] Corbett, Steve, Brian Fikkert, John Perkins, and David Platt. *When Helping Hurts How to Alleviate Poverty Without Hurting the Poor … and Yourself.* Chicago: Moody Publishers, 2014.Page 54

the failure to wisely steward natural resources. Broken relationships in general often manifest in addiction and substance abuse, which have serious economic consequences.

Myers says *"Poverty is the result of relationships that do not work, that are not just, that are not for life, that are not harmonious or enjoyable. Poverty is the absence of shalom in all its meanings."*[309]

These comments provide insight on how the gospel touches the issue of poverty. They clarify how we can hold a full-gospel position without judging people's spirituality by financial standing. Bringing reconciliation to the four relationships, the gospel carries prosperity to many once-impoverished households and societies.

Many who teach tithing treat poverty as a manifestation of a broken relationship with God, and they promote tithing as the way to remedy that. By doing so, they obscure the message of the gospel! Poverty can have roots in any of those four broken relationships, but for many people, the primary cause of material poverty is societal injustice. That has no reflection on the spiritual state of the individual.

The same gospel which mends relationship also brings division. The same gospel which lifts people out of material poverty can result in material poverty for others. Yet the one who is walking with Christ is rich no matter how much money they have. Jesus said:

> **Matthew 10:34-36 Do not suppose that I have come to bring peace to the earth. I did not come to bring peace, but a sword. For I have come to turn "a man against his father, a daughter against her mother, a daughter-in-law against her mother-in-law—a man's enemies will be the members of his own household."**

Many Christians live in the context of heavy religious persecution. For them, following Christ means being rejected by their families

---

[309] Bryant L. Myers, Walking with the Poor: Principles and Practices of Transformational Development (Maryknoll, NY: Orbis Books 1999)

and society at large. Sometimes it even means being enslaved. They are experiencing material poverty at the moment due to injustice, but they are rich!

Hebrews 10:34 You suffered along with those in prison and joyfully accepted the confiscation of your property, because you knew that you yourselves had better and lasting possessions.

What Is a Poverty Spirit Versus Prosperity Mentality?

We've heard much talk about a *"poverty spirit."* Certainly, there are patterns of thinking and habits that keep people struggling financially. Yet judgments about who is operating in a *"poverty spirit"* are often erroneous. Ministers who shun using pressure to bring in money or who are employed part time sometimes get labeled as having a *"poverty spirit!"* Yet Paul had the same attitude, and he certainly didn't operate under a *"poverty spirit."* He quoted Jesus's words *"It is more blessed to give than to receive"*[310] in the context of paying his own way as he did apostolic ministry!

The person who doesn't have money but is full of joy and giving away God's riches is moving in prosperity. We can't define a prosperous mindset or *"poverty spirit"* in financial terms. We must define them in terms of heavenly riches, which Jesus called *"true riches."* Corrie and Betsie Ten Boom were moving in prosperity even as they wore rags in a Nazi concentration camp, and they experienced supernatural multiplication of vitamin drops as they gave them away![311]

Philippians 4:4 Rejoice in the Lord always; again I will say, Rejoice.

---

[310] Acts 20:35

[311] Boom, Corrie Ten; Elizabeth Sherrill; John Sherrill (2006-01-01). The Hiding Place (p. 213-214). Baker Publishing Group. Kindle Edition.

Philippians 4:11-13 Not that I am referring to being in need; for I have learned to be content with whatever I have. I know what it is to have little, and I know what it is to have plenty. In any and all circumstances I have learned the secret of being well-fed and of going hungry, of having plenty and of being in need. I can do all things through him who strengthens me.

Being content doesn't mean you don't want to improve your financial situation. It doesn't mean you don't want to prosper and have money. Rather, contentment means this: you are in God's presence now and because of that, you have fullness of joy, no matter what the circumstances. You can say *"Thank you God that you're with me, you're for me, and you'll never leave me! Thank you, God, that you've cleansed me from sin, made me righteous, and given me the Holy Spirit and the privilege of representing you to the world!"* You know that you're immeasurably rich with heavenly riches and always have something to give by the Spirit of God to those around you.

As soon as our joy is hinged on how much we have or the circumstances we face, we have fallen to idolatry. We must learn to be subject to the heavenly reality that is in God's presence. Knowing who my Father is determines how I'm doing! Like the apostle Paul, even in times of hardship, don't let your face stop glowing with God's love and glory. Don't become subject to mammon.

The person whose joy is not altered by finances is truly rich and walking in prosperity. The rich man who is suicidal is walking in a poverty spirit. The penniless one who is full of joy and giving away heavenly riches is walking in prosperity, not in a poverty spirit. Although walking in a prosperity mindset can certainly result in financial miracles and material blessing, it cannot be defined by them.

Mammon, not being true riches, can never satisfy our souls. Seeking satisfaction for our souls in mammon is a manifestation of a poverty mindset.

Many Tithe Teachings Promote a Poverty Spirit

When we identify poverty's root issue as broken relationships, we can see how most modern tithe teachings promote a poverty spirit. They encourage people to judge their relationship with God by their financial status, and disqualify church people who can't fully support their families and pay a tithe. Such teachings undermine the family model that Jesus taught for his church. They apply shame and the fear of punishment as motivations for so-called *"giving."* Shame is a major factor in broken relationships and a manifestation of poverty!

Dr. Abel Damina, the African preacher we mentioned who repented from the give-to-get teaching he once espoused, confessed how miserable he was as he taught that doctrine. He didn't even have an assurance of salvation! He had plenty of money, but he was walking in a poverty spirit![312]

Tithing and any other form of *"give to get"* teaching is rooted in a poverty mindset of lack. The prosperity mindset says *"I have all I need in Christ!"* It focuses on releasing God's riches to the world. Financial giving from a prosperity mindset is about blessing other people, because I have all I need!

We've shared stories of people who are tithing and not properly caring for their families. If that is happening so often in the United States, how much more is it happening in third-world countries influenced by our tithe teachings and give-to-get theology? This is currently a big issue of in African nations like Nigeria. Elderly parents in much of the world rarely have savings or investments and therefore rely on their children to sustain them. An African brother recently told me that many people are tithing to get God's blessing yet neglecting to care for aging parents! This surely does not reflect God's heart or reflect what *"kingdom*

---

[312]Online:https://www.youtube.com/watch?v=GVZZDsfuTiA&fbclid=IwAR2WOwUcALcB hP1ZPo4M9N3lM8CoDFByLMKpWwTNR4AcFvcJ613QM_g2-Ws Accessed August 2nd, 2019

prosperity" looks like. Christians whom the early church would have assisted are instead told to tithe in order to resolve their financial situation!

Christians with money often wrongly think they are walking in prosperity. Sometimes they are giving a lot to the church because they've been taught they'll get a financial return from it, but they sure aren't treating employees very well! They are still operating in a mindset of lack. Consider the business woman whose salespeople we caught in various lies and whose business wiped out our operating capital through gross negligence; when confronted with proof of those injustices she concluded that we must not be tithing like she was! She was walking in a poverty spirit! Her wisdom was corrupted by mammon.

Corrupted wisdom seeks justification to support tithing so faulty reasoning applies a *"logic"* we would not apply to any other issue. This irrationality extends to the point of inventing reasoning like, *"Adam's sin in the garden of Eden was failing to tithe."* The issue boils down not to *"Does the Bible teach tithing?"* but *"How would we support our church without this?"* The root issue is that *"we need to teach tithing because we are afraid that not enough money would come in if we didn't."*

Corrupting our wisdom and losing our integrity because of worry about lack is walking in a poverty mentality and not a prosperity mindset! Can we not trust the Holy Spirit to lead God's people to give? Can we believe that the love of God shed abroad in our hearts is what motivates us to give? Instead of using external compulsion, let us teach people to walk in communion with the Holy Spirit, so that the things which move God's heart will move theirs! And if we can't pay for it without compromising our integrity, let's be content without it! God is a radical giver, and the gospel unites us with him in Spirit![313] Giving is an aspect of God's grace and can be a thrilling journey as we grow in faith and believe God for seed to sow.

---

[313] 1 Corinthians 6:17

Come, All You Who Have No Money!

Isaiah 55:1 Come, all you who are thirsty, come to the waters; and you who have no money, come, buy and eat! Come, buy wine and milk without money and without cost.

This is Isaiah proclaiming the gospel! Doesn't it seem strange that we could readily pay so much attention to a scripture from the law given on Mount Sinai saying *"Nobody shall come before me empty-handed"*[314] yet not notice how great the contrast with the gospel scripture *"You who have no money, come, buy, and eat!"*

Galatians 4:21-31 Tell me, you who want to be under the law, are you not aware of what the law says? For it is written that Abraham had two sons, one by the slave woman and the other by the free woman. His son by the slave woman was born according to the flesh, but his son by the free woman was born as the result of a divine promise.

These things are being taken figuratively: The women represent two covenants. One covenant is from Mount Sinai and bears children who are to be slaves: This is Hagar. Now Hagar stands for Mount Sinai in Arabia and corresponds to the present city of Jerusalem, because she is in slavery with her children. But the Jerusalem that is above is free, and she is our mother. For it is written: "Be glad, barren woman, you who never bore a child; shout for joy and cry aloud, you who were never in labor; because more are the children of the desolate woman than of her who has a husband."

Now you, brothers and sisters, like Isaac, are children of promise. At that time the son born according to the flesh

---

[314] Exodus 23:15

persecuted the son born by the power of the Spirit. It is the same now. But what does Scripture say? 'Get rid of the slave woman and her son, for the slave woman's son will never share in the inheritance with the free woman's son.' Therefore, brothers and sisters, we are not children of the slave woman, but of the free woman.

The law given on Sinai said *"Nobody shall come empty-handed"* but the gospel says *"Come, all you who have no money!"* Which message are we getting across to the world? Have we come to Sinai, or to the heavenly Jerusalem? Will we lead people into slavery or into freedom? Are we going to operate according to the flesh or by the power of the Spirit? The gospel is good news for the poor. The law isn't good news for anybody, for *"by the works of the law no man shall be justified!"*[315]

When we minister healing, some people think *"I don't deserve healing"* or *"that person deserves healing."* Either attitude is pride. Humility comes with empty hands to receive, not based on any of our merit of lack thereof, but on what Jesus has done. I recently heard the Lord shouting *"Come to me with empty hands"* as God opened up the scriptures to me contrasting the law given on Sinai with the gospel. The glory I felt as my understanding was opening to this manifested so strongly that I fell back in my seat. A pure gospel message brings a manifestation of God's glory, often with people weeping, feeling the weight of God's goodness, or being healed as they listen.

When *"Come you who have no money"* becomes *"Don't come without your tithes and offerings,"* we no longer have a pure gospel message. I've seen God's glory and I've seen people weep as they received his grace. I don't have time to waste with powerless religion. I want the pure message that manifests in power to transform people.

Now, of course by saying *"Come to God empty handed,"* I'm

---

[315] Galatians 2:16

not saying *"Don't bring money to church!"* Participate in giving, but don't hold your money in your hand as something of merit with which you approach God in order to receive his grace. Come in humility with your eyes on who God is rather than the proud, self-centered attitudes of *"I deserve something from God"* or *"I don't deserve anything from God."* Those who approach God in humility will receive grace.[316]

---

[316] James 4:6

Chapter 15
When Not To Accept an Offering

Don't Try To Approach God in the Same Way a
Sorcerer Communes With Evil Entities!

God is so serious about the integrity of our gospel message and communicating clearly how he relates to mankind, that there are times we should not accept an offering because of the intention of the one giving it! We see one example of this in Acts.

> **Acts 8:18-23 When Simon saw that the Spirit was given at the laying on of the apostles' hands, he offered them money and said, "Give me also this ability so that everyone on whom I lay my hands may receive the Holy Spirit."**
>
> **Peter answered: "May your money perish with you, because you thought you could buy the gift of God with money! You have no part or share in this ministry, because your heart is not right before God. Repent of this wickedness and pray to the Lord in the hope that he may forgive you for having such a thought in your heart. For I see that you are full of bitterness and captive to sin."**

Paul recognized that Simon the sorcerer was attempting to buy what could only be received by God's grace. He wanted nothing to do with it! People in pagan religions offer sacrifices of money, food and other items to the sea goddess or some other entity in order to gain prosperity, then come into the church and try to approach our

Heavenly Father in the same way! It's not surprising that Simon, with his background in sorcery, tried to buy God's gift.

Once someone with a background in witchcraft offered me something after I prayed and all the pain left her body. I didn't want anything to do with receiving a *"gift"* that would obscure the revelation of Jesus Christ to this lady! Here in Brazil, many church people still cling to the old mentalities they had while in witchcraft. My heart cries, *"Come out of darkness and into God's wonderful light!"*

I can't help thinking of the similarity between the above scenario and hearing a famous conference preacher state, *"I'm not saying you can buy your healing,* **but...**" This distortion of God's message grieves me.

What Can I Do To Thank You?

I've heard the response *"What can I do to thank you?"* more than once after seeing Jesus heal people. I appreciate the desire to reciprocate with blessing. But I have only one answer when people ask *"what can I do?"* after God heals them.

Please, go and tell other people what Jesus has done for you. Go and give the same gift to others. Lay hands on the sick in Jesus's name! If you want to do something for me, nothing will make me happier than if you catch a hold of the revelation of Jesus and minister the same to others! This ministry is for all Christians because it is the nature of Jesus.

Curry Blake holds *"Divine Healing Technician"* training in various countries. I remember him saying that they take an offering on the training days, but he does not take an offering on the day they minister to the sick. He's found that some people have the mindset of hoping they can *"deserve"* for Jesus to heal them, and give with that motivation. If Curry receives a check to the ministry with a prayer request on it, he tears up the check. He wants to make it clear that we freely receive healing only by God's grace, and not by our works. That is commendable, and it's a great example for situations where people are attempting to buy God's gift or otherwise approach the Father by works.

T.B. Joshua has repeatedly refused to accept a monetary gift from a sick person coming to receive healing. An elderly woman in need of healing came to a pastor's conference where he spoke in Cali, Colombia. After rising from her wheelchair and walking, she proceeded to offer a $1,000 gift she'd been saving for a year to give to Joshua's ministry. He replied *"Look, help me give it to the needy and the orphans."*[317] Explaining to the crowd, Joshua said *"When she goes back home, she can give anything to the ministry, but not now. Now, it would look like the miracle was exchanged for money."* His words were met with cheers and applause.

Preaching at a pastor's conference in South Korea, T.B. Joshua stated *"Healing, deliverance, prophecy, and all of God's blessings are hindered by money....even if the richest man in the world is sick and you pray for him, don't expect anything....so it will not look as if healing is for sale...I stopped traveling the world from country to country for the last five years, because, when I saw the challenges...and I realized that the gift of God that was coming from me was not completely delivered, and I'm asking what is the cause of not being able to deliver ninety percent of the gift? The Lord said to me that money is the hindrance.... this person you are praying for: they have collected money from him. And you want to sell the gift?"*[318]

Why is T.B. Joshua saying that money hinders God's blessings? As soon as people get caught up in trying to buy what can only be received by grace, they are no longer approaching God with humility or honoring what Jesus has done for us. I disagree with T.B. Joshua that tithes are in any way relevant. However, the heart of his teaching is much closer to the biblical model of giving, including his emphasis on where to give. I honor his integrity with

---

[317] *Why TB Joshua Refused to Collect $1000 Offering* Online: https://www.youtube.com/watch?v=FG_ewp_J4G4 Accessed January 7th, 2020
[318] *Do Not Collect Money From The Sick* Online: https://www.youtube.com/watch?v=OJn0VbQb-8I Accessed January 7th, 2020

the gospel message and thank God for the example he is showing for other pastors and leaders to follow.

Support From Unbelievers

The apostle John mentioned some brothers on a mission refusing support from unbelievers:

3 John 7 (NRSV) ... for they began their journey for the sake of Christ, accepting no support from non-believers.

I don't think it's always wrong to accept a gift from a non-Christian. However, sometimes the Holy Spirit leads us to refuse a gift. There may be various reasons. Sometimes a gift comes with strings attached, or sometimes a person is attempting to approach God from a position of self-righteousness.

God wants to show people that his gift is free, at least free for the receiver. Our forgiveness and healing are free for us, but they cost Jesus dearly. He paid in blood! Wanting to pay for them is often a manifestation of pride, and that pride must be dealt with if the person is going to come to Christ. Come to God with humility, and you will receive grace.[319]

Pride

2 Kings 5:9-15 (NRSV) So Naaman came with his horses and chariots, and halted at the entrance of Elisha's house. Elisha sent a messenger to him, saying,"'Go, wash in the Jordan seven times, and your flesh shall be restored and you shall be clean." But Naaman became angry and went away, saying, "I thought that for me he would surely come out, and stand and call on the name of the Lord his God, and would wave his hand over the spot, and cure the leprosy! Are not Abana and Pharpar, the rivers of Damascus, better than all the waters of

---

[319] James 4:6

Israel? Could I not wash in them, and be clean?" He turned and went away in a rage.

But his servants approached and said to him, "Father, if the prophet had commanded you to do something difficult, would you not have done it? How much more, when all he said to you was, 'Wash, and be clean'?" So he went down and immersed himself seven times in the Jordan, according to the word of the man of God; his flesh was restored like the flesh of a young boy, and he was clean. Then he returned to the man of God, he and all his company; he came and stood before him and said, "Now I know that there is no God in all the earth except in Israel; please accept a present from your servant." But he said, "As the Lord lives, whom I serve, I will accept nothing!" He urged him to accept, but he refused.

Naaman almost didn't follow Elijah's instructions because of his pride. But his servants convinced him to humble himself and he was completely healed! It also humbled Naaman, who was an important official, to receive healing from the God of Israel and give nothing in return. That showed him that the God of Israel is the Most High God and is not a respecter of persons.[320]

2 Kings 5: 19-27 (NRSV) But when Naaman had gone from him a short distance, Gehazi, the servant of Elisha the man of God, thought, "My master has let that Aramean Naaman off too lightly by not accepting from him what he offered. As the Lord lives, I will run after him and get something out of him." So Gehazi went after Naaman. When Naaman saw someone running after him, he jumped down from the chariot to meet him and said, "Is everything all right?" He replied, "Yes, but my master has sent me to say, 'Two members of a company of

---

[320] Acts 10:34

prophets have just come to me from the hill country of Ephraim; please give them a talent of silver and two changes of clothing.'" Naaman said, "Please accept two talents." He urged him, and tied up two talents of silver in two bags, with two changes of clothing, and gave them to two of his servants, who carried them in front of Gehazi. When he came to the citadel, he took the bags from them, and stored them inside; he dismissed the men, and they left.

He went in and stood before his master; and Elisha said to him, "Where have you been, Gehazi?" He answered, "Your servant has not gone anywhere at all." But he said to him, "Did I not go with you in spirit when someone left his chariot to meet you? Is this a time to accept money and to accept clothing, olive orchards and vineyards, sheep and oxen, and male and female slaves? Therefore, the leprosy of Naaman shall cling to you, and to your descendants forever." So he left his presence leprous, as white as snow.

Naaman was a rich and powerful man, and he wanted to give a gift worthy of his position. **But God's blessings of healing and forgiveness humble us. Jesus paid the greatest price for them. To imagine that we could buy them with anything else is an insult to the price that Jesus paid. It is devaluing Jesus's blood.**

The story of Gehazi shows us how seriously God takes this matter. How we represent God to others may be a matter of life and death for them. The man who came to God in pride, boasting of his tithe and how often he fasted, left without being justified!

Luke 18:14 I tell you that this man, rather than the other, went home justified before God. For all those who exalt themselves will be humbled, and those who humble themselves will be exalted.

If we ever feel uncomfortable about receiving a gift or offering, the Holy Spirit may be revealing pride in the equation. Bertie Brits related a time when he was a guest speaker and he felt uncomfortable about accepting the offering. He felt that they were giving to get; according to the law and not according to God's grace. Since it was Mother's Day, he had the entirety of the offering given to the oldest women in the congregation instead of receiving it himself![321]

A few people and churches use the word *"tithe"* very loosely, as another word for giving, and not even necessarily 10%. Such a loose usage of the word *"tithe"* isn't accurate and causes confusion. We need to understand the significance tithing has for many people who come holding a tithe in their hand as something with which to approach God. That is the primary reason to avoid such language.

That is also why it's a bad idea to teach tithing even as a *"good, but not mandatory, model for giving."* We want to see people giving, not as a way to approach God, but as the outflow of fellowship with God, having already approached him with empty hands and having entered through our open heaven, which is the torn body of Christ.

If We Love the Lord's Flock, We Want To See Them Giving As Led by the Spirit—Motivated by Love!

We mentioned Dan Mohler, who led Todd White to the Lord and has impacted so many Christians. Dan has often refused offerings when he felt it would violate his conscience to accept them. In one sermon, he said the following:

> **I'm here because I believe this. I'm not here for an offering. I've probably stopped 8, 10 pastors a year when they're receiving an offering for me, and take nothing, because of the way they took the offering—without exposing them, and without them even knowing what I did—'cause it violates me.**

---

[321] Brits, Bertie *Healing For The Financially Abused (Tithing Can Kill You)* 1 hour, 17 minutes, 8 seconds into the message. Online: https://www.youtube.com/watch?v=VcyYnrQp7YA&t=424s Accessed December 21, 2019

'Cause I'm not here for that…See, 'cause some pastors compel for an offering…You say 'The laborer's worth his hire'… Nobody hired me!

When Dan says the Lord told him not to receive the offering, people often try to preach giving sermons to him. He says:

I've already read my Bible! One of the biggest lines I hear is "Well brother, you need to receive it! You ain't robbing us of our blessing!" And I'm like "If you're giving to me for your blessing, why don't you stop being self-centered and don't give anymore until you get your heart right? You're just giving to get? That's weird!"

"Well you ain't robbing me of my blessing." I think you're already robbed by just the way you're thinking. You give because you love. You give because you appreciate. You give because you sincerely want to empower.

I can't tell you how many times I've done it. A pastor gets on that tune and crosses a line to my conscience and I'll stand up and cry. "Pastor, I'm so sorry to put you in this position pastor. Listen, I should have said something sooner, it's been on my heart just sittin' here that I should just…let's just…man I'm not here for an offering… I know you guys love and you wanna give, and some of you already feel like 'I'm supposed to give,' but listen…let's not do that. In fact, you have a building fund, let's pour it into that. I don't feel like I'm here for an offering, and don't let anybody try to preach to me, I'm following my conscience, what I believe is the Lord. Man, I'm just blessed to be here." And I'll sit down and the pastor will go "OK…well"[322]

Why would Dan care so much about people's attitudes when they

[322] Online: https://www.youtube.com/watch?v=RSJYozIXsXg Accessed December 21, 2019

take an offering for him? Dan loves the church and he wants to see it thriving. I believe he knows that when there is a pride issue, as there was with Naaman, it hinders the church from reflecting God's glory and receiving God's grace.

Chapter 16
Mothers Are Pleading for Someone To Tell Their Children the Truth

I recently read a dream I wrote down two years ago. Reading it again brought tears to my eyes as I remembered all the young people and unbelievers I've talked to who didn't want to hear the gospel because Jesus had been misrepresented to them. It stirred the drive in my heart to keep praying for the churches and for the young people whose mothers are pleading for someone to tell their kids the truth. I had shared this with my mom and she gave an interpretation.

I don't often remember my dreams, but this one was especially vivid and contained a lot of symbolism. I believe it's prophetic and especially relevant as to what's happening in the church right now. The weeds are being separated from the wheat and God is dealing with the church concerning a compromised gospel message. I would not be writing this book as a plea to pastors if I did not believe there are many pastors who are *"wheat"* and sincerely love God's flock but have gotten their roots entangled with weeds, especially concerning tithing.

The Old House Dream

In the dream, I saw a show on the Discovery Channel or History channel about an old house and realized it was in Lancaster country. I was excited and wanted to visit it.

I drove to the place and introduced myself to the owner. He had another guest whom he was talking with and seemed very uncomfortable with my presence. I felt like I wasn't wanted there. After a while, when I explained to them that I saw the show and wanted to see the house, he said it really wasn't that house I'd seen, but another house, and it was having work done on it. I asked, but he said it wouldn't be available for showing even after the work was done. I thanked him for his time.

The homeowner had been impersonating a young healing minister I know named Art Thomas, but in secret he opposed and slandered Art. As I was leaving his house, I passed through part of it when he was distracted elsewhere and I saw that he had a shrine to four Hindu gods.

As I was leaving, a delivery to the house from Art Thomas arrived. It was three things, like teaching CDs and books or something. The delivery man gave it to me. I offered it to the homeowner, who it was addressed to. He rejected it and said, *"You might as well keep it."*

When I went to leave, my car key was on the ground behind the car. I was surprised and wondered how it got there and wasn't on my keychain. I got in the car, and the wife and two (or three) kids of the man who owned the house, were in my car! The wife was fervently preaching the gospel to her children. That really surprised me because her husband, who was impersonating a minister, was so against the gospel. I had wrongly assumed that she was in the same place of cold idolatry as he was.

The kids didn't want to hear their mom. When I got in the driver's seat, I started telling the kids (young teens) that what their mom was saying was true, and I told them about what God had done in my life. When I spoke, the kids were convinced. Then I prayed with great passion and they felt God's presence in my car.

Mom's Interpretation

My mom prayed over the dream and responded. Following is her response, with slight edits. I wept when I read her response, as her words rang true!

Dear Jonathan,

After reading, praying and processing, this is what I see in your dream:

The old house in Lancaster represents the church of Lancaster, which has historical roots for our whole nation. The owner of the house represents church leaders. The homeowner was uncomfortable with your presence because he was not operating in the Holy Spirit but was of a different spirit. The church has been trying to get the work done; to fix itself up. This has been for the sake of "show;" outward appearance and the glory of man. That minister was not genuine; he had an outward show of religion but denied the power of it.

The leadership was, in fact, worshiping other gods; idolatry; spiritual adultery. The church of Lancaster (representing the American institutional church) has compromised with this world's belief systems, becoming perverse, tainted and corrupt. Sound doctrine has been offered to the leadership, but they have not embraced it or put it into practice, even if they have preached it. Neither have they (overall) been able to receive you or the unadulterated gospel that you preach and live by.

However, the Lord has given you a vehicle, a ministry, by which to reach people that the institutional church has not been helping. You had temporarily lost this key, but the Lord let you find it again. It has to do with your calling, Jonathan. The sound doctrine, (orthodoxy) that you teach, married to the power of the Holy Spirit is mighty to the pulling down of strongholds; opening blind eyes and releasing people from their prisons. This is the manifest presence of the Spirit of God.

287

This was why the children in the car were able to receive from you, when they had not been able to receive in the church settings they had known. Women are pleading with and praying for their children, but the children want a man to tell them the truth. The younger generations want to hear the gospel not just from their mothers but also from men."

My Thoughts

I'm not sharing to encourage judgment against certain Christian groups because they are *"institutional."* God is doing a mighty work in many different contexts, among people from many different backgrounds. Wherever I go, I want to have eyes to see what the Holy Spirit is doing and to recognize sincere love regardless of people's tradition or background. However, the purpose of Christian institutions must be to serve people, who are the true temple of God.

I also don't want this to be misunderstood as casting a one-sided negative slant on the church in Lancaster or in the US. A lot of great things are going on in Lancaster and the United States, with some churches in the United States having a strong positive impact in other nations. Lancaster PA is the oldest inland city in the United States and is where I lived before moving to Brazil. It's well known for strong religious foundations.

But the church, or old house, in Lancaster is symbolic of religion that holds to human traditions at the expense of people. It is self-serving. There is certainly a portion of ministers in the American church who are self-serving and living in idolatry.

Art Thomas represented ministers who are moving in supernatural power and motivated by sincere love. He represented a movement of the Holy Spirit today among many like him. The owner of the old house was a religious leader who was impersonating Art because it was the trend. It got him followers and popularity if he went along with it. But his true motivation was really self-serving. Under the facade, he secretly hated Art and opposed him because the sincere love that rejected control and manipulation was a threat to what he had built. It was also why he was so uncomfortable with me being in his house.

Although he pretended to be on board with the move of the Holy Spirit, the healing, and the miracles, he actually rejected Art's teaching that came in the mail. The four Hindu gods he brought into the house revealed where his heart really was.

The apostle Paul talked about this. Some preached the gospel for wrong motives and were actually hostile to him. He had a hard time finding co-workers in Christ who were genuinely concerned for the churches.

Philippians 1:15-18 It is true that some preach Christ out of envy and rivalry, but others out of goodwill. The latter do so out of love, knowing that I am put here for the defence of the gospel. The former preach Christ out of selfish ambition, not sincerely, supposing that they can stir up trouble for me while I am in chains. But what does it matter? The important thing is that in every way, whether from false motives or true, Christ is preached. And because of this, I rejoice.

Philippians 2:19-22 I hope in the Lord Jesus to send Timothy to you soon, that I also may be cheered when I receive news about you. I have no one else like him, who will show genuine concern for your welfare. For everyone looks out for their own interests, not those of Jesus Christ. But you know that Timothy has proved himself, because as a son with his father he has served with me in the work of the gospel.

Look for people with sincere love. Look for people who have a heart to serve the church. Some are self-serving and even if they appear to be going along with the move of God, they feel threatened by those who truly give themselves in sincere love for the church without control or manipulation. Don't stay in the houses of those self-serving ministers!

So many pagans come in to Christianity and are taught to relate to God in the same way they did to their idols. Watch out for those who encourage you to attempt to relate to God like Hindus do! Hindus and other pagans bring sacrifices of money, food, and animals to their idols, but we come to God through Jesus's torn body which is the only way into the Father's presence.

Two years after the aforementioned dream, I was astounded to learn of four entities which different branches of Hinduism consider their primary deities. I had known that Hinduism had millions of gods, but I hadn't known there were four most prominent ones when I had the dream showing four Hindu idols in the man's house.

In that dream, I'd thought the mom was on board with her husband, who impersonated a minister but worshipped Hindu gods. Then I was surprised to find her in my car trying to convince her kids of the gospel. We may have easily misjudged some people because they were in the house of an idolater, but they love Jesus and are yearning for truth.

That was the part of the dream that brought me to tears. Women are pleading with their kids, and pleading for somebody to tell their kids the truth about Christ. I've talked to so many young people. I've heard and felt their moms' pleas for someone to convince their kids that Jesus is real. Those kids have been sickened by what they've seen of religion that looked nothing like Jesus. Let's pray for those kids. They will only listen when they sense earnest, sincere love combined with a testimony and demonstration of the Holy Spirit's power.

What comes through in the Apostle Paul's writings to the churches is passionate love for people and such sincerity that his motives could not be questioned. Let us throw off everything that is not the gospel or truth but is the tradition of men and is creating a stumbling block for people to come to Christ. The tithe tradition is one of those stumbling blocks. May we not fight to sustain the religious status-quo at the cost of truth.

Let's get rid of the leaven so we don't end up with children who don't want to hear their moms telling them about Jesus. May there be no question that our motivation is anything but pure love and care for the well-being of God's flock. I was just watching another interview of Benny Hinn speaking about his repentance, and it was so sincere. He wept as he talked about how precious God's love is and how he never again wants to grieve the Holy Spirit.[323] He said *"I'm done with it!"*

I pray that likewise, a wave of repentance will sweep through the Body of Christ and many will say *"I'm done with it! No more pagan, works-centred religion mixed in with the gospel! No more teaching people to relate to the Heavenly Father in the same way as pagans sacrifice to the sea goddess!"* I pray that the church will be set free to truly give freely, out of communion with the Holy Spirit, and that many whose hearts have been hardened against Christ would be drawn again by the sincerity and purity of our gospel message.

1 Corinthians 5:6-8 Don't you know that a little yeast leavens the whole batch of dough? Get rid of the old yeast, so that you may be a new unleavened batch—as you really are. For Christ, our Passover Lamb has been sacrificed. Therefore, let us keep the Festival, not with the old bread leavened with malice and wickedness, but with the unleavened bread of sincerity and truth.

If the message of this book has moved your heart, please help me to share it with as many people as possible! Help me get it to pastors and leaders.

---

[323] *Benny Hinn Opens His Heart During A Very Special Interview* Online: https://www.youtube.com/watch?v=BSnHbZqmqM4&t=19s Accessed December 19th, 2019 Starting at 1 hr, 2 minutes and 30 seconds

Check out www.gotoheavennow.com for more edifying writing. I'd love to hear how this book has impacted you. You can contact me by email: jonathan@gotoheavennow.com

Recommended Reading

Bertie Brit's messages on money are so on-target that I highly recommend listening to them all. Just search *"Bertie Brits money"* on YouTube. They are especially helpful for pastors, since he is approaching the topic as a pastor who receives his living from free-will giving. They are full of wisdom for people who've been burnt-out on tithing, guilt-motivated, and give-to-get messages. Besides Bertie's online sermons, I recommend the following books for anyone who wants to look into the subject more:

***Should The Church Teach Tithing: A Theologian's Conclusions about a Taboo Doctrine* by Dr. Russel Earl Kelly**
The strongest point of Dr. Kelly's book may be explaining the nuts and bolts of what tithing was to the Jews. He also goes into a few arguments in more detail than I have. Among other things, he argues that the context of Malachi 3 is found in Nehemiah 13, that Melchizedek was historically a pagan priest but prophetically a type of Christ, and that *"honor"* in 1 Timothy 5 is not a salary for elders. Dr. Kelly's book contains a great overview of the history of tithing. He espouses the view that there were three different tithes.

Dr. Kelly's website, www.tithing-russkelly.com, also contains a wealth of additional information in articles. He has great compilations of quotes from history, from theologians, and from Biblical commentary works about tithing. His book as well as Dr. Croteau's book are more academic.

You Mean I Don't Have To Tithe?: A Deconstruction of Tithing and a Reconstruction of Post-Tithe Giving by Dr. David Croteau

Dr. David Croteau's book is really strong on the history of tithing. He also examines the levirate law as a parallel to tithing and does a good job of explaining the fulfillment of the tithe in the New Covenant. He does a great job of explaining why the tithe is not consistent with different major theological systems. Dr. Croteau presents the position that there were three tithes. This is an academic work loaded with footnotes and well worth reading.

Jesus Is The Tithe: The Message of God by Gysbert Brits

Bertie writes with prophetic authority and does a great job of laying out how tithe and give-to-get doctrine hurts Christians and destroys the purity of our gospel message. He shares his own powerful testimony of how such teachings were destroying him, how he walked away, and how he found freedom to go beyond the hurt so as to radically give and receive.

One of Bertie's best contributions is explaining *"family logic"* and how it is incompatible with tithing. He also does an unparalleled job of explaining how the tithe prophetically pointed to Christ and cuts straight to the heart issues behind the corrupted wisdom which goes to such lengths in attempts to support tithing. Bertie speaks with wisdom as a pastor and TV preacher in full-time ministry, and parts of the book are especially directed towards pastors.

Eating Sacred Cows: A Closer Look At Tithing by Graeme Carlé

This is the book that convinced Derek Prince to change his position on tithing. Derek bought 20 copies of to share with his international council to help prevent burn-out. It presents the single-tithe with three uses view rather than the view that there were three tithes. It also emphasizes how the ancient tithe teaches us the need to rest. *Eating Sacred Cows* is especially helpful for pastors, as Graeme shares his experience pastoring and not teaching tithes.

Tithing: Low-Realm, Obsolete & Defunct by **Matthew E. Narramore**

Matthew Narramore's book is really strong in pointing out how the modern tithe doctrine misrepresents how we relate to God and how he relates to us in the New Covenant. He presents the weakness and uselessness of teaching tithing as compared to the glorious realities of life in Christ, and explains how tithing distorts people's view of fundamental topics such as righteousness, grace, salvation, and blessing.

Supernatural Provision: Learning to Walk in Greater Levels of Stewardship and Responsibility and Letting Go of Unbiblical Beliefs by **Michael Van Vlymen**

Michael encourages radical, Spirit-led giving, and inspires faith for miracles of provision. He has literally had an angel hand him cash! His teaching contrasts with the storehouse tithing doctrine and other forms of manipulation. This book also contains an *"activation exercise"* of believing God for seed to sow in Spirit-led giving. Free-will giving becomes an adventure of growing in faith and growing in God's grace!

Provision of Heaven by **Reinhard Hirtler**

Reinhard is a missionary and a friend I met in Brazil. He has developed a deep trust in God's nature as our provider, and has hundreds of amazing testimonies of God's provision. His teaching promotes radical generosity and faith for supernatural provision based on the revelation of our Heavenly Father's nature, rather than being tithe or principle-based.

All profits from Reinhard's books go towards caring for orphans in Brazil. He also has several hours of teaching on kingdom finances on YouTube. The four parts are under the Portuguese title: FINANÇAS NA NOVA ALIANÇA - PR. REINHARD HIRTLER – However, all four videos are bilingual with Reinhard speaking in English and being translated to Portuguese. These teachings will challenge you, and they contain a lot of solid scriptural truth.

About the Author

Jonathan Brenneman was born in Rochester, New York and raised in Pennsylvania. Although a very troubled child he was at the same time very religious. He read the Bible from cover to cover when he was seven years old, all the while questioning and wondering about the existence of God.

When Jonathan was nine years old, he woke up one morning with bad back pain. His mother prayed for him, and to his surprise, he felt something like a hot ball of energy rolling up and down inside his back, and the pain melted away. It was shocking to say the least, but it convinced him God did exist! He later told his friends, "I know that God is real. I felt his hand on my back."

In spite of this experience, Jonathan still had no peace. He prayed the "sinner's prayer" but with no change until two years later when he had a "born again" experience. It felt like heaven opened and unexplainable joy and peace descended upon him! He was different, and knew it! The things he had felt so guilty about that he tried unsuccessfully to change, were simply gone. After this time, Jonathan dedicated his life to the Lord as a missionary, going on his first mission trip at age fourteen. As a teenager and young adult he continued to travel and learn languages. Then, when he was twenty-one and during a time of desperation, Jonathan went to a Christian conference where he was very encouraged and touched by the Lord. It was a start of a supernatural lifestyle and growing in spiritual gifts during which time many amazing miracles and healings began to happen.

Jonathan worked in construction, but in between jobs he began to visit churches in the United States and Canada as well as in Latin America and Eastern Europe. His ministry journeys have included Russia, Ukraine, Poland, Italy, Canada, Mexico, Belize, and Brazil. In these places Jonathan has encouraged the believers and shared testimonies, and spoken with unbelievers and prayed for them. He also worked with children and seniors. He dedicated a lot of time to talking with, praying for, and encouraging people wherever he went, all the while growing in an experience of a love for people that is beyond understanding—for it is God's love. Jonathan believes it is a wonderful and tremendous privilege to be able to serve the people for whom Jesus gave his life.

Jonathan now lives in Rio de Janeiro Brazil with his wife Elizabeth, and baby daughter Rebekah. He loves people very much, enjoys being with them, and rejoices at seeing what the Holy Spirit does in their lives. He likes to minister in the role of caring for people, laying hands on the sick, visiting the elderly, and working with children—always with the intention of loving them so they in turn will learn to love others with the love of God.

Contact

Amazon reviews are the author's tip jar! They also help to get the message out to more people. If you have enjoyed this book, please consider leaving a review at Amazon.com

You can contact Jonathan through his Facebook author page, *Jonathan Brenneman,* or by email: jonathan@gotoheavennow.com

You can read his blog at: www.gotoheavennow.com

Other Titles By Jonathan Brenneman:

I Am Persuaded: Christian Leadership As Taught By Jesus

The Power And Love Sandwich: Why You Should Seek God's Face AND His Hand

Present Access To Heaven (Heaven Now Book 1)

I Will Awaken The Dawn (Heaven Now Book 2)

Jesus Has Come In The Flesh (Heaven Now Book 3)

What Really Causes Needless Casualties Of War?: Why We Do Have Authority Over All Satan's Power, And Why People Really Get Hurt

Evergreen Life: Flourish In Every Circumstance

Are You My Spiritual Father?: Spiritual Fathers And Spiritual Sons, Or Brothers?

Printed in Great Britain
by Amazon